Criminal Investigation
An introduction to principles and practice

Peter Stelfox

WILLAN
PUBLISHING

Published by

Willan Publishing
Culmcott House
Mill Street, Uffculme
Cullompton, Devon
EX15 3AT, UK
Tel: +44(0)1884 840337
Fax: +44(0)1884 840251
e-mail: info@willanpublishing.co.uk
website: www.willanpublishing.co.uk

Published simultaneously in the USA and Canada by

Willan Publishing
c/o ISBS, 920 NE 58th Ave, Suite 300
Portland, Oregon 97213-3786, USA
Tel: +001(0)503 287 3093
Fax: +001(0)503 280 8832
e-mail: info@isbs.com
website: www.isbs.com

First published 2009

ISBN   978-1-84392-337-4 paperback
       978-1-84392-338-1 hardback

British Library Cataloguing-in-Publication Data

A catalogue record for this book is available from the British Library.

FSC
Mixed Sources
Product group from well-managed
forests and other controlled sources
Cert no. SGS-COC-2482
www.fsc.org
© 1996 Forest Stewardship Council

Project managed by Deer Park Productions, Tavistock, Devon
Typeset by GCS, Leighton Buzzard, Bedfordshire
Printed and bound by T.J. International Ltd, Padstow, Cornwall

Contents

List of figures and tables

Figures

Tables

Chapter 1

Crime and investigative practice

Introduction

Criminal investigation is one of the key functions of the police service. It contributes to the achievement of a wide range of objectives at every level of policing, from the investigation of anti-social behaviour in neighbourhoods to international counter-terrorism operations. Whatever level of offending it is directed at, criminal investigation involves locating, gathering and using information to bring offenders to justice, or to achieve one of the other objectives set for it by the police service, such as victim care, intelligence gathering or managing crime risks.

Despite the importance of criminal investigation, there has been little study of how it is practised by individual investigators and how the knowledge, skills and understanding they bring to the task might be improved. Indeed, the recognition that the scope and complexity of criminal investigation is such that it requires a range of knowledge, skills and understanding which is distinct from other areas of police work is relatively recent. The professional model within the police service has always been that of the 'omni-competent constable'. This was held to be an individual who could turn their hands to any of the many problems that present themselves to the police service to be dealt with. Criminal investigation was seen as being simply one of these problems and all officers were expected to be able to carry it out as part of their routine duties. While police forces had a Criminal Investigation Department (CID) of one sort or another to deal with the most serious crimes, they rarely constituted more than 10 per cent of a force's staff and the dominant view was that investigation required few skills in addition to those possessed by all officers.

This may have worked well enough in an era when the legal and technical aspects of criminal investigation were relatively straightforward and when there was a general consensus in society about the objective of criminal investigation and the means by which it was to be achieved. However, during the last quarter of a century, the legal framework of criminal investigation has changed beyond recognition and now encompasses a range of legislation which must be mastered by investigators if they are to carry out their role effectively within the law. Scientific and technical advances have been equally great and mean that investigators must have a far broader knowledge of the techniques of investigation than was previously required.

The objective of criminal investigation has also changed. At one time, its sole purpose was to bring offenders to justice and investigative practice was shaped only by the need to identify suspects and gather evidence to support prosecutions. Now, victim care, community reassurance, intelligence gathering, disruption of criminal networks and managing a wide range of crime risks are also seen as fundamental objectives of the process. All of these developments have increased the complexity of the task of criminal investigation and mean that those who engage in it require high levels of professional competence if they are to perform their role effectively.

The police service's capacity to carry out investigations across the wide spectrum of offending it deals with, and its ability to respond to new challenges as they emerge, consists entirely of the knowledge, skills and understanding that individual investigators have of investigative practice. Legal, procedural, scientific and technical provisions are, of course, important, but without the individuals who are competent to apply them in individual cases, they would have little effect. Therefore, the training and the continued professional development of investigators is of the highest importance to the police service. The model by which they are achieved is fast evolving away from internal police training schools towards further and higher education establishments, and increasingly involves external bodies in the development and accreditation of standards. These developments are entirely in keeping with the professionalisation of the role of police investigators. But past failures to recognise investigative practice as a distinct area of police work means that there has been little investment in practitioner-focused research and there is no tradition within the police service of practitioners taking responsibility for the development of a literature on investigative practice. As a result, there is something of a gap between the ambition to have investigators trained and developed according to a professional model and a literature that enables this to be achieved.

This is not to say that there is no material available at all. As will be seen in Chapter 2, many police forces, government departments and the Association of Chief Police Officers (ACPO) have produced policy and procedural guidance on various aspects of criminal investigation, and police training schools still provide students with much useful material. But the coverage of this material is far from comprehensive and the quality is variable. Furthermore, little of it is available outside of the police service and so those delivering the many external courses and other development opportunities for investigators often have no direct access to it. Taken overall, such material cannot be considered to be the type of peer- reviewed professional literature that is available to other professional groups.

To some extent this gap in the professional literature has been filled by social scientists, academic lawyers, psychologists and others within the various academic fields that have an interest in policing. But because this literature reflects the research interests and methodologies of a wide range of disciplines, its relevance to investigative practice is variable. Much of the legal literature does have a direct bearing on practice, as does the sub-branch of psychology that is concerned with investigative interviewing. The forensic science literature is probably the most advanced in respect of practitioner involvement and relevance, but much of this is naturally aimed at forensic practitioners rather than police investigators. Some of the literature is based on research carried out to underpin policy or managerial objectives, and this applies to much of the social science literature sponsored by the Home Office and the ACPO. This has some relevance to investigators but when the aims and recommendations of such work are examined it can be seen that they generally relate to broader policy or managerial issues rather than the skills and knowledge that investigators need in order to carry out their role.

This is not to say that either academic or policy-based research is of no value to practitioners. Much of it is highly relevant and practitioners can gain a lot from it. However, the situation is analogous to engineers having access to a literature about the role that bridges play in society but not on how to build them, to nursing literature focusing on the policy and management challenges of the

NHS rather than on patient care, or to builders having access to a literature on planning law but not on construction. Of course, the value to society of engineers, nurses and builders lies in the fact that they can build bridges, care for patients and construct buildings. As a consequence, and in common with many other occupational groups such as lawyers, accountants, teachers, social workers and many more, they have developed a professional literature in which they can be trained and developed and which can help them respond to evolving challenges. But a practitioner-focused literature such as this is only just emerging within criminal investigation.

The aim of this book is to contribute to that literature by providing practitioners and those undergoing training in the many disciplines that support criminal investigation with an introduction to the principles and practice of criminal investigation. It does this by exploring some of the key elements of investigative practice in the police service of England and Wales and how they are applied in the many situations where the police are called on to carry out criminal investigations. In particular it looks at the factors that shape investigative practice and how they influence the outcomes that are achieved.

Because the evidence base for investigative practice is still limited, much of this book is based on practice drawn from official policy and procedure rather than from an independent professional literature. As a consequence, I have not referenced the text extensively but have included all the material I have drawn from in the Further reading sections at the end of each chapter. As the focus of this book is very much on what individual practitioners need to know about the principles of investigative practice, many of the critical debates around policing within the social science, criminological, legal and psychological literature are not directly addressed. This is partly because others within the relevant disciplines are better equipped to explore them and partly because they are often not central to how individual crimes are investigated. They may nonetheless be of interest to practitioners and so at the end of each chapter I have tried to steer readers in the direction of further material on the wider questions of policing and criminal investigation.

Although the focus is limited to the police in one jurisdiction, much of what is covered is relevant to criminal investigations carried out by other public and private agencies and in other jurisdictions.

The remainder of this chapter examines the relationship between investigative practice, crime and the criminal justice system, together with the objectives that are sought through the investigation of crime.

Chapter 2 looks in more depth at the development of investigative practice within the police service of England and Wales. The focus is on early developments, when the investigation of crime was merged with other policing functions and so acquired its role in delivering multiple objectives within a complex policing structure. Chapter 3 looks at how some behaviour comes to be defined as criminal and the legal and policy framework within which investigations are carried out. But the investigation of crime is not simply a matter of the police enforcing the law. Chapter 4 is concerned with information and how it is generated by a crime and the unique information profile that each crime gives rise to. Chapter 5 looks at the techniques that are available to investigators to locate, gather and use this information, and Chapter 6 explores the strategies that investigators use to deploy these techniques in individual cases. Chapter 7 looks at how the work of investigators is managed within the police service. Chapter 8 looks at how law and policy, information profiles, techniques of investigation and the strategies used by investigators to deploy them all come together to solve crime. Finally, Chapter 9 draws together the themes discussed throughout the book to examine how investigative practice is likely to develop in the future.

Investigative practice

It is difficult to overstate the importance that criminal investigation has assumed in contemporary society. During the first years of the new millennium, over five million crimes were reported to the police in England and Wales each year and crime control has become a significant social and political issue. As a consequence, society expects the police to be competent in criminal investigation at all levels, from the local to the transnational, and across all types of offending from the minor to the most serious. This competence lies in the investigative practice of individual police officers and police staff engaged in the investigation of crime.

The professional practice, sometimes also called the expert knowledge, of any occupational group consists of 'the particular competences, specialised knowledge and practices used by occupations claiming autonomy and authority to solve specific types of problem' (Flynn 1999: 34). Professional practice of this sort has been developed by other occupational groups which have traditionally been seen as having a broad and ill-defined public service remit similar to investigators, for example nursing (Bernhard and Walsh 1995;

5

Benner 1984; Laurenson 1995) and social work (Davies 1994; Malin 2000). It is generally contained in a literature written specifically for practitioners and has to be mastered before one can be considered to be professionally competent. Such competency is usually recognised by a qualification or by entry on to a professional register, both of which function 'as a trademark does, promising a certain level of performance to those who rely on it' (Davis 2002: 4). It is often described in terms of the knowledge that practitioners need in order to provide the service, the skills and abilities they need apply that knowledge and the understanding they need to do so. Investigative practice can, therefore, be thought of as encompassing the knowledge, techniques and understanding that those tasked with carrying out criminal investigation need to do their job effectively.

The knowledge, skills and understanding required by investigators is shaped by the complexity of the investigative task. The law defines certain types of behaviour as criminal, it provides a framework of rules and regulations within which investigators must work and it determines the standard of evidence that is required before a prosecution can be brought against someone. The law, therefore, frames the type of problem that criminal investigation is for investigators and the way in which they can address it. But the law cannot describe the wide range of circumstances in which criminal behaviour occurs or the situations in which investigators will operate. Nor can it anticipate the type, volume or distribution of information generated by the unique circumstances in which each crime is committed. Some offences generate a large amount of information that is widely distributed, while others generate very little. Locating and gathering this information is the key focus of investigations, but the way in which offenders, victims, witnesses and communities react after a crime has been committed determines how easy or difficult this is. Not all crimes are reported to the police. Even where they are, the accounts given by victims, witnesses and suspects can be unreliable, partial or false and it is often difficult for investigators to know with any degree of certainty which of these applies in any situation. Investigative practice equips them with the techniques they need to locate and gather information, the knowledge they need to apply these techniques to the many different situations in which investigations are carried out and the understanding needed to interpret the information they gather and use it to further the investigation.

The main problem of criminal investigation is therefore one of matching the dry certainty of the law to the messy, unpredictable and complex reality of the human behaviour called crime. In order to do this effectively they require:

- Knowledge of law, information profiles, human behaviour, investigative techniques, and investigative strategies.
- Skills in applying the techniques of criminal investigation such as interviewing and searching.
- Understanding of how to apply their knowledge and skills to solve the specific type of problem with which they are faced. This includes understanding the social context in which the investigation is taking place and the way it will impact on victims, witnesses and the wider community.

Crime

Understanding investigative practice requires an understanding of the phenomenon it is aimed at addressing. Crime is first and foremost about how people behave towards each other and so it has always been a feature of the human experience. Ancient myths are shot through with tales of those who transgressed the legal boundaries of their society, and recorded history documents countless crimes against individuals, groups and states. Today, no news bulletin would be complete without crime-related reports. Crime is even invented for entertainment and a high proportion of books, films, plays and television dramas have fictitious crimes as their central theme. Whether our experience of crime is first-hand, from news reports or from fiction, most people are aware of crime on a daily basis. These experiences shape how we live. For example, fears over the vulnerability of children to crime sometimes lead parents to restrict activities such as playing out or online surfing, airports are designed to minimise the potential for terrorists to commit crime, many people voluntarily lock themselves into their homes at night for no other reason than their fear of crime, and as a society we spend millions on CCTV cameras in an effort to minimise crime in our streets. In contemporary society, crime even influences the political agenda, with all parties seeking to demonstrate competence in managing crime and those who commit it.

One of the difficulties faced by anyone who wants to address the problem of crime in society, as either legislator, policy-maker or police officer, is simply the complexity of the behaviour that comes

7

to be termed crime. Most people will readily identify that murder, rape, burglary and robbery are crimes, but it is doubtful that they could name more than a small proportion of the more than 8,000 acts that are against the criminal law in England and Wales. Many of these behaviours have nothing whatsoever in common other than the fact that they are against the law. The teenage girl who conceals her pregnancy and whose baby dies from neglect after a secret birth commits a crime; the prospective employee who lies about their qualifications to get a job commits a crime; the dealer who sells heroin commits a crime; the man who assaults his wife commits a crime; the accountant who launders money commits a crime and the drunk who drives a car commits a crime. These behaviours are so diverse as to defy easy categorisation, other than to call them all criminal.

If the range of behaviour that is criminal is wide, then the range of circumstances in which it is committed is even wider. If we take a very common form of offending, such as theft, it can be seen that people commit it alone and in groups, some of which are highly organised for the purpose. It can be committed spontaneously in response to an opportunity, such as a handbag left unattended in a bar, or it can involve months of careful planning. It can be a local affair or it can involve international conspiracies. It can involve minor thefts or millions of pounds and can be committed once or be part of an ongoing pattern of offending. The same is true of most types of offending. The legal definition of the behaviour does not generally describe the wide variety of circumstances in which the offence can be committed.

Nor is there any easy explanation of why people commit crime. Criminology is the academic discipline most closely associated with attempts to discover why people commit crime and in doing so it draws on a variety of other disciplines such as sociology, psychology, psychiatry, law, history and anthropology (Garland 2002: 15). While it has produced many theories about the causes of crime, there is no single factor that can explain why people commit it. Explanations have been sought in factors such as poverty, social relationships, drug and alcohol abuse, mental health, psychological conditions, genetics, parenting, masculinity and many more. All of these things can be shown to be associated with some offending behaviour but there is no general causal explanation of why people commit crime.

In addition, many people take a moral view of the causes of crime. They hold that people commit crime because they are bad, anti-social or whatever other label fits the moral framework being used. This approach is as limited as any other in explaining why some people are bad or anti-social in the first place. The best we appear able to do at the moment is to say that crime is a highly complex phenomenon that is not easily categorised in terms of the behaviour involved, the circumstances in which that behaviour occurs or the reasons why people do it.

Many people commit crime at some point in their lives. For many this will be infrequent, minor and undetected, or at least unreported to the police. The 2003 Crime and Justice Survey was a self-reporting survey carried out by the Research, Development and Statistics Directorate of the Home Office. It estimated that there were 3.8 million active offenders aged between 10 and 65 in England and Wales. The majority of these (2.4 million) were under 25 years of age and a higher percentage of males surveyed said they had offended (13 per cent) than females (7 per cent). Thus, offending behaviour was far more prevalent in the young than in older age groups and among males than females. But most of those who were surveyed had given up offending by their early twenties (Home Office 2005b).

The response to crime

Running alongside our experience of crime, whether real or fictional, is society's concern for justice and restoration. Society reflects these concerns through the criminal justice system, which can be thought of as encompassing a set of values, agencies and practices that enable society to formulate and implement a response to crime. This response has two aims: the first is symbolic and expresses society's view that crime is a moral wrong that requires offenders to be brought to justice; the second is instrumental, in that it is intended to reduce crime and society's fear of crime. Criminal investigation is central to the achievement of the first of these and plays an important role in the second by enabling detected offenders to be diverted from future criminal behaviour and by producing intelligence that enables other crime prevention and crime management measures to be implemented.

Views vary as to the ways that these objectives can best be met and the ways in which the interests of victims, offenders and society as a whole can be balanced. The criminal justice system seeks to accommodate these differences, which are mainly played out at the political level in the legislature, but which are also reflected in the way in which criminal justice agencies develop their policies and in the way in which individuals choose to use the criminal justice system. These three elements – the legislature, criminal justice agencies and the ways in which individuals respond to crime – are considered in detail below.

The legislature

The legislature is the political institution that determines what behaviour will be defined as criminal and the laws by which investigations are carried out. In relation to the jurisdiction of England and Wales, the legislature is the two Houses of Parliament: the House of Commons and the House of Lords. England and Wales is a common law jurisdiction, which means that some offences, together with the doctrines of the criminal law and some legal practice, are derived from the rulings of judges rather than from the legislation of politicians. However, in recent times all law has been made by the legislature and it is they who consider all proposals for new laws and debate and amend them in relation to political arguments. The process by which this occurs is discussed in greater detail in Chapter 3, but for now it is sufficient to note that the legislature is essentially a political institution which is governed by the political considerations of the day. In a democracy, this, in theory at least, gives members of society access to the legislative process through membership of political parties, campaigning groups or simply through their Member of Parliament. This access is one of the means by which the various tensions between different views about the objectives of the criminal justice system and how it should operate are mediated.

Criminal justice agencies

The criminal justice agencies are the means by which the laws passed by the legislature are implemented. The police are the largest of the criminal justice agencies, both in terms of the number of people employed and the proportion of the criminal justice budget allocated to them by the government. They are also the agency that has the most direct role in criminal investigation. They are therefore considered first and in the greatest depth.

Police

The police are the main state agency with responsibility to carry out criminal investigations and have a remit to investigate all types of crime falling within their area. The police service of England and Wales is made up of 43 independent police forces:

Avon and Somerset
  Constabulary
Bedfordshire Constabulary
Cambridgeshire Constabulary
Cheshire Constabulary
City of London Police
Cleveland Police
Cumbria Constabulary
Derbyshire Constabulary
Devon and Cornwall
  Constabulary
Dorset Police
Durham Constabulary
Dyfed-Powys Police
Essex Police
Gloucestershire Constabulary
Greater Manchester Police
Gwent Police
Hampshire Constabulary
Herefordshire Constabulary
Humberside Police
Kent Police
Lancashire Constabulary

Leicestershire Constabulary
Lincolnshire Police
Merseyside Police
Metropolitan Police Service
Norfolk Constabulary
Northamptonshire Police
Northumbria Police
North Wales Police
North Yorkshire Police
Nottinghamshire Police
South Wales Police
South Yorkshire Police
Staffordshire Police
Suffolk Constabulary
Surrey Police
Sussex Police
Thames Valley Police
Warwickshire Police
West Mercia Constabulary
West Midlands Police
West Yorkshire Police
Wiltshire Constabulary

Within these police forces criminal investigation is carried out by sworn police officers and police staff. Sworn officers hold the office of constable and have a set of unique powers granted under various statutes, such as those of arrest and entry. Confusingly, the office of constable also includes those who have been promoted into supervisory and management roles within the service. The police force includes the following ranks:

- Constable
- Sergeant
- Inspector
- Chief Inspector
- Superintendent
- Chief Superintendent
- Assistant Chief Constable (Commander and Deputy Assistant Commissioner in the Metropolitan Police)
- Assistant Commissioner (Metropolitan and City of London Police only)

- Deputy Chief Constable (Deputy Commissioner in the Metropolitan Police)
- Chief Constable (Commissioner in the Metropolitan and City of London Police).

Police staff is the term used to describe those employed by the police organisation who are not sworn constables. A wide range of roles in relation to criminal investigation are carried out by police staff. For example, call centre staff receiving the initial report of a crime, police community support officers (PCSO) carrying out patrol work, plus crime scene investigators (CSI), analysts, intelligence officers, surveillance officers and many more.

In 2007, there were 139,710 sworn officers within the police service of England and Wales and 76,721 police staff, although it is not possible to say how many of each are deployed on crime investigation at any one time.

Forces are typically divided into Basic Command Units (BCU) aligned with local authority areas and the largest proportion of sworn officers and police staff are deployed on BCUs. They are involved in uniformed patrol, either as part of a neighbourhood team serving the needs of a particular community or as part of a team providing a response to calls from the public over a larger area. A great deal of the work done by all uniformed officers is crime investigation, and contrary to what may be expected from popular literature and drama, the majority of criminal investigations are carried out by them rather than by detectives or other specialists.

Police forces also maintain a specialist crime investigation capacity. This generally involves specialists working in Criminal Investigation Departments, domestic violence units and child abuse units on BCUs, and squads of officers at a force level who specialise in the investigation of organised crime, fraud, homicide and terrorism. The size of these squads and the focus of their attention vary from force to force and depends to a large extent on the priority that each force gives to particular types of crime.

Criminal Defence Service (CDS)

If the police are the gatekeepers to the criminal justice process, then defence solicitors must be next in line in terms of both the sequence in which they become involved in criminal investigations and the influence they have on the outcomes of individual cases. Until very recently, defence solicitors acted as independent agents, and have not often been considered to be part of the criminal justice system. This seems odd in view of the central role they play in the process of criminal investigation and the fact that they are, by and large, paid for by the government under the legal aid scheme. Everyone is entitled to free legal advice if they are arrested and taken to a police station for questioning, although the degree of assistance they receive if they are charged and have to appear in court is means tested. The Criminal Defence Service (CDS) administers this system and, as their website states (www.legalservices.gov.uk), they help the police and the courts operate fairly and efficiently by ensuring that people accused of crimes have access to legal advice and representation. They are funded by the Legal Services Commission, which is a non-departmental public body sponsored by the Ministry of Justice. Individual solicitors, or their representatives, acting for suspects under investigation are still likely to be independently employed in their own or a joint legal practice, but many specialise in defence work. A small number are employed directly by the Legal Services Commission and provide their services through the Public Defender Service, but this is still a small organisation and is not widely represented throughout England and Wales.

Although defence solicitors act independently for each client, they are formally considered to be officers of the court and have a responsibility to conduct their cases in the interests of justice. They are also bound by the Solicitor's Code of Conduct issued by the Law Society, which seeks to ensure that in acting for individual clients they do so with integrity and in the wider interests of society.

Most defence solicitors first become involved in a criminal investigation when a suspect is arrested and taken to a police station. The police are obliged to inform suspects of their right to free independent legal representation and to make the necessary arrangements to ensure that a solicitor of their choice is requested to attend. At the police station the solicitor's only role is to 'protect and advance the legal rights of their client' (6D PACE Code of Practice C).

Crown Prosecution Service (CPS)

The Crown Prosecution Service (www.cps.gov.uk) was established in 1986 under the Prosecution of Offenders Act 1985. The original role of the CPS was to prosecute the cases sent to them by the police, having first satisfied themselves that the cases had a realistic chance of leading to a conviction. This replaced the previous system whereby the police themselves prosecuted cases. Under this new arrangement the police still retained responsibility for deciding what charges should be brought in individual cases, but in 2003 the CPS took over this responsibility as well. Their role is now to consider the evidence collected by investigators, decide on the appropriate charge and manage the prosecution. Where the case is prosecuted in a magistrates' court, they generally prosecute the case using a directly employed solicitor, but they brief independent barristers to prosecute in the Crown Court. There is generally a close working relationship between the police service and the local CPS and in serious cases many CPS solicitors provide a range of advice on the legal aspects of the investigation well before the requirement to formally consider the evidence.

Courts

Courts hear the cases being prosecuted by the CPS. There are essentially three levels of courts that are relevant to criminal investigation: magistrates' courts, the Crown Court and the Court of Appeal (Criminal Division). These are all administered by Her Majesty's Court Service, which is an executive agency under the Ministry of Justice (www.hmcourts-service.gov.uk). The majority of criminal cases are dealt with in the magistrates' courts. Magistrates are local people who generally have no legal training and are unpaid, although they get expenses relating to their role. They usually sit in panels of three, called the Bench, and can try cases themselves or, if the cases are serious, can refer them to the Crown Court. Most towns of any size have a magistrates' court. More serious cases are tried in Crown Courts in front of a judge who is a qualified lawyer and a jury selected from the community. Crown Courts can also hear appeals from those who believe that there has been some fault in the way their cases have been dealt with in a magistrates' court. The Court of Appeal is composed of senior judges who hear appeals about cases tried in the Crown Court. The House of Lords is the highest court of appeal, where cases are heard by the twelve Law Lords, who are selected from among the most senior judges.

All courts hear the evidence put before them according to rules laid down both by legal tradition and in statutes passed by the legislature. Their role is to hear the evidence according to these rules, to determine if someone is guilty or not and, if they find them guilty, to impose an appropriate sentence, which is generally designed to both punish the offender and deter them from further offending. Many sentences are administered by the courts themselves. These include fines and orders such as suspended sentences or conditional discharges. Other sentences are administered by Her Majesty's Prison Service and the National Probation Service.

Prison and Probation Service

Her Majesty's Prison Service (www.hmprisonservice.gov.uk) and the National Probation Service (www.probation.homeoffice.gov.uk) are both administered by the Ministry of Justice. Their roles are to carry out the sentences of the courts, to work towards rehabilitating offenders and to keep communities safe. These two criminal justice agencies play a limited role in the process of criminal investigation.

Individual responses to crime

The legislature and the criminal justice agencies are the most visible elements of the criminal justice system. Their policies, together with the values and working practices of those employed within them, are naturally highly influential in shaping the type of criminal justice system we have, but so too are the choices made by those who use the system and those who seek to influence the local and national response to crime. In other words, the criminal justice system is not simply about how the institutions of criminal justice work, it is also about how society as a whole uses them. This is particularly important when considering criminal investigation. As will be seen throughout this book, crime investigation is a collaborative activity which requires the active participation of the police, other relevant agencies and the community. What the police and other criminal justice agencies bring to this collaboration are certain capacities and competencies, but on their own they are unlikely to have much effect. The choices that individual members of society make are also important.

It is all too easy to view the criminal law and its application as a mechanistic function of society. Laws are passed, people break them; some are caught and processed through the criminal justice system, which it is hoped has an effect on their future behaviour. In this model, the law, and the institutions that are there to apply it, operate as objective elements of a largely neutral criminal justice system.

The reality is, however, that most people experience crime as a far more personal phenomenon than this model allows. Victims of crime are not simply the starting point of an investigation or essential witnesses in court. They are people who may have suffered physical or emotional harm as a consequence of another's behaviour. Even where this is not the case they may feel cheated, embarrassed, humiliated or shamed. Some can even feel a sense of guilt, believing that they may have provoked the crime or at least not done enough to prevent it. For these reasons, most crimes generate an emotional response in those who are most immediately affected by them. This can intersect with their religious, political or social values to produce a complex and sometimes contradictory response to the crime. Experienced investigators will recognise that the old joke that a conservative is a liberal who has been mugged often has the ring of truth about it.

Witnesses and the wider communities within which crimes occur can also respond emotionally. This is not simply a response to seeing or hearing the details of distressing events. The type and frequency of crime in a neighbourhood can be experienced by the people living there as a statement about them and their values. Communities that have suffered disadvantage or prejudice may view crimes against members of their community as an index of wider social attitudes towards them. For example, homophobic crime can be seen by some as not simply about attacks on individuals, or levels of crime in a particular location. Its prevalence may be interpreted by gay men and lesbians as indicating something about how they personally are viewed and how safe they are. People's experience of crime, whether as victims, witnesses or communities, their emotional response to it and their wider social, political and religious values, are all important elements in shaping the criminal justice system.

The role of criminal investigation in the response to crime

Criminal investigation is important for other agencies in the criminal justice system because it is virtually the only source of the material they need to play their role. If the CPS, defence solicitors and courts are to make effective decisions about the cases that pass through their hands, it is important that both the quantity of material gathered about a crime and its quality are maximised by investigators.

There is now an expectation, and indeed a legal requirement under the Criminal Procedure and Investigations Act 1996 (CPIA), that investigators will pursue all reasonable lines of enquiry in an investigation. This is because it is now understood that the criminal investigation is usually the only chance to identify and collect the material needed by courts to hear a case. If material is not identified during an investigation, it is unlikely that it can later be recovered. This is certainly the case with most forensic evidence, which is likely to degrade if not located quickly after the events. Even in the case of more traditional types of material such as witness accounts, if investigators fail to identify them during the investigation phase, it is unlikely that they will become available later. Even where they do, it may be difficult for courts to assess their quality because of the time that elapsed between the events and the witness's account of them (see Chapter 4 for more detail about how information degrades over time).

Criminal investigation is not only carried out solely to bring offenders to justice. There are a number of important ancillary objectives, such as victim and witness care, community reassurance, intelligence gathering, crime reduction, disruption of criminal networks and asset recovery, all of which rely on effective investigations.

Judgements about the quality of criminal investigation do not rest solely on the effectiveness with which its various objectives are met. Society is also concerned about the way in which criminal investigations are carried out. This has been a concern from the earliest days of policing. One of the main objections to the introduction of plain clothes police officers to detect crime during the first decades of the Metropolitan Police in the middle of the nineteenth century centred not on the legality or the effectiveness of the proposals but on the methods the police would use, which some felt would amount to spying on the population (Emsley 1996: 236). This has been a recurring theme in policing in general and in criminal investigation in particular. While society wants the effective detection of crime, it also wants the methods used to be proportionate and to be implemented with respect for all concerned, including suspects and offenders. These things are not incompatible with effectiveness and are actually likely to improve the willingness of people to co-operate with and support individual investigations. The importance of criminal investigation to society lies both in its effectiveness in bringing offenders to justice and in the way in which it achieves this. How crimes are investigated is seen by many people as being symbolic of wider social relations and for this reason they expect investigators to exercise the legal powers they have with discretion.

How these various purposes of criminal investigation and the way in which they are met are explored in more detail below.

Bringing offenders to justice

The formal purpose of a criminal investigation in England and Wales is defined by the Code of Practice under Part II of the CPIA, which defines a criminal investigation as:

An investigation conducted by police officers with a view to it being ascertained whether a person should be charged with an offence, or whether a person charged with an offence is guilty of it. This will include:

- Investigations into crimes that have been committed;

- Investigations whose purpose is to ascertain whether a crime has been committed, with a view to the possible institution of criminal proceedings; and

- Investigations which begin in the belief that a crime may be committed, for example when the police keep premises or individuals under observation for a period of time, with a view to the possible institution of criminal proceedings;

- Charging a person with an offence includes prosecution by way of summons.

On this definition, a criminal investigation is the means by which the material required to bring offenders to justice is identified and gathered. It is the first stage in the criminal justice process and provides the information required by the CPS to undertake prosecutions and for those acting for suspects to take the course of action they believe is in a suspect's best interests. Where investigations are successful, they achieve public policy aims in that victims receive justice and society is protected from further harm by either rehabilitating offenders or inhibiting their ability to offend further by measures such as imprisonment.

In addition to taking offenders to court, there are a number of other measures the police can take to bring them to justice. The cautioning of young offenders by the police has a long history. Many young people commit minor crime at some point and get caught, but it is known that the majority are unlikely to become repeat offenders. It is widely accepted that in these cases warning them of the consequences of their behaviour together with parental support is a more constructive approach than prosecution. The system of cautioning has gradually expanded and now covers a wide range of measures. These are:

- *Reprimands.* These are given by the police to those aged 10 to 18 years old who have committed minor crime.

- *Final warnings*. These are given by the police to those aged 10 to 18 years old who have committed a subsequent minor crime or a more serious offence for the first time.

- *Simple caution*. These are given to those over 18 years old and are designed to divert them from future offending.

- *Conditional cautions*. Conditional cautions are the same as cautions but they include provisions for rehabilitation, such as attending drug treatment programmes and making reparation to victims.

- *Cannabis warnings*. As the name suggests, these can be given by police officers to those they find in possession of small amounts of cannabis.

- *Penalty notices for disorder*. These are fixed penalty notices that can be issued to anyone over 16 years old who engages in anti-social behaviour.

In issuing cautions and fixed penalty notices investigators are required to make a judgement that the material they have gathered is sufficient to prove the case. The suspect must also admit the offence and agree to the particular method of disposal.

While bringing offenders to justice has traditionally been the purpose of criminal investigation, there are now a number of other objectives it is expected to achieve.

Reassurance and care

Victims, witnesses and communities are not a homogeneous group. They differ widely in their needs and expectations. These will also change according to the type of crime under investigation and the characteristics of individual offences. Some victims and witnesses will require a great deal of help and support following a crime and they will look to investigators to provide at least some of this; others will not welcome the intrusion. As noted earlier in this chapter, crime does not just affect those most closely involved; it also impacts on communities, and one of the objectives the police seek to achieve when carrying out criminal investigation is to reassure communities.

Identifying the needs and wishes of victims, witnesses and the communities in which crimes are committed is not easy, and has not always been done well by the police. But there is now recognition that it forms an important part of investigative practice.

Crime prevention and reduction

Criminal investigation is one of the main ways in which the police seek to control crime. There is some doubt as to the general effectiveness of criminal investigation as a means of crime control because of the relatively small numbers of offenders caught in comparison to the number of offences reported to the police. Even where the police do bring an offender to justice, they are not in control of the measures taken to divert or prevent them from further offending. These are determined by judicial sentencing decisions and by the effectiveness of agencies such as the Probation Service and the Prison Service.

However, it is recognised that there is much that investigators can do in individual cases to promote crime reduction and prevention during the course of investigations. Research has established that those who are victims of crime once are more likely to be victimised in the future and so one of the objectives of investigative practice is to minimise the chance of re-offending against individual victims.

Disruption

In recent years, using criminal investigation as a means of disrupting criminal activity, rather than bringing offenders to justice, has been advocated by those engaged in counter-terrorism work and the investigation of organised crime. The concept of disruption is not well developed within the police service but it has been used to describe two different situations. The first is where investigators obtain material that indicates that a specific harm is about to occur. In such cases, they make a tactical decision to intervene and prevent the harm. In doing so, they risk losing investigative opportunities that may have led to the gathering of sufficient material to bring offenders to justice. In the case of counter-terrorism, such intervention may involve arresting suspects to prevent them from carrying out a bombing attack. In organised crime enquiries, investigators may learn of a plan to carry out a violent robbery and intervention will be aimed at preventing it from occurring. The logic in both cases is obvious: the prevention of serious harm is a higher priority than gathering material to prosecute those involved after the event. Where such interventions are made, investigators will try to maximise the gathering of material, but this is secondary to preventing the harm. What is significant about such cases is that the disruption occurs in response to a specific threat; in the absence of such a threat investigators would have sought to bring the offenders to justice.

The second way in which disruption is used differs from the first because disruption, rather than bringing offenders to justice, is the object from the outset. Disruption of this type arises from the difficulty of gathering material to mount a prosecution against many of those involved in organised crime or terrorism. The types of outcome that will lead to significant disruption of organised crime networks are more difficult to identify than the type of tactical interventions that will prevent a specific harm. For example, interdicting a drugs shipment makes sense where it is possible to do so, but it is unlikely to cause major disruption to a trafficking network. Those involved expect to lose a proportion of their drugs in this way and price them to reflect the risk. Bringing members of the network to justice on the grounds that this will disrupt the remainder may be viable, but differs little from the conventional outcome sought through criminal investigation and so hardly merits being described as an outcome in its own right. Seizing the assets of those involved in organised crime is often proposed as a method of disrupting their criminal activity, but much of the legislation which enables this to be done requires a conviction for some offence before the assets can be seized and so can properly be thought of as an ancillary measure to bringing offenders to justice, and is considered separately below. The difficulty of identifying the specific measures that may serve to disrupt organised criminals does not negate the value of the approach; it simply reflects the lack of research into this particular outcome. What is important to note at this point is simply that criminal investigations may be carried out for the purpose of disruption rather than bringing offenders to justice.

Asset recovery

Like disruption techniques, asset recovery is primarily aimed at those who are involved in terrorism or organised crime. It involves identifying the assets that criminals have accumulated through crime and using various legal instruments contained in the Proceeds of Crime Act 2002 (POCA) to recover them. The origin of this strategy is the belief that some criminal will be discouraged from committing crime if there are no financial profits involved. Many also believe that there is a moral imperative to ensure that criminals do not benefit from their crimes and asset recovery is aimed at this end.

Kidnap, extortion and hostage negotiation

Resolving situations where someone has been kidnapped and is being held for ransom, or where individuals or companies are being subject to extortion to stop an offender from doing some harm such as contaminating products or releasing damaging information (often called blackmail), or where individuals are being held hostage by terrorists for political reasons, all require the skills of criminal investigation. The outcome that is desired in such cases is principally the safe release of the individuals or the reduction of the harm that will result from the product contamination or the release of the information. In such cases, investigators will try to establish a channel of communication with the offenders to negotiate a safe outcome and will endeavour at the same time to carry out investigations to identify them and gather evidence to bring them to justice. Offences of this type are rare and this is a highly specialised area of criminal investigation. As a consequence, few practitioners will become directly involved in such cases, but the safe resolution of kidnap and extortion crimes, together with the safe release of hostages, is an outcome of the criminal investigation process.

Intelligence gathering

The National Intelligence Model (NIM) is the business process used by all police forces to gather and analyse information that is then used for a wide variety of purposes around business planning, crime reduction initiative and criminal investigation. The effectiveness of the NIM depends on the quality of information fed into police intelligence systems, and in most cases this is a by-product of criminal investigations. For example, crime reports provide a detailed picture of offending patterns in particular locations and enables patrol patterns for officers to be decided. In some cases investigations are carried out for the specific purpose of developing police knowledge of specific people or types of offending and this is often referred to as 'operational intelligence'. Whether done for business planning or to gain operational intelligence, providing information for intelligence purposes is now a key objective of criminal investigation.

Objectives of the law and ethics

Criminal investigation has a wide range of strategic objectives, and in any given case investigators will have to make choices about which of these outcomes has priority. What all of them have in common is that they require investigators to use the techniques of criminal investigation described in Chapter 5 to locate, gather and use information to achieve the particular objective being sought. This has to occur within the legal framework that governs the gathering of material and the treatment of individuals. Investigators cannot ignore the law simply because they have selected an outcome that will not involve bringing an offender to justice. For example, they cannot mount an operation to interdict a shipment of drugs with the object of disrupting a criminal network, and work outside of the legislation on the grounds that they have no intention of prosecuting anyone. Similarly, when dealing with victims and communities, they must ensure that they deal with the release of information about an investigation in ways that will not jeopardise a fair trial of someone in the future, even if at that moment they have no suspect and their main objective is calming public anxiety about a crime.

For historical reasons that will be examined in more detail in Chapter 2, the rational underlying criminal investigation has always been that of bringing offenders to justice. In some locations, at some times and for some types of offences, the statistical probability of this occurring has been very low, but it had important implications for the oversight of the investigative process. This is because investigators had to meet standards that would stand scrutiny in court. They may not have always achieved this and on occasions some may have taken the decision to circumvent these standards, but they were nonetheless real and had an important effect on the way investigations were carried out. This was because the oversight that the judiciary gave to the cases that went before them influenced the way in which every crime was investigated. The increasing use of methods of disposal and objectives that do not involve courts means that bringing offenders to justice has diminished as an underpinning rationale for the conduct of investigations. Some cases do still get to court, but it is now one option among a number. These developments have not been accompanied by the adoption of any independent alternative to judicial oversight and so there is a heavy reliance on the internal quality control mechanisms of the police and the integrity of individual investigators. Oversight arrangements are examined in Chapter 7.

In relation to individual integrity, the police service has adopted a number of ethical standards to guide investigators. The first is the *Police Service Statement of Common Purpose*, which lays down a number of basic principles that apply to all police officers. This states that the purpose of the police service is to:

- uphold the law fairly and firmly;
- prevent crime;
- pursue and bring to justice those who break the law;
- keep the Queen's Peace;

- protect, help and reassure the community;
- be seen to do this with integrity, common sense and sound judgement.

An additional ethical framework for investigators is provided by ACPO's *Core Investigative Doctrine* (2005), which states that:

- when a crime is reported, or it is suspected that one may have been committed, investigators should conduct an effective investigation;
- the exercise of legal powers should not be oppressive and should be proportionate to the crime under investigation;
- as far as operationally practical and having due regard to an individual's right to confidentiality, investigations should be carried out as transparently as possible; in particular, victims, witnesses and suspects should be kept updated with developments in the case;
- investigators should take all reasonable steps to understand the particular needs of individuals including their culture, religious beliefs, ethnic origin, sexuality, disability or lifestyle, see 3.11 Race Relations (Amendment) Act 2000;
- investigators should have particular regard for vulnerable adults and children;
- investigators should respect the professional ethics of others. This is particularly important when working with those whose role it is to support suspects.

One of the objectives of investigative practice is to equip investigators with the knowledge, skills and understanding they need to carry out investigations to the highest possible standards and to make choices about the objectives that are being pursued and the method of disposing of cases that are driven by considerations of the public good rather than expediency.

Conclusion

Crime presents society with a set of complex problems which it seeks to address through the criminal justice system. Criminal investigation plays an important role within this system, but the range of objectives it seeks to achieve is wider than simply bringing offenders to justice. It also provides care for victims and witnesses, reassurance for communities and contributes to the reduction of crime and the management of many of the risks society faces as a consequence of criminal behaviour. This is entirely consistent with the wider social role played by the police service in the UK, which seeks to achieve its objectives through a range of measures, only one of which is the enforcement of the law.

The original aims of policing were to prevent crime and disorder through police patrols, which were nothing more than an institutionalised version of the citizen watch systems that they replaced. As such, patrolling police officers needed no additional powers, and indeed, for a long time it was believed that to give them specific law enforcement powers would in some way undermine their relationship with the communities they served. This led the police to work with communities and other agencies to identify how social control could be achieved in ways that are acceptable to the majority of the community and the doctrine of policing by consent became a key feature of this style of policing. Law enforcement, on the other hand, suggests an approach to achieving social control only through the enforcement of the law. The investigative practice that is developing can be seen to be in the tradition of policing by consent. The achievement of the range of outcomes discussed in this chapter depends on the active participation of individuals as well as the competence of investigators. Investigative practice seeks to equip investigators with the skills, knowledge and understanding they need to work effectively in this complex environment. Although developing in the tradition of policing, investigative practice is a far cry from the traditional concept of the omni-competent constables, and Chapter 2 explores in more detail how this change came about.

Further reading

The role that the police play in society and the organisation and governance of police forces has been extensively studied. A key text is R. Reiner, *The Politics of the Police* (3rd edn, Oxford: Oxford University Press, 2000), which deals with the history, sociology and politics of the police in England and Wales. A. Wright, *Policing: An Introduction to Concepts and Practice* (Cullompton: Willan Publishing, 2002) examines policing through its key functions, including criminal investigation.

T. Newburn (2008) *Handbook of Policing* (2nd edn, Cullompton: Willan Publishing, 2008), covers a range of subjects relevant to policing in general. Part IV is particularly useful to those interested in the many critical debates about the police and policing. T. Newburn, T. Williamson and A. Wright, *Handbook of Criminal Investigation* (Cullompton: Willan Publishing, 2007) provides in-depth coverage of the field of criminal investigation. T. Newburn and P. Neyroud, *Dictionary of Policing* (Cullompton: Willan Publishing, 2008) is an excellent source of short summaries of many of the key features, functions and issues relating to policing in general, and a large proportion of the entries relate specifically to criminal investigation.

Crime as a social phenomenon has been extensively researched in the criminological literature. An excellent introduction is provided by M. Maguire, R. Morgan and R. Reiner, *The Oxford Handbook of Criminology* (4th edn, Oxford: Oxford University Press, 2007), which gives an overview of many of the key topics and, in Section Four, some of the forms that crime takes. E. McLaughlin, J. Munchie and G. Hughes, *Criminological Perspectives: Essential Readings* (2nd edn, London: Sage, 2003) is a good source for the various theories on why people commit crime as well as the forms it takes and society's response to it. These sources should enable practitioners to identify further works in the particular crime types or communities within which they are working. The range of crime types and the extent of the criminological literature makes it impossible to provide a representative sample of what is available here. However, F. Brookman, (2005) *Understanding Homicide* (London: Sage, 2005) and D. Hobbs, *Doing the Business: Entrepreneurship, Detectives and the Working Class in the East End of London* (Oxford: Clarendon Press, 1988) together with D. Hobbs, *Bad Business* (Oxford: Oxford University Press, 1995), are examples of the type of criminological studies that investigators should be familiar with. They provide valuable insights into crime, the communities and circumstances in which it occurs and the individuals involved as offenders, victims and witnesses.

The criminal justice system is explored in P. Joyce, *Criminal Justice: An Introduction to Crime and the Criminal Justice System* (Cullompton: Willan Publishing, 2006), and all the agencies involved have their own websites which are good sources of information. The three tripartite partners to policing have websites that provide information on their structure, geographical area and policies. The Home Office website can be found at www.homeoffice.gov.uk. Individual police force and police authorities each have their own websites.

Chapter 2

The development of investigative practice

Introduction

The police service has only recently recognised that the investigation of crime requires a distinct occupational practice. Of course, those responsible for the investigation of crime have always had a practice in the sense that they have used their knowledge, skills and understanding of crime and its investigation to carry out their role. But there was never common agreement about what this practice consisted of and it was not documented in ways that enabled practitioners to be trained and accredited in it. It was more like a craft, which was passed down from practitioner to practitioner, and shot through with individual and local variation. This is not to say that it was necessarily ineffective. Far from it; there is plenty of evidence that it could be very effective and highly responsive to local needs. But the practice of criminal investigation and the training and accreditation of investigators has become more standardised over time and the police service is seeking to put it on a more professional footing. This chapter sets contemporary developments in investigative practice in the context of the longer-term role that criminal investigation has played in the police service.

The starting point is the century immediately before 1856, which was the year when it became compulsory for every town to have a professional police force. During that century, the investigation of crime and the instigation of prosecutions was a matter for individual victims. Policing, where it was done at all, was a separate, civic function, carried out for the benefit of the whole community. The

27

development of police forces brought these two functions under the control of chief constables, who took over responsibility for the investigation of crime and the prosecution of offenders. The professional model that developed to carry out these two key functions was the omni-competent constable. This individual could carry out all the functions of the police service equally well. These functions were wide-ranging and included, among many others, patrolling a beat, dealing with traffic incidents, investigating crime and policing sporting events. This model persisted until very recently, when legal and social changes highlighted the need for a more professional approach to the investigation of crime.

The development of investigative practice

The historical perspective

Reiner (2000: 1) has noted that the concept of 'the police' and the functions that they perform are so familiar that we take them for granted. It seems obvious now that the police service should be responsible for carrying out criminal investigations and for developing investigative practice. But it was not always the case. There is no general history of the development of investigative practice in the United Kingdom, although many works on the history of criminal law and the police organisation touch on relevant issues. A key period in the development of investigative practice is the century between 1750, the year in which the Bow Street Runners were established, and 1856, when the County and Borough Police Act made it compulsory for all areas of England and Wales to have a police force. These years saw the transition from a system of justice where the responsibility for investigating crime and prosecuting offenders lay with individual victims, to one where publicly funded police forces received reports of crime, carried out investigations and brought offenders to justice.

At the beginning of this period the public officials most closely associated with responding to crime were Justices of the Peace. These were the local representatives of the Crown who were empowered to enquire into crimes committed in their area. This was a judicial function, carried out in a court, and lacked any formal administrative system for making enquiries into crimes that were not already detected. Justices of the Peace could hear allegations of crime and could try some lesser offences themselves or send more serious cases to be heard by a judge. How they discharged these duties was very much a matter for them and the degree of assistance a victim could expect following a crime, together with the effectiveness of the investigation process, differed from area to area.

Some Justices of the Peace appear to have been relatively passive and to have simply tried those cases that were brought before them by victims who already knew the identity of the offender. In such cases they could issue arrest warrants and could hear the testimony of all parties before deciding whether to deal with the case themselves or to send it to a higher court. Others appear to have been a lot more proactive and to have undertaken, or at least directed, investigations into crimes that were reported to them. In doing this they were supported by a range of officials, the nature of which varied according to local tradition. Some of these officials were paid, while others were performing unpaid civic functions.

In addition to the formal posts associated with criminal investigation, there developed a group of individuals who earned a living by acting independently of the courts to assist victims in the investigation of crime and the recovery of property. Where they were involved in prosecutions, they also benefited from the fees that courts paid as part of the prosecution process. These individuals were generally known as 'thief takers' and had a pretty poor reputation because many were undoubtedly corrupt. They staged thefts to charge a fee for recovering the stolen property and gave perjured evidence to earn court fees. But Emsley (1996: 19) notes that some were effective and could have been better than any of the available alternatives.

As a consequence of these arrangements, the efficiency of criminal investigation varied considerably. In some places it was reported to be effective, but in the towns and cities, particularly London, it was considered to be poor. Detection rested to a large extent on whether the victim knew the identity of the offender or could discover it themselves. Furthermore, prosecution could be expensive and inconvenient and so, even when a crime was detected, victims often settled for the recovery of their goods or other forms of reparation rather than taking the matter to court.

The best-known example of effective local action by a Justice of the Peace is the establishment in 1750 of the Bow Street Runners by Henry Fielding. Fielding was an early advocate of improved arrangements for controlling crime, which included full-time paid officials, the centralisation of records and the publication of information that would lead to the detection and apprehension of offenders. Fielding was what was known at the time as a 'trading justice', that is, he lived mainly from the fees he earned as a Justice of the Peace, and the Bow Street Runners were professional 'thief takers'. Thus, the Bow Street Runners present an early example of a full-time, professional body concerned with the investigation of crime.

Running alongside these arrangements for the investigation of crime and the prosecution of offenders were the equally varied civic functions that were concerned with preventative patrol and watch-keeping. These had been organised by communities for centuries and involved posts such as constables, beagles and watchmen, although the titles varied over time and in different locations. The functions they performed also varied: some, such as the night watch, were essentially what we would today describe as security guards, while others had a range of functions from apprehending known offenders to administering local arrangements for poor relief. Those involved in these civic functions inevitably became involved in criminal investigation because they had crimes reported to them or were on hand to help victims of crimes that had just occurred. Many were also under the direction of the local Justice of the Peace and so were available to assist them if required.

There was, therefore, a very close relationship between the civic functions aimed at safeguarding communities and the private functions of the investigation and prosecution of crime, but there were also significant differences. The first was a local government issue aimed at protection and administering local regulations; the second was a private matter aimed at justice and restoration. While there were overlaps between the two, it was not inevitable that they should have eventually come together under the umbrella of single organisations. For example, the Bow Street Runners and the Metropolitan Police coexisted for ten years carrying out their different functions and could have continued to do so as separate organisations. But, during the century between the formation of the Bow Street Runners and the passing of the County and Borough Police Act 1856 these various strands of local criminal investigation and patrol functions coalesced into police forces. As they did so, the many types of local official who had previously been involved in them were absorbed into the new police forces and all became constables under the direction of a chief constable. As part of their overall objective of suppressing crime, chief constables assumed responsibility for receiving reports of crime and carrying out investigations independently of Justices of the Peace. The role of Justices of the Peace became confined to hearing allegations against offenders once they had been detected.

These developments did not happen overnight and there was much experiment and local variation along the way. The Thames River Police were established in 1798; in June 1829, the Cheshire Police Act enabled the employment of professional constables in the county; and later that same month the Metropolitan Police Act authorised the establishment of a professional police force in parts of London. The Parish Constables Act of 1842 made it compulsory for all areas to maintain a list of those eligible for duty as constables and made provision for their payment and supervision. By 1856, there was sufficient confidence that locally managed police forces could effectively respond to crime and deliver a range of other local services that the government made it compulsory for all local authorities to establish one. There was no single model by which they did this. Many, perhaps the majority, simply built on what already existed and appointed a chief constable to manage the force. Many of these were men with a military background or were professional police officers with experience in another force and the Royal Irish Constabulary together with the Metropolitan Police were popular, but by no means exclusive, recruiting grounds for senior officers.

This model of police forces led by a chief constable under local political control set the pattern of policing that continues to the present. As criminal investigation and prosecution passed from being an essentially private issue to an administrative process, police forces established procedures for receiving reports of crime, for instigating investigations and for mounting prosecutions. Over time, investigators developed improved knowledge about how this system could be used to investigate crime and developed improved techniques for gathering material. In short, investigative practice developed. This did not happen all at once and was not the result of a conscious decision on the part of the police service. Investigative practice evolved slowly, and because of the local nature of policing in the UK, different ways of approaching the problems presented by criminal investigation developed in different forces. The developments that took place in the century before 1856 are important to our understanding of investigative practice because it was during this period that criminal investigation became embedded in the wider police function.

In thinking about these developments, it is important to make a distinction between the development of investigative practice, which all police officers use because they come into contact with crime on a routine basis, and the development of Criminal Investigation Departments (CID), which are a sub-set of police officers who specialise in criminal investigation. From its formulation in 1829, the Metropolitan Police sought to control crime through the use of uniformed officers patrolling the streets and did not establish a Detective Branch until 1842. There is little information about the working practice of other forces, but it seems certain that officers in police forces throughout the country were involved in criminal investigation from the outset. For many this would simply have been a continuation of what they previously did before they were called a police force. The formal adoption of criminal investigation as a technique of crime control therefore predates the establishment of a Criminal Investigation Department in any force.

The omni-competent constable

Although criminal investigation was a feature of policing from the outset, it was not viewed as an activity that was sufficiently distinct from general policing to require a separate professional practice. The police role in general was not considered to be complex (Dale 1994: 211). It was thought to require the application of a common-sense approach to the wide range of situations that the police were faced with, but little specialist ability. The model was that of the 'omni-competent' constable who was able to deal with all policing problems equally well and criminal investigation had no special status within this range of problems.

The model of the omni-competent constable was supported by the fact that, until relatively recently, the process of criminal investigation was not subject to specific legislation. The view of the police as 'citizens in uniform', who had few powers above and beyond those available to any member of the community, meant that the role of the police in investigating crime was poorly defined by legislation simply because their role in general was not regarded as being legally distinct. The position was summarised in the report of the 1929 Royal Commission on Police Powers: 'The police of this country have never been recognised, either in law or by tradition, as a force distinct from the general body of citizens' (quoted in Hitchens 2003: 51). In carrying out a criminal investigation and presenting evidence to courts, the police were being paid to do what, in theory at least, anyone could have done and so they required little specialist knowledge to do it. The regulation that did exist was not difficult to understand or apply and the consequences of non-compliance were negligible for the individual officer.

The view that the investigation of crime required few skills additional to those of policing in general was reinforced by research carried out in the late 1970s and early 1980s. This showed that as a general rule crimes are solved because members of the public supply the police with the necessary information during the early stages of the investigation. Where this information is not available, it is unlikely that the crime will be detected by additional police activity (in the UK, Zander 1979; Steer 1980; Bottomley and Coleman 1981; Banton 1985; Burrows and Tarling 1987; in the US, Greenwood *et al.* 1977; Eck 1982). The implication usually drawn from these studies is that because detections are primarily determined by the willingness of the public to pass information to the police, changes in police activity or an increase in resources make little difference (Burrows and Tarling 1982: 14).

As a consequence of the above, the police service did not develop a separate professional practice of criminal investigation that could be taught to officers. Some work was done by individuals, usually located in force training schools, but this was un-coordinated and was not subject to any formal evaluation to ensure its quality. Even where training was provided, it did not lead to any specific qualification by which individuals could demonstrate competence.

The drivers for change

There appear to be three main reasons why criminal investigation has now come to be seen by the police service as an activity that requires its own professional practice. These are:

- Changes to the legal framework of criminal investigation
- Technological and procedural changes to the investigation process
- Concerns over police effectiveness and conduct in criminal investigation.

None of these factors have occurred in isolation and they sit in a complex relationship to each other. For example, changes to the legal framework were largely influenced by concerns over police effectiveness in investigating major crime, which arose from a series of miscarriages of justice, and many technological and procedural changes were driven by a desire to improve effectiveness. However, these three headings provide a convenient way to discuss the range of factors involved.

Changes to the legal framework of criminal investigation

A series of miscarriages of justice were uncovered during the 1970s and 1980s, and the two subsequent Royal Commissions they gave rise to triggered a series of legislative changes to the process of criminal investigation. These were aimed at defining the rights of suspects and others, delimiting the powers of the police and assuring the quality of evidence through procedural compliance. A consequence of these developments was to introduce a specialist body of law which has to be mastered before criminal investigations can be conducted with any competence. The main legislative changes and the affect they have on the criminal investigation process are shown in Table 2.1.

Taken together, these developments clearly envisage the role of criminal investigation as one of gathering material about the crime in a non-partisan, inquisitorial way and making it available to both the prosecution and the defence, who argue the case according to the adversarial procedures of a criminal trial. The overall effect has been to create a complex legal framework within which investigations are carried out. As a result, when the police are investigating crime they no longer have the role of 'citizens in uniform', exercising a general

Table 2.1 Legislative changes to criminal investigation

Date	Legislation	Change to the investigation process
1984	Police and Criminal Evidence Act (PACE)	Defined police powers, laid down investigative procedures and defined suspects and others' rights.
1985	Prosecution of Offences Act	Established the Crown Prosecution Service to take over responsibility for prosecution from the police.
1996	Criminal Procedure and Investigation Act (CPIA)	Provided a legal definition of criminal investigation and the role of investigator. Placed a duty on investigators to investigate impartially. Provided statutory disclosure process.
2000	Regulation of Investigatory Powers Act (RIPA)	Defined processes of investigation and placed them within a regulatory regime.
2003	Criminal Justice Act	Gave the Crown Prosecution Service responsibility for selecting charges (they previously reviewed police charges).

set of duties and responsibilities that apply to all members of society. They are now implementing an investigative process that has been designed specifically with them in mind.

Technical and procedural changes to the investigation process

Developments in DNA and other forensic techniques, the availability of material from CCTV cameras, telephone data, automatic number plate recognition, internet traffic, improved intelligence analysis: all these and more provide investigators with sources of material that their predecessors could only dream of. Furthermore, developments in legislation, such as those covering the right to silence contained in the Criminal Justice and Public Order Act 1994, also mean that older techniques, such as interviewing suspects, are now a richer source of material. These developments require investigators to expand the range of investigative techniques they are able to use in order to fully exploit the possibilities that are open to them.

There has also been a growth in the number of specialists involved in criminal investigation and it is now likely that even in the most straightforward of cases investigators will have to co-ordinate the work of a range of specialists such as crime scene examiners, forensic scientists and intelligence analysts. In more complex cases, the list of specialists and experts may be considerable. Investigators must know what specialists are available to them, how they can contribute to the investigation, what information is required to deploy them and how to use the material they provide. They must also have the management skills necessary to co-ordinate the work of all the specialists used in the investigation.

Concerns over police effectiveness in investigation

The third factor that has helped to define the need for a professional practice of criminal investigation is concern over police effectiveness in the investigation of both major crime and volume crime. The investigation of major crimes, such as murder, are seen by the public as an index of police competence overall (Innes 2003: 276). It is also seen within the police service as a model for the way in which other investigations should be conducted. Her Majesty's Inspector of Constabulary (HMIC 2000: 115) has stated that 'the investigation of murder should set clear standards of excellence that all other criminal investigation can follow'. But the police have not always succeeded in living up to public expectations or their own aspirations in this area. Corruption scandals, miscarriages of justice and organisational and individual blunders have occurred in major crime investigation throughout the history of the police service (Maguire 2003: 375). These failures are generally followed by the introduction of new procedures aimed at ensuring that they do not re-occur.

There is, however, a growing realisation that the service's best defence against failure in investigation lies not just in the introduction of such procedural measures, but also requires improving the skills of investigators. This is because the high level of variation in the way in which individual crimes are committed makes it difficult for the police organisation to lay down hard and fast rules about the type of activity that may be effective in any given case. Investigators must adapt to the unique circumstances that each case presents them with. This means that they must be competent in the techniques of criminal investigation and have experience in applying them to a wide range of cases. Management structures and procedures do, of course, need to be adequate and Bowling and Phillips (2002: 155) make the valuable point that often too little attention is paid to them when seeking to understand the outcomes of police work, particularly adverse outcomes such as racism. However, the competence of investigators is a key determinant in the success of criminal investigation. The police service has already identified that there is a lack of senior detectives with the necessary skills to carry out the role of senior investigating officers (SIO) in more serious crimes (Flannery 2004: 26) and making improvements in this area was one of the original drivers behind the professionalisation of criminal investigation, which is discussed in more detail below.

In addition to its role in relation to major crime, criminal investigation is also viewed as an important element in the drive to reduce crime in general: 'Detecting, convicting and punishing criminals appropriately are at the heart of long-term crime reduction' (Home Office 2001: 17). But Her Majesty's Inspector of Constabulary (HMIC) (Flannery 2004: 26) found that in some areas there was a lack of adequate investigative skills among patrol officers. The same report also found that their managers did not understand the processes of investigation either and did not check that the routine procedures of investigation were carried out adequately. Addressing these shortcomings has been one of the key drivers for change in investigative practice.

Changes to the legislative framework of criminal investigation, developments in the techniques and procedures used to carry them out and concerns over the effectiveness of criminal investigation have, between them, served to identify criminal investigation as an area of policing that requires the development of a professional practice which can be taught to investigators and against which they can be tested. As HMIC (2004: 173) has noted:

> Policing is now highly complex and spans a massive spectrum of activities requiring a similarly extensive range of skills and competencies in those taking up the challenge. The omni-competent officer has been a traditional icon and supposed mainstay of the service. It is debatable whether effective omni-competence has ever actually been achieved but it is now abundantly clear that such an aim is no longer viable, or indeed appropriate, for 21st century policing needs.

The Professionalising Investigation Programme (PIP)

The recognition that investigative practice needed to change in response to these drivers led, in September 2005, to the Association of Chief Police Officers of England, Wales and Northern Ireland[1] (ACPO) launching a national training and development programme intended 'to enhance the crime investigation skills and ability of police officers and staff involved in the investigative process and to drive through new standards of investigation at all levels' (NCPE 2005: 1).

The term 'professionalising' appears to have been deliberately chosen by those designing PIP to signal that it intended to bring about improvements in criminal investigation through training and development rather than through alternative strategies, such as re-engineering business processes or improving management systems. While there is little agreement in the general literature on the meaning of terms such as 'professional', or the attributes that define a particular occupation group as a profession (Beckley 2004: 92), the term professionalisation is widely used within the police service as shorthand for improved training and development (Perrier 1978: 212, Allgood 1984: 676, Small 1991: 315, Phillips 2003: 5) and it is in this sense that it is used by those designing PIP.

The training of investigators, like most police training, had been based on a craft model where officers receive some basic formal training but learn the majority of what they knew 'on the job'. In addition, and possibly because of the above, the police service never formally examined the competence of investigators against an objective standard. Judgements about competence were generally made by line supervisors based on their experience of working with the individual, usually once a year during formal performance appraisal. This system was heavily reliant on the experience of the individual supervisor who may have had difficulty in explaining the standards they use.

PIP addressed these shortcomings by providing a cradle to grave training curriculum for investigators that takes them from the basic levels of investigation through to the most complex. The PIP programme focuses on the qualities of investigators at three levels, as shown in Table 2.2.

All police officers attend the Initial Police Learning and Development Programme (IPLDP), which is developed for the service as a whole but delivered by individual forces, sometimes in conjunction with a local university. The full programme takes two years to complete and consists of formal classroom-based training and work experience. The latter is gained on a BCU, in the company of a tutor constable who will patrol with the officer and instruct them on the practical application of a range of policing skills, including criminal investigation. In the latter part of their training they carry out independent patrol to gain experience of dealing with cases on their own.

They will then be subject to independent assessment against the National Occupational Standards (NOS). NOS have been developed by Skills for Justice, an organisation funded by the government to identify learning needs in criminal justice organisations and to link

Table 2.2 PIP investigative levels

Investigative level	Example role	Description of typical investigative activity
Level 1	Patrol constable/Police Staff/Supervisors	Investigation of anti-social behaviour and volume crime.
Level 2	Dedicated investigator, e.g. CID officer Specialist investigative roles,	Investigation into more serious and problem offences including road traffic deaths.
	e.g. Child abuse investigation, Special Branch, Family Liaison, Major Crime	Child abuse investigations, Special Branch, Family Liaison, Force Intelligence Bureau.
Level 3	Senior Investigating Officer	Lead investigator in cases of murder, stranger rape, kidnap or complex crimes.

Source: NCPE 2005: 1.

these to qualifications. The NOS describe competent performance in relation to the outcomes of investigations and the knowledge, skills and understanding investigators need to perform effectively. They, therefore, provide a benchmark against which an individual investigator's competence to practise can be tested. Assessment has three elements: competent performance of investigations against the NOS; proving the required level of understanding of the specialist knowledge of criminal investigation; and demonstrating appropriate core behaviours, including community relationships and diversity (NCPE 2005: 10). Investigators undergo periodic reassessment and mechanisms exist to suspend the registration of those who are found not to be competent.

Following initial training and development, officers may receive a range of training in specific aspects of criminal investigation, for example surveillance training, exhibit handling and so on. The training specifically associated with the three levels of PIP is shown in Table 2.3.

PIP is aimed at ensuring that the professional practice of criminal investigation being developed by the service is backed up by a training and development programme and, perhaps most importantly, by a means of assessing the competence of investigators.

Developing investigative practice

The professionalisation of investigation is dependent on an authoritative investigative practice that forms the basis of training, continued professional development and accreditation. Professional practice is usually developed by bodies that are independent of those who employ individual practitioners. The result of this arrangement is that practices can be developed that are in the best interest of clients and the public good rather than in the best interests of the employers, who may be more interested in issues of profitability, productivity or minimising expenditure in training rather than the maintenance of professional standards. Table 2.4 lists some of these professions with the bodies that develop their professional practice.

This division between the bodies that develop professional practice and employers has not always been seen in a positive light. The claim of professionals to know what is right for customers has been increasingly questioned (Exworthy and Halford 1999: 5) and professional bodies have sometimes been seen to be more concerned

Table 2.3 PIP training

Course	Summary
PIP Level 1	
Initial Police Learning and Development Programme (IPLDP)	The basic training course that all police officers go through and it forms the basis of their accreditation to PIP Level 1.
Sexual Offences – Specially Trained Officer Development Programme (STODP)	Provides training for those involved in the initial response to sexual offences and the interview of complainants in such cases.
Investigative Interviewing for Volume and Priority Investigations	Provides enhanced training in investigative interviewing techniques for officers investigating crime at PIP Level 1.
PIP Level 2	
Initial Crime Investigators Development Programme (ICIDP)	The basic training course for all police officers who carry out investigations at PIP Level 2.
Initial Management of Serious Crime (IMSC)	Aimed at supervisors who manage the initial response to serious crime incidents.
Detective Inspectors Development Programme (DIDP)	Trains officers to conduct complex investigations at PIP Level 2 and to manage others during such investigations.
Specialist Child Abuse Investigator Development Programme (SCAIDP)	Trains those involved in the investigation of child abuse.
Family Liaison Officer (Major Crime and Mass Fatality)	Trains those who are carrying out the role of family liaison officer in homicide and other incidents involving the loss of life.
Investigative Interviewing for Serious and Complex Investigations	Develops investigators' abilities in investigative interviewing.
Managing and Co-ordinating Interviews for Complex or Major Investigations Interview Advisor Development Programme	Aimed at those managing others involved in investigative interviewing in complex investigations or who are advising SIOs in such cases.
PIP Level 3	
Senior Investigating Officers Development Programme (SIODP)	This programme provides training for those who will be leading homicide and major incident investigations.

Table 2.4 Professions and professional bodies

Profession	Professional body
Medical Doctors	General Medical Council
Chartered Accountants	Association of Chartered Certified Accountants
Nurses	Nursing and Midwifery Council
Social Workers	General Social Care Council
Solicitors	Law Society
Barristers	General Council for the Bar
Psychologists	British Psychological Society

with protecting their professional position than serving the public good (Flynn 1999: 19).

The police service has no single body that defines professional practice independently of chief constables or the Home Office. Prior to 2007, the most common way in which practice was developed for the service was through working groups of ACPO, through research commissioned by the Home Office or through the efforts of individual forces. In addition, a range of bodies including Her Majesty's Inspector of Constabulary (HMIC), the Policing Standards Unit (PSU) and others, developed professional practice for areas of policing within their remit. In many cases these organisations had no full-time staff dedicated to the role and so it was done by working groups of individuals in addition to their other duties. Despite the difficulties, a great deal of policy, guidance and advice for practitioners was produced. Examples include the *Murder Investigation Manual*, first published by the ACPO Homicide Working Group in 1998, *Vulnerable Witnesses: A Police Service Guide*, produced by the Home Office in 2001 and *Domestic Burglary: National Good Practice and Tactical Options Guide*, published by the Policing Standards Unit in 2003.

In 2007, the Home Office brought together a range of the national agencies that played a role in supporting policing into the National Policing Improvement Agency (NPIA). One of NPIA's responsibilities is the production of professional practice for the police service and this is accomplished within its Professional Practice Unit. Within this unit, there is team responsible for the development of investigative practice. The NPIA Investigative Practice Team adopted the definition of investigative practice contained in the Core Investigative Doctrine, which is the knowledge, techniques and understanding that investigators require to carry out their role, and this is explored further below.

Knowledge

The knowledge required for professional practice is generally produced by an academic community with strong links to practitioners and is contained in a professional literature. In the case of criminal investigation, this should contain all the knowledge investigators need to make sense of the wide variety of situations they are presented with (Ormerod *et al.* 2005: 1) and should draw on a diverse academic literature. Despite the central role that investigative practice plays in delivering the police service's strategic aims, investigators have a relatively modest professional literature and there is a pressing need to develop it further. Such academic research as there has been has focused on a narrow band of issues with a limited methodological palette and few studies have focused on the knowledge, skills and experience that investigators require to carry out their role.

In describing what she calls 'crime science', Laycock (2005: 6) draws an analogy with the medical profession, which uses the disciplines of chemistry, biology, physics, epidemiology and biochemistry to provide a body of knowledge described as 'medical science'. A literature for investigators is likely to be equally multi-disciplinary and will include the criminal law, psychology, the forensic sciences, sociology, criminology, operations management and media, among others. The ways in which various disciplines could contribute to investigative practice are shown in Table 2.5.

In order to study criminal investigation in the round, it is necessary to draw on all the above disciplines. But studies of investigative practice are still relatively rare, with the exception of investigative interviewing where there is an active group of practitioners and academics which promotes research and develops practice. Research, such as that by Milne and Bull (1999) and Bull and Milne (2004) has been developed into practice in the ACPO *Investigative Interview Strategy* (2001) and guidance for practitioners in the *Practical Guide to Investigative Interviewing* (2003). There are now national training courses in investigative interviewing and an ongoing programme of evaluation of the effectiveness of the technique. Those involved in these developments believe that the key to success has been the existence of a national infrastructure under the leadership of the ACPO National Investigative Interviewing Strategic Steering Group, which is supported by regional co-ordinators and lead officers within each force. The work done by this group provides a model of what can be achieved in relation to investigative principles, but it remains the exception rather than the rule.

Table 2.5 Academic disciplines relevant to criminal investigation

Discipline	Contribution
Law	Interpretation of the criminal law and legal practice.
Psychology	The behaviour of offenders, witnesses and groups affected by crime. Particular sub-disciplines are: • Investigative interviewing • Behavioural sciences • Investigative decision-making
Criminology	An understanding of why crime occurs and the way in which society responds to it. Analysis of crime trends.
Criminal justice	How criminal justice agencies work. Particular sub-disciplines are: • Probation • Prison • Police • Court systems
Sociology	The role of policing in society and the way it impacts on communities and individuals.
Media	The way in which policing is portrayed in the media and the way in which the police use the media to achieve various organisational aims.
Management	The application of developments in management to the processes of criminal investigation.
Sciences, Technology and Engineering	The application of scientific, technical and engineering developments to the gathering, analysis and interpretation of material in criminal investigation (often referred to collectively as Forensic Science).
Medicine	The application of medical science to criminal investigation. The two main sub-groups are: • Pathology • Forensic medical examination

Core Investigative Doctrine divides the knowledge required by investigators into three basic areas, each of which has leanings towards different academic disciplines.

Legal knowledge

Investigators are expected to take action to secure relevant material in operational situations when 'they must depend on instinct, habit, or memory, rather than library research' (Davis 2002: 187). In order to do this they need a working knowledge of the legislation that governs the conduct of investigations, together with the main types of offences they are likely to have to investigate. Lack of this knowledge could lead them to take action that is unlawful or to gather material in ways that make it unlikely that it will be accepted as evidence. Of all the areas of knowledge required by investigators, the literature on criminal law is perhaps the most developed and readily accessible. Online access to the Police National Legal Database (PNLD) is available to all officers and there are a number of publications written specifically for them (Wilson 2004, English and Card 2005; Johnston and Hutton 2005). NPIA have also published guides to specific areas that are judged to be problematic, for example:

- ACPO, *Practice Advice on the Use of Immigration Powers Against Crime* (2005)
- ACPO, *Practice Advice on Part 4 of the Anti-social Behaviour Act 2003* (2007)
- ACPO, *Practice Advice on Evidence of Bad Character* (2005).

National and local policies

The local structure of policing and the complexity of its strategic remit led to the development of a great deal of national and local policy. The reasons for producing policy include:

- Ensuring compliance with the law
- Procedural good practice
- Improving service delivery
- Resource management
- Managing inter-agency co-operation.

Many of these policies impact on criminal investigation and so investigators need to know those that are relevant to the type of investigations they are involved in. This enables them to comply with legislation, follow procedure and gain access to the most appropriate resources or level of inter-agency co-operation required to carry out an investigation.

Investigative principles

There is no tradition in the police service of recording the experience of investigators or of analysing the reasons for success or failure (West 2001: 13) As a consequence, empirical research has not focused on comparing and evaluating criminal investigation techniques in ways that would inform the choices made by investigators. Nonetheless, investigative principles are available to them in the ACPO *Core Investigative Doctrine* (2005) and other official manuals, some of which are listed below.

- ACPO, *Practice Advice on Core Investigative Doctrine* (2005)
- ACPO, *Practice Advice on Evidence of Bad Character* (2005)
- ACPO, *Practice Advice on Search Management and Procedures* (2006)
- ACPO, *Practice Advice on Financial Investigation* (2006)
- ACPO, *Practice Advice on House to House Enquiries* (2006)
- ACPO, *Practice Advice on Stop and Search in Relation to the Terrorism Act* (2006)
- ACPO, *Guidance on the Management of Covert Human Intelligence Sources* (2006)
- ACPO, *Practice Advice on The Right to Silence* (2006)
- ACPO, *Practice Advice on Dealing with Legal Advisors* (2006)
- ACPO, *Practice Advice on the Management of Expert Advisors* (2006)
- ACPO, *Practice Advice on Family Liaison* (2008)
- ACPO, *Guidance on the Use and Management of Specialist Surveillance Techniques* (2008)

Skills

The skills that investigators require can be thought of in three groups:

1 *Investigative techniques.* Some of the techniques of criminal investigation, such as forensic examination, are applied by others, but the majority, such as interviewing, searching and viewing CCTV images, can be applied directly by investigators and they need to be skilled in their use. These techniques will be examined in more detail in Chapter 5.

2 *Communication.* As was seen in Chapter 1, crime is essentially about how people behave to each other and within society. Carrying out a criminal investigation is therefore primarily about

dealing with people, and often at times when they are distressed, frightened or angry. Well-developed communication skills are essential if investigators are to gather information from those involved in crimes, whether as victims, witnesses or offenders. Furthermore, the material they gather generally has to be shared with others involved in the investigation process or presented in briefings or to courts, and these activities involve a high degree of communication.

3 *The management of investigations.* A range of management skills are required by investigators. They must manage their caseloads by deciding on priorities and allocating time and resources to achieve them. They must manage the material they gather, making sure that exhibits are correctly labelled and catalogued and that the correct procedures have been followed for storing them. They must task others to carry out various activities associated with the investigation and must integrate their work into the overall effort of the investigation. Finally, they must keep good records of what they have done and why, for their own benefit and that of other investigators who may have to take over the investigation from them, or supervisors who may need to carry out management functions, or courts, which may wish to audit the decisions they have made. Investigators need to be skilled in all these generic management functions to enable them to keep control over the process of investigation.

Understanding

Understanding how to apply the knowledge and skills of investigations to the many situations in which crimes are committed and to the many different people encountered is an essential element of investigative practice. This is not simply a case of maximising the material they gather, it is equally about knowing how and when to exercise discretion and judgement. Investigators' understanding of criminal investigation and how to do it well comes mainly from experience, but official manuals provide guidance to them in various areas. Some examples are listed below.

- ACPO, *Guidance on Investigating Child Abuse and Safeguarding Children* (2005)
- ACPO, *Guidance on Investigating Serious Sexual Offences* (2005)
- ACPO, *Guidance on the Management, Recording and Investigation of Missing Persons* (2005)

- ACPO, *Practice Advice on Investigating Harassment* (2005)
- ACPO, *Murder Investigation Manual* (2006)
- ACPO, *Guidance on Investigating Domestic Abuse* (2008)

Investigators

Since the establishment of the modern police service in 1856, much has changed, including the professional knowledge, skills and understanding required by police officers. But despite this, one thing has remained constant: the importance of uniformed constables to the policing function. The overwhelming majority of all police functions, including criminal investigation, are delivered by uniformed patrol officers, who make up the majority of the workforce. Uniformed officers are organised to provide a twenty-four hours a day patrol function. Their main purpose is to provide a visible uniformed presence in a community and to respond to calls for service from members of the public. Their patrol duties mean that they occasionally come across criminal offences, which require them to initiate an investigation there and then, but it is more common for them to be sent to a crime as the consequence of a report being made by a member of the public to a police call centre. Telephone reports are graded to assess the level of response required, and where this involves police attendance at a scene or to the person making the report, a uniformed patrol officer will be sent. Their role in these cases is to carry out an initial investigation, aimed at gathering any material that is immediately to hand, such as victim and witness accounts and CCTV images and to arranging a crime scene investigation if required. In more serious cases they may call addition resources to the scene and others will take over the investigation from them.

Officers' initial reports are subject to a screening process that is designed to quality assure the initial investigation and make decisions about the level of further investigation required. Many investigations do not progress beyond this stage because it is judged that nothing further of any value can be done. Where additional investigation is required, the case may be sent back to the original officer to complete enquiries, or if they are not available, one of their colleagues. Most reported crime is investigated in this way and uniformed patrol officers spend about 20 per cent of their time on crime-related work such as investigation, processing prisoners and preparing prosecution files (PA Consulting 2001: 14). Although uniformed patrol officers will be involved in the initial response to virtually all types of crime, each police force has its own policy on what type of crime should be allocated to them for follow-up investigation. Typically these will include offences of theft, assault, vehicle crime, damage and burglary, although most forces will allocate such investigations to specialists if considerable harm has been caused to victims or high values are involved.

Where the crime is judged to be serious or complex, the investigation is likely to be allocated to a detective or other specialist investigator. Unlike uniformed patrol officers, who carry out a range of policing functions, the main role of detectives and other specialist investigators is the investigation of crime. There is no definition of a detective within the police service. It has traditionally described those who work in Criminal Investigation Departments (CID) and although some forces now use different titles for such departments, the term detective is still widely used. Generally speaking about 10 per cent of BCU staff will be in the CID. These will be officers with specialist training who investigate those cases that are deemed to be more serious or complex and therefore need a higher level of skill and experience. Sometimes they are also allocated crimes because the cases simply require a greater degree of focus than would be possible for a uniformed patrol officer to provide, given the reactive nature of their role and the fact that they usually work shifts, which often makes it difficult for them to complete enquiries quickly. Whatever the underlying rationale for allocating cases to them, detectives usually carry a mixed caseload of investigations, ranging across crime types and degrees of complexity. Typically this may include serious wounding, sexual offences, other serious or series crimes and investigations involving prolific or persistent offenders. In addition, they will also investigate offences of the type allocated to uniformed patrol officers where there has been considerable harm to a victim or where the value involved is high.

In some forces there will also be investigators on BCUs who specialise in cases of child abuse, domestic violence and hate crime. Such cases require a high level of inter-agency work and training in particular techniques and so it is sometimes deemed necessary to provide specialist units at a local level. In some forces specialist investigation of this sort is provided at a force level. Officers in these roles will generally only be allocated crimes of the relevant type for investigation.

Police forces also maintain a force-wide specialist crime investigation capacity. This generally involves squads of officers who specialise in the investigation of organised crime, fraud, homicide, terrorism, and sometimes child abuse and domestic violence. The size of these squads and the focus of their attention vary from force to force and depend to a large extent on the priority that each force gives to particular types of crime. The reason forces specialise in this way is twofold. Some squads, such as those targeting various types of organised crime and terrorism, are formed because such crimes tend to transcend the limited geographical remit of a BCU. In most cases they also transcend the boundaries of the force, and squads are necessary to provide a capacity that is able to operate over these larger areas. In the case of child abuse and homicide, the reason for having central squads is the degree of specialisation required to carry out the investigation.

In addition to uniformed patrol officers and specialist investigators on BCUs or at the forces level, all forces have a small number of Senior Investigating Officers (SIO) who the ACPO *Murder Investigation Manual* describes as 'the lead investigator in cases of homicide, stranger rape, kidnap or other complex investigations.' It goes on to define the role of the SIO as being to:

- Perform the role of officer in charge of an investigation as described in the Code of Practice under Part II of the Criminal Procedure and Investigations Act 1996;
- Develop and implement the investigative strategy;
- Develop the information management and decision-making systems for the investigation;
- Manage the resources allocated to the investigation;
- Be accountable to chief officers for the conduct of the investigation. (ACPO 2006a: 25)

SIOs are generally of the rank of detective inspector (DI), detective chief inspectors (DCI) or detective superintendent (Det Supt). In most forces, crimes of the type allocated to SIOs are infrequent and so they generally have management responsibility for investigative units and only perform the role of SIO when required. Some larger forces have a sufficient number of serious cases to make it worthwhile having a small number of officers performing the role full-time, although this is still uncommon.

At a national level, police forces seek to co-operate on issues of common interest through collaborative arrangements for the investigation of terrorism and other types of cross-border crime. They sit alongside other national agencies with an independent policing or law enforcement remit, such as:

- British Transport Police (BTP)
- Civil Nuclear Constabulary
- Independent Police Complaints Commission (IPCC)
- Ministry of Defence Police and Guarding Agency
- Serious and Organised Crime Agency (SOCA)
- Serious Fraud Office (SFO)
- Secret Intelligence Services (MI5, MI6 and GCHQ).

These national agencies are supplemented by the in-house criminal investigation departments maintained by many public authorities such as Her Majesty's Revenue and Customs, the Department of Work and Pensions and the military.

Organising investigators

Irrespective of whether investigators are uniformed patrol officers or specialists, or whether they work on BCUs or in force squads, there are three main ways in which they are organised. They can work as single investigators, in squads, or in temporary teams brought together for a single investigation.

Single investigators

Few, if any, investigations rely solely on the actions carried out by one person. As well as the officer in charge of the investigation, others such as crime scene investigators, forensic scientists, financial investigators, analysts, forensic medical examiners and so on, may work on a case. However, responsibility for tasking these resources, interpreting the material they produce and integrating it with what has already been gathered is the responsibility of the officer in charge of the investigation. Section 2.1 of the Code of Practice under Part II of the Criminal Procedure and Investigations Act 1996 defines the officer in charge of an investigation as 'the police officer responsible for directing a criminal investigation. He is also responsible for ensuring that proper procedures are in place for recording information, and retaining records of information and other material in the investigation.' Officers in charge of investigations are often referred to in the police service as investigating officers (IO), or in the case of homicide and other major investigations, senior investigating officers (SIO). They are accountable for the conduct of the investigation and are the key decision-makers who develop the investigative strategy and assess the material gathered during the investigation.

It may be that at different times the case is allocated to different individuals, as would happen if a uniformed patrol officer carried out the initial investigation into a report of a burglary which was later allocated to a detective to carry out further enquiries. What characterises a single investigator enquiry is the fact that although it may pass through a number of hands, one individual at a time is responsible for making the decisions relating to the investigation.

The allocation of a crime to a single investigator is by far the most common way of carrying out a criminal investigation. All types and seriousness of crime are investigated in this way and they involve the use of all types of investigative strategy. As has already been noted, the majority of investigators are uniformed patrol officers who are responding to reports of crime from the public. Only a small percentage of reported crime is allocated to detectives or other specialist investigators. As a consequence, most operational police officers carry a caseload of investigations. Within specialist units it is also customary for managers to carry a caseload and they will tend to have the more complex investigations. Most police officers will therefore have some experience during their career of working on a caseload of single investigator enquiries.

Squads

Squads or permanent teams of investigators are a common feature in most police forces. They provide a way of pooling resources to focus on a particular kind of crime and are of two types. The first is where the squad specialises in a particular type of investigation, but investigators carry individual caseloads. This enables the squad to develop its collective knowledge of particular types of crime and to build networks with other investigators working in the same field and other relevant agencies. Such squads are generally found to be involved in the reactive investigation of reported crime. For example, a team specialising in investigating child abuse will quickly acquire a high level of knowledge of the relevant legislation, the ways in which child abuse is committed, the types of information profile generated and the way in which victims, witnesses and offenders are likely to react. In addition, they will also build up relationships with the specialist resources used in the investigation of child abuse, such as forensic medical examiners, social workers and health visitors, and the agencies that are likely to become involved in such investigations. In principle, this enhanced level of knowledge, which is only really acquired by specialising in a particular type of investigation, should enable them to carry out more focused investigations than would be the case if they were carrying a mixed case load.

The second type are squads where investigators work collectively on the same investigations. This typically occurs where the squad is focused on the proactive investigation of crime identified through the police analysis of intelligence. An example would be investigations carried out by a drug squad, where a number of officers will work as a team on a range of actions, such as surveillance, before making arrests and carrying out searches of property and vehicles.

As has been noted elsewhere, the distinction between reactive and proactive techniques should not be overstated, as investigators in both types of squad will use a combination of techniques. Furthermore, it is not unusual for officers in squads to sometimes work as individuals on a caseload and sometimes as a team focused on one investigation. However, the general distinction can be made between those squads where the main working model is single investigators and those where it is usual for investigators to be deployed in teams. Typical examples of the two types of squad are shown in Table 2.6.

Temporary teams
Some investigations are conducted by teams that are brought together temporarily in response to a single event. The most common type of investigation carried out by temporary teams is homicide investigation, although they are sometimes also used to investigate other types of crime that have been given a high priority, such as rape and kidnap. Such teams are generally led by a senior investigating officer (SIO). They will have the support of a major incident room (MIR) and the HOLMES computer system, both of which are designed to provide support in managing the high volume of information generated by this type of investigation.

Temporary teams can also be established for more modest ends, such as to address a particular problem at a local level, like car crime and vandalism. In cases such as this they will generally be led by a sergeant or inspector.

Table 2.6   Types of squad

Individual caseloads	Teams
Child abuse	Counter-terrorism
Fraud	Organised crime
Domestic violence	Drugs
Sexual offences	Vehicle crime
Computer crime	Organised robbery

Conclusion

The recognition that criminal investigation requires a distinct set of knowledge, skills and understanding is relatively recent within the police service. But PIP, the emerging literature on investigative practice and the growing interest being shown by researchers in criminal investigation provide a foundation for the professionalisation of the role of investigator. Although in the public mind this role is associated with that of detective, in reality most investigations are carried out by uniformed patrol officers as part of their routine duties and the overall success of the criminal investigation is dependent on them having an effective investigative practice. More complex crime and incidents that have caused significant harm tend to be investigated by a relatively small number of specialists at PIP Levels 2 and 3, and these are estimated to make up less than 10 per cent of a typical police force.

There is no single model for how investigators are deployed. Most work as single investigators, drawing in the additional expertise that is required as they need it, but maintaining overall responsibility for the decisions that are made. Some work in squads, where the combined efforts of a number of investigators are focused on a single objective, and some work in temporary teams to tackle a specific problem, usually a murder or other serious crime.

Whatever level of PIP they are working at and no matter how they are deployed, all investigators require a high level of knowledge, skill and understanding if they are to carry out their roles successfully. This is contained in an investigative practice, some of which is taught, some contained in the various manuals published by the police services, but most derived from the experience of carrying out criminal investigations.

Further reading

The history of policing has been well documented in C. Emsley, *The English Police: A Political and Social History* (2nd edn, London: Longman, 1996), and P. Rawlings, *Policing: A Short History* (Cullompton: Willan Publishing, 2002). Both provide a broad overview covering long periods and deal with criminal investigation as a function of the wider policing mandate. The practice of criminal investigation has not been covered as extensively but an accessible overview of the key historic developments is provided in B. Morris, 'History of Criminal

Investigation', in T. Newburn, T. Williamson and A. Wright (eds), *Handbook of Criminal Investigation* (Cullompton: Willan Publishing, 2007).

P. King, *Crime, Justice and Discretion in England 1740–1820* (Oxford: Oxford University Press, 2000) provides an account of how the criminal justice system developed during this important period and is particularly good at portraying how the system was used to achieve outcomes for victims and communities as well as for the various officials involved.

Many original sources on crime as a social problem and criminal investigation as one of the responses to it are readily available. A selection of Henry Mayhew's journalism in V. Neuburg (ed.), *London Labour and the London Poor* (London: Penguin, 1985) provides first-hand accounts of the social conditions within which early policing was carried out, while the title of Mayhew's *The London Underworld in the Victorian Period: Authentic First-Person Accounts by Beggars, Thieves and Prostitutes* (London: Dover Publishing, 2005) speaks for itself. Charles Dickens, writing in the same era is also an excellent source and selections of his journalism are available in *Sketches by Boz* (London: Penguin, 1995) and *Selected Journalism 1850–1870* (London: Penguin, 1997). Many newspapers and journals from the late nineteenth century onwards are now available in facsimile and provide first-hand accounts of crimes, investigations and trials.

Those with access to good library facilities may be able to access some early original material, such as *The First Report of the Commissioners Appointed to Inquire as to the Best Means of Establishing and Efficient Constabulary Force in the Counties of England and Wales*, which was published in 1839. Such material not only provides a fascinating insight into the structure of the criminal justice system of that time, but also shows how enduring the problems of crime and its detection are.

Many police forces have museums or historical societies that provide local sources of information, and the Police History Society exists to 'advance the public education in police history' (www.policehistorysociety.co.uk). The memoirs of detectives, forensic scientists, lawyers, pathologists and other professionals involved in criminal investigation, as well as criminals themselves, are often written as 'ripping yarns' but nonetheless provide a fascinating insight into how their authors saw their world, or at least how they wanted others to see it. Most go out of print quickly and so no particular recommendations are made here, but searches in good second-hand bookshops usually uncover some examples at bargain prices.

As noted in this chapter, the drivers for change in investigative practice have not occurred in isolation and they all sit in a complex relationship with each other. A good starting point is to examine miscarriages of justice from 1970 onwards as these illustrate both the problems and the nature of the solutions that have been sought. C. Walker and K. Starmer (eds) *Miscarriages of Justice: A Review of Justice in Error* (Oxford: Oxford University Press, 1999) examines some of the main problems within the criminal justice system that have led to miscarriages of justice, and the adequacy of some of the measures put in place to address them. Although now somewhat dated in terms of legal provisions and investigative practice, M. McConville, A. Sanders and R. Leng, *The Case for the Prosecution: Police Suspects and the Construction of Criminality* (London: Routledge, 1993) still provides a useful illustration of the relationship between routine investigative activity and the circumstances that can lead to miscarriages of justice. A more up-to-date examination of the relationship is provided by S.P. Savage and B. Milne, 'Miscarriages of Justice', in T. Newburn, T. Williamson and A. Wright (eds), *Handbook of Criminal Investigation* (Cullompton: Willan Publishing, 2007).

The technical and procedural developments related to investigative practice are too numerous to list in any great detail but C. Beavan, *Fingerprints: Murder and the Race to Uncover the Science of Identity* (London: Fourth Estate, 2002) provides a very readable account of the early development of fingerprinting written by a journalist, while C. McCartney, *Forensic Identification and Criminal Justice* (Cullompton: Willan Publishing, 2006) provides analysis of more recent developments in both fingerprint and DNA technology. An issue of the *Journal of Homicide and Major Incident Investigation* (Vol. 3 Issue 2, Autumn 2007) was given over to papers on a range of new technologies and how they are being increasingly integrated into the investigation process. One of the key developments in investigation in recent years has been the adoption of intelligence-led policing, which is explored in J. Ratcliffe, *Intelligence-led Policing* (Cullompton: Willan Publishing, 2008).

Concerns over the effectiveness of criminal investigation were outlined in the Audit Commission, *Helping with Enquiries: Tackling crime effectively* (London: HMSO, 1993), which detailed the failure of reactive investigations to keep pace with increased reporting and advocated a more proactive approach by the police. This was highly influential in promoting intelligence-led policing. Concerns about the effectiveness of individual practice tend to emerge during public inquiries into individual investigations and reports such as Sir

W.M. Macpherson, *The Stephen Lawrence Inquiry: Report of in Inquiry by Sir William Macpherson of Cluny* (London: HMSO, 1999) and Dame J. Smith, *The Shipman Inquiry Second Report: The Police Investigation of March 1998* (London: HMSO, 2003) are valuable sources for the type of problems that have been identified in individual cases.

The professionalisation of criminal investigation has not yet been well documented, but P. Stelfox, 'Professionalising Criminal Investigations', in T. Newburn, T. Williamson and A. Wright (eds), *Handbook of Criminal Investigation* (Cullompton: Willan Publishing, 2007) provides a recent overview of the issues.

Note

1 Within the United Kingdom, Scotland is a separate jurisdiction and has its own policing arrangements under the leadership of the Association of Chief Police Officers of Scotland (ACPOS).

Chapter 3

Criminal law and policy

Introduction

The idea that some types of behaviour are defined as criminal is such a familiar feature of modern societies that we rarely consider how this comes about. The way in which laws get made is important for investigators because the provisions of statutes, and the ways in which they are interpreted by judges, determine the type of information that must be located to bring offenders to justice. The law also lays down the rules by which evidence can be gathered by investigators and the standards required before a prosecution can be mounted. The nature of the task of criminal investigation is therefore largely shaped by the criminal law, and understanding the type of task that investigation is for practitioners requires an understanding of how laws are made. But every law cannot be enforced all the time and choices have to be made about what crimes police forces should focus on and the resources that should be applied to them. Furthermore, how investigators apply the law is considered to be important. Society expects them to operate to high ethical standards, to be civil, to be fair and to exercise discretion in the use of the powers that the law gives them. Setting the objectives for criminal investigation, allocating resources and defining the methods by which investigations are to be carried and how discretion is to be exercised is achieved through the development of policy. This chapter examines how law and policy come to be made, the complex relationship between them and how they influence investigative practice.

The law

Making laws

The United Kingdom is a common law jurisdiction. This means that the law is comprised of the rulings of judges in relation to cases brought before them, and by laws made by politicians in the form of Acts of Parliament. Until about the seventeenth century, most laws were made by judges, but since then the balance has shifted towards Acts of Parliament and all new law is now made that way. Judges still have an important role to play in interpreting Acts of Parliament, when cases come before them, and the decisions they make can be influential because they set precedents for how other judges may interpret the law in future cases.

Proposals to make a particular type of behaviour a criminal offence are contained in a 'Bill' which is introduced into either of the two Houses of Parliament by a member. This will be an elected politician in the House of Commons or a peer in the House of Lords. Most Bills are introduced by the government and are based on the manifesto they put before the electorate at the time they are voted into office. Before introducing a Bill, the government may publish a consultation paper, called a 'Green Paper', or a policy paper, called a 'White Paper'. Both of these have the intention of generating wider consultation about the proposal. It is possible for any member of either House of Parliament to put forward a Bill on their own, known as a 'private member's Bill', but in reality it is difficult for such Bills to make progress without government support.

The proposals contained in a Bill are subject to debate in Parliament in the form of 'readings', during which politicians can argue for changes to be made to the clauses of the Bill. Once the House into which it was introduced agrees the terms of the Bill, it is sent to the other House where it goes through a similar process. When both Houses of Parliament have agreed the content of the Bill it receives Royal Assent and becomes law. It is generally during the various readings of a Bill that debate centres on the specific provisions. The provisions that are most relevant to investigators are:

1 The behaviour that is deemed to be illegal, which is often known by its Latin name of *actus reus*.

2 The state of mind of the offender at the time the act was done, which is often known by its Latin name of *mens rea*. There are essentially three types of *mens rea*:

- *Intention.* The act was done deliberately, e.g. wounding someone with intent to cause grievous bodily harm (Section 18, Offences Against the Persons Act 1861).
- *Knowingly.* The act was done in the knowledge of some relevant circumstances, e.g. knowing that goods were stolen (Section 22, Theft Act 1968).
- *Negligence, carelessness or recklessness.* The act was done irrespective of the risks involved, e.g. manslaughter.

Some offences are known as *strict liability* because no *mens rea* is required for them to be committed. These tend to be minor offences and are often related to road traffic law. An example is the offence of exceeding the speed limit, where it does not matter whether the offender knew they were doing it or not, or whether they intended to do it or not. The evidence required by a court is simply that they did it.

It is during the passage of a Bill through the Houses of Parliament that precise details of the *actus reus* and *mens rea* are decided. How they are decided and the way in which they are drafted into law determines the type of information that investigators must locate and gather before a prosecution can be brought under that particular law. An example of how this works in practice is the Terrorism Bill, which received its first reading in Parliament on 13 October 2005. The Bill contained a range of measures that were intended to strengthen the law on terrorism in the wake of the bombings on 7 July that year. In its original form, Section 2 contained the offence of 'dissemination of terrorist publications', which proposed making it an offence to carry out acts such as distributing or circulating terrorist publications. The aim of this measure was to stop people glorifying or assisting terrorism through the publication and distribution of material. A number of defences were included which amounted to the fact that the person disseminating the material did not know its content. Significantly, there was no mention of any intent in the Bill and so anyone who distributed such material knowing what its content was committed the offence, irrespective of their intention.

Had the Bill gone through Parliament unchanged, the investigation of such offences would have only involved finding evidence that someone had disseminated material falling within the definition of terrorist publications, which was fairly wide-ranging. During the parliamentary debates members of both Houses objected to this section of the Bill. Some pointed out that books about Nelson Mandela or those describing the establishment of the Irish Republic could fall within its definition. They argued that an important element of the offence must be the intent behind the dissemination. Special interest groups such as internet service providers also argued that they could unwittingly commit the offence if people posted such material to their sites. As a consequence, the section was amended and when the Bill became the Terrorism Act 2006, Section 2 included a new clause that required *intent* to encourage or assist terrorism or that the person was *reckless* as to whether it would do so. From an investigator's point of view, this significantly changed the type of information that would be required to bring a prosecution. Not only would information about the dissemination be required, but now information as to the intention of the person disseminating it would have to be gathered. Such information is generally much harder to acquire and usually is only available as a result of admissions made during interviews with the police. This offers a typical example of how the parliamentary process determines the type of information that investigators must gather.

Judicial decisions

Although the rulings of judges no longer make law, they are nonetheless influential in determining how the law is applied in practice. Decisions made in higher courts set precedents for lower courts to follow and so are highly influential on the way in which the lower courts deal with the individual cases that come before them. There is a hierarchy of courts: the House of Lords is the highest, followed by the Court of Appeal (Criminal Division) then the Divisional Court, a judge in the Administrative Court, then the Crown Court and magistrates' court. Only judgements in the first four of these count as precedents and the general rule is that rulings in a higher court set precedents that lower courts must follow.

Investigators need to be aware of the relevant legal judgements because the way that a law is interpreted will be as influential in determining the type of information that is required as the drafting of the law in the first place.

Points to prove

It is common for investigators to break down laws into the elements that require to be proved in court. This enables them to understand the type of evidence they are looking for and to focus investigations on gathering it. It also helps them in ensuring that the evidence they gather is as comprehensive as possible. The elements they focus on are usually called *points to prove*. An example of how points to prove are used in practice is taken from Section 1(1) of the Theft Act 1968, which gives a definition of theft: 'A person is guilty of theft if he dishonestly appropriates property belonging to another with the intention of permanently depriving the other of it; and thief and steal shall be construed accordingly.'

Investigators need to gather evidence to prove every element of this definition in court. The first part, referring to a person, is not generally considered to be a point to prove for theft because it is common to all offences. However, the prosecution may have to prove that the accused is over ten years of age, because the law holds that no one under that age is capable of committing a crime, and that the accused had the mental capacity to form the intent necessary to commit the theft. These things will usually only need to be proved if they are raised as specific defences, which is rare.

The points to prove for the specific offence of theft are:

- Dishonesty
- Appropriation
- Property
- Belonging to another
- Intention to permanently deprive.

The Act defines each of these elements and this is supplemented in a literature written for practitioners, such as *Blackstone's Police Manual, Volume 1: Crime*. Practitioners also have online access to the Police National Legal Database (PNLD), which provides information on the points to prove in a particular case. These are often complex and are influenced by recent case law.

Although the law provides the framework within which criminal investigations take place, people rarely report specific breaches of the law to the police. In practice what happens is that people report behaviours to the police that they believe to be wrong or that have caused them harm. Thus, they may report that they have been assaulted or robbed, without any specific notion on the particular offence that has been committed, merely a belief that they have been harmed and they want the police to take action. It is generally up to the police to decide what type of offence may have been committed and to gather information with a view to bringing the offenders to justice. Once the evidence has been gathered the CPS decides the exact charges but the reality is that investigators choose the information that is gathered and this determines the type of charges that can be brought against an individual. The same is true of investigations instigated by the police themselves. For example, they may identify drug-dealing as a specific problem in an area, but the choice of the offences that will be used to investigate it is largely tactical, and may depend as much on the type of material they can gather as the type of behaviour they are seeking to curb. Investigators may therefore address the problem of drug dealing by arresting offenders for possession of illegal drugs, by using money-laundering legislation, or they may focus on the weapons they carry or even the fact that they are committing anti-social behaviour in the area.

One of the tasks for investigators then is to decide which law is applicable to a particular complaint or crime control problem. Clearly, it is not expected that investigators will know the points to prove in relation to each of the many thousands of offences contained within the criminal law. However, they are expected to know the more common ones. They are also expected to have a sufficient knowledge of legal theory and practice to be able to identify the points to prove in relation to any crime so that they can apply them to operational situations.

As noted in Chapter 1, bringing an offender to justice is not always the primary objective of an investigation. Intelligence-gathering, disruption and other forms of risk management may be to the fore in individual cases. However, the justification for all such objectives must be that they are in some way concerned with managing behaviour that is a criminal offence. There is a wider public policy assumption that police action is aimed at preventing and investigating criminal behaviour, and it is difficult to see how operations that focus on behaviour that cannot be defined as criminal could be justified, even if as a matter of expediency or policy the case is not subsequently taken to court. It is therefore important that all investigators have a thorough understanding of the way in which individual behaviours are deemed to be criminal, the points to prove and the influence that case law has on the way judges will interpret individual cases.

The investigatory framework

As well as defining individual crimes, the law also provides a legal framework within which investigators must work as they locate and gather material. The legislation that makes up the investigatory framework has developed incrementally and is a much smaller body of law than that which creates individual offences. Table 3.1 lists the key legislation in this area.

Table 3.1 Key legislation on the process of criminal investigation

Date	Legislation	Relevance to the investigation process
1984	Police and Criminal Evidence Act (PACE)	Defined police powers, laid down investigative procedures and defined suspects' and others' rights.
1985	Prosecution of Offences Act	Established the Crown Prosecution Service to take over responsibility for prosecution from the police.
1996	Criminal Procedure and Investigation Act (CPIA)	Provided a legal definition of criminal investigation and the role of investigator. Places a duty on investigators to investigate impartially. Provided statutory disclosure process.
1998	The Human Rights Act	Gives legal effect to the European Convention on Human Rights (ECHR), and requires domestic courts to take account of the rulings made by the European Court of Human Rights.
2000	Regulation of Investigatory Powers Act (RIPA)	Defined processes of investigation and placed them within a regulatory regime.
2003	Criminal Justice Act	Gave the Crown Prosecution Service responsibility for selecting charges (they previously reviewed police charges).

The investigatory framework has three main functions. It defines the rights of individuals during a criminal investigation, it ensures the integrity of the information gathered and it facilitates access to information. There is a great deal of overlap between these functions, but it is usually possible to see one or other of them as being the foundation of a particular legal measure within the investigatory framework. For example, people have a legal right not to incriminate themselves. This means that the prosecution should have sufficient evidence to prove its case without the participation of the suspect. This has led to a requirement that investigators tell those they suspect of being responsible for an offence that they have the right to remain silent during police questioning (Section 10, Code of Practice C, PACE 1984). The form of words used is designed to alert suspects to this right so that they can exercise it if they wish. If investigators do not caution suspects before questioning them, the information they gather may be excluded by a judge. Breaches of the provisions of PACE may also leave investigators open to disciplinary action. The caution has no bearing on the quality of the information gathered by investigators – it is no more likely that words said by a suspect will be true or false simply because they have been cautioned – it is simply a matter of ensuring that their legal rights are upheld.

Some rules are designed to ensure the quality of information. For example, the Turnbull Rules, which arise as a consequence of a decision in the case of R v Turnbull (1977, QB 224, CA), are designed to ensure that information gathered from eyewitnesses to a crime reach a minimum level of quality. The rules provide a range of factors against which courts can evaluate eyewitness testimony. These are:

- How long did the witness have the accused under observation, at what distance, and in what light.
- Was the observation impeded in any way.
- Had the witness ever seen the accused before, and if so, how often.
- If only occasionally, had he any special reason for remembering the accused.
- How long had elapsed between the original observation and the subsequent identification to the police.
- Was there any material discrepancy between the description of the accused given to the police by the witness when first seen by them and his actual appearance.

Legal rules that give access to information generally seek to clarify what type of information investigators can look for, and often what they cannot legitimately look for, and place limits on the means they can use. For example, Section 7.2 of Code B, PACE 1984 states that 'No item may be seized which an officer has reasonable grounds for believing to be subject to legal privilege, as defined in PACE, section 10, other than under the Criminal Justice and Police Act 2001, Part 2.'

The Human Rights Act 1998 (HRA)

This Act gives legal effect to the European Convention on Human Rights (ECHR), and requires domestic courts to take account of the rulings made by the European Court of Human Rights in Strasbourg. The ECHR guarantees the following rights:

Article 2:   The right to life.
Article 3:   Freedom from torture or degrading treatment or punishment.
Article 4:   Freedom from slavery.
Article 5:   The right to liberty and security of the person.
Article 6:   The right to a fair trial.
Article 7:   The right not to be convicted under a retroactive penal stature.
Article 8:   The right to respect for one's private and family life, home and correspondence.
Article 9:   Right to freedom of thought, conscience and religion.
Article 10: Freedom of expression.
Article 11: Freedom of assembly and association.

Some of these rights are absolute, such as Article 3, the prohibition of torture, but others are limited or qualified in some way. For example, Article 8, which on the face of it would make it difficult for investigators to gather a wide range of material relevant to an investigation is qualified in the following way:

> There shall be no interference by a public authority with the exercise of this right except such as is in accordance with the law and is necessary in a democratic society in the interests of national security, public safety or the economic well-being of the country, for the prevention of disorder or crime, for the protection of health or morals, or for the protection of the rights and freedoms of others.

This qualification makes it possible for investigators to breach this particular Article, provided:

- There is a clear legal basis for doing so.
- The breach seeks to achieve a legitimate aim as set out in the qualification.
- The action they take is no greater than is necessary to achieve the legitimate aim.

The Act has been highly influential in relation to investigative practice. All officers receive training in human rights legislation and there are few manuals on investigative practice that do not explore the link between practice and human rights.

Common law powers

ECHR means that many intrusive investigative techniques, such as placing surveillance devices in a suspect's home or car, would contravene the individual's human rights unless it was explicitly allowed under domestic law. As a consequence, a great deal of investigative practice is now covered by legislation. However, investigators can still rely on common law powers in some circumstances. The term common law powers, although widely used, is something of a misnomer because there are no powers as such. What there is, is an absence of a legal barrier to some types of action and an acceptance by courts that they are part of the investigatory process. For example, investigators can ask questions of anyone without recourse to any specific law, although they cannot detain them for the purpose or search them. Investigators can therefore do things like carrying out house-to-house enquiries in the area of an offence although there is no statute that says they may do so. Similarly, they can define crime scenes and exclude people from them while they carry out forensic examinations. So long as they do not enter private premises against the wishes of the occupier or use force, they are acting legally, although, again, there is no specific statute covering their actions.

Such common law powers are gradually diminishing but it seems likely that the complexity of human behaviour means that investigators will always be required to undertake activities that are not explicitly covered by the law. Where such activity has a long history of acceptance by the courts and society at large, there should be no difficulty in this. But as investigators respond to new technologies or social processes, there is a danger that legislation lags behind and so they resort to common law powers.

An interesting example is the use by investigators of technology to reveal the faces of paedophiles who have posted photographs of themselves abusing children on the internet. The offenders use technology to distort their features in the belief that they will not be recognised. The police have had some success in reversing this distortion process and have made arrests as a consequence. There is no legal provision specifically allowing them to take images off the internet and manipulate them in this way. In England and Wales, they could claim to be acting on a common law power. As few people like paedophiles, or understand the technology involved, this is unlikely to be challenged unless, or until, cases start to arrive in the courts where wrongful identifications have been made or an offender successfully claims that their human rights have been violated. Such an eventuality could lead to the introduction of specific legislation covering this type of activity. Common law powers can therefore be seen as fulfilling two purposes: they legitimise long-standing and accepted investigative practice, and they fill a gap between technological and social change, and the legal framework.

The Criminal Procedure and Investigations Act 1996 (CPIA)

The main purpose of the CPIA is to ensure that there is a level playing field at a trial by placing a legal duty on investigators to disclose all the material they gather to both prosecution and defence. The need for this arose because there have been cases where investigators and prosecutors failed to disclose material that could have helped the defence case, and so created miscarriages of justice. In some instances, such behaviour may have been influenced by the adversarial nature of the legal system and the police organisation's strategic remit to bring offenders to justice. The CPIA overrides such considerations by, in effect, making the gathering of material for both parties the primary aim of investigations. It does this by defining a criminal investigation and the roles of the investigator in it. It place obligations on them to:

- Maintain records of the investigation.
- Pursue all reasonable lines of enquiry.
- Disclose the material they uncover to all parties in the trial.

These provisions make the conduct of the investigation a relevant issue in a trial. For example, if the investigation did not pursue a reasonable line of enquiry or did not disclose some of the material gathered, the defence could argue that the defendant could not receive a fair trial.

The Act is supplemented by a Code of Practice that defines the roles of the officer in charge of the case, the disclosure officer, the investigator and supervisors. It also sets out the duties and responsibilities of the officers regarding the recording and retention of material obtained in the course of a criminal investigation.

The CPIA has undoubtedly been highly influential in the development of investigative practice insofar as it has put the recording of decisions and the retention and disclosure of material at the centre of the investigative process. In a more subtle way, it has influenced how many investigators view their role. They no longer see themselves on the prosecution side of the adversarial system, but as neutral gatherers of material for the process as a whole.

The Police and Criminal Evidence Act 1984 (PACE)

Prior to the introduction of PACE, many of the powers that the police relied on to carry out investigations, particularly those concerned with stop and search, arrest, interview and the entry to premises, relied on the provisions of a wide range of legislation. Some of this was very old, some was contained in Acts that only applied locally, and some relied on common law. There was, therefore, a great deal of variation in practice and many gaps in the legal definitions of what was, and was not, permissible. This patchwork of provision failed to protect the rights of individuals, and a number of miscarriages of justice that came to light during the 1970s led to the establishment of the Royal Commission on Criminal Procedure, which reported in 1981. It made recommendations that tried to balance the competing needs of the investigation and prosecution process against those of the individual subject to investigation. These recommendations became the basis of PACE, which for the first time in English and Welsh history (Northern Ireland and Scotland had different legislation) sought to comprehensively define what police powers were and how they should be used. The Act was reinforced by the publication of Codes of Practice, which provide guidance to investigators on the provisions of the Act and its use. These Codes of Practice are:

- Code A Stop and Search and Recording of Public Encounters
- Code B Search of Premises and Seizure of Property
- Code C The Detention, Treatment and Questioning of Suspects
- Code D Identification Procedures
- Code E Audio Recording of Interviews with Suspects
- Code F Visual Recording of Interviews
- Code G Arrest
- Code H The Detention, Treatment and Questioning of Persons Under Section 41 and Schedule to the Terrorism Act 2000.

The last of these codes is necessary because some of the provisions of the Terrorism Act differ from those of PACE, for example, detention times.

PACE underpins much of investigative practice and all investigators should be fully conversant with its provisions.

The Regulation of Investigatory Powers Act (RIPA) 2000

RIPA regulates four areas of investigative practice:

- The interception of communications.
- The acquisition by investigators of communications data.
- Covert surveillance, including the use of covert human intelligence sources.
- Access to encrypted data.

As with PACE, practice in these areas was previously covered by various statutes or by police custom and practice, and RIPA sought to provide overarching legislation to ensure that police action in this area was lawful under human rights legislation.

RIPA is overseen by the Office of Surveillance Commissioners (OSC) (www.surveillancecommissioners.gov.uk). There is a chief surveillance commissioner and six surveillance commissioners, all of whom are retired judges. Their prior consent is required for certain types of surveillance that are considered particularly intrusive and they must be informed of all surveillance falling within the Act. They also have powers to inspect police forces to ensure compliance with the Act. By defining the circumstances in which the acquisition of communications data and surveillance can take place, and putting a regulatory framework around it, RIPA has significantly shaped investigative practice in this area.

Balancing people's human and legal rights, ensuring the quality of information and facilitation access to information needed by investigators is never likely to be a straightforward task. There are many conflicting interests and the situation on the ground sometimes makes it difficult to know which rule applies to novel or complex situations. For this reason, the legal provisions governing investigations are often the subject of contention within a trial. It is important, therefore, that investigators have a thorough grasp of the legislation that goes to make up the investigatory framework. Without that, they risk infringing individuals' rights, of mishandling information so as to make it likely that courts will exclude it and committing breaches of the law for which they may be liable.

Standards of proof

The final area where the law is significant for investigators is in defining standards of proof and how they are to be achieved. The standard of proof that has to be achieved during a trial is that of *beyond reasonable doubt*. In applying this standard, courts operate to a complex set of rules and provisions that are collectively called the *rules of evidence*. These define what has to be proved, the types of material that may be brought before a court as proof and how it is to be dealt with. Some of these rules are complex and their interpretation is often a contested area within a trial. Evidence usually takes one of four forms (May 1999: 3):

1 Testimony, oral statements by witnesses given on oath
2 Documents produced for the inspection of the court
3 Real evidence, i.e. exhibits and other material
4 Admissions of facts by either party so that the other does not have to prove them.

The rules of evidence mean that not all the information gathered during an investigation can be used in court. This applies particularly, although not exclusively, to testimony evidence. For example, testimony evidence must be first-hand and given under oath. It cannot be reported to the court by a third party. This rule means that information passed third-hand to the police is of no evidential value. As a matter of practical convenience testimony can often be presented in the form of a written statement, if all parties agree. But this is only on the understanding that unless they fall within one of the exceptions to this rule, the witness would be able to attend court and give evidence in person under oath if required. Perhaps the most widely known rule of evidence is that the defendant's previous criminal history cannot be used as evidence (although as with most things legal there are exceptions). The rules of evidence mean that not all the material gathered during an investigation can attain the status of evidence. The type of evidence that courts will allow to be used in a trial and the standard of proof they require are highly influential in determining the volume and type of information that investigators gather when the objective of their investigation is to bring offenders to justice.

When investigators have objectives other than bringing offenders to justice, they may have to apply other standards when making judgements about the material they gather. For example, the issuing of an anti-social behaviour order (ASBO) under the Crime and Disorder Act 1998 and some of the provision of the Proceeds of Crime Act 2002 (POCA), use the civil standard of 'on the balance of probabilities', which is a lower test than the criminal one and subject to a different set of legal rules. While on the one hand this makes it easier for investigators to meet the standard, it also requires them to know the type of material that is acceptable in such situations and the rules that courts will apply in reaching the standard.

Further difficulties arise when investigations are mounted for the sole purpose of risk management. The gathering of the material needed to provide intelligence to interdict illicit goods or products, to disrupt organised criminal behaviour or to prevent terrorist activity is a legitimate end of criminal investigation, but the end result is not subject to the same oversight or quality control as cases brought to courts. Although investigative practice must still be within the law, the absence of any external oversight carries the obvious danger that standards will be applied differently by individual investigators or by those in different forces or organisations. This has the obvious potential for loss of quality, misunderstanding of meaning and general confusion. The history of criminal investigation also provides numerous examples of situations where the importance of the ends were used by investigators to justify unacceptable means. The absence of an explicit standard to be applied in those cases that do not go before a court means that society is wholly reliant on investigators themselves applying high ethical standards.

The policy framework

While it is easy to see how the criminal investigation process is shaped by the law, it is also influenced by policy. Unlike the law, policy does not have a well-defined authoritative source, language and literature. It is made by a number of bodies, some of which are discussed below, it takes many forms and there is no index of policy that provides practitioners with easy access to it all. It is an ill-defined body of material that has often been overlooked by researchers, but is highly influential on investigative practice.

Sources of policy

There are three main sources of policy for investigators: the Home Office, ACPO and individual police forces. They sit in a loose hierarchy and are influenced by various other agencies and interest groups. The relationship between the three main sources of policy and the type of bodies which influence them is illustrated in Figure 3.1.

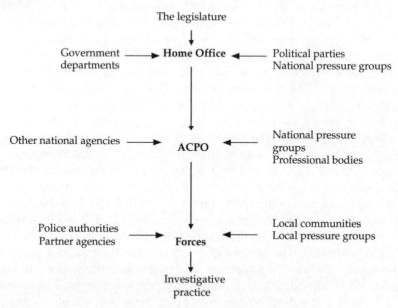

Figure 3.1 Influences on the three main sources of policy

Home Office

As the government department with responsibility for the police, the Home Office plays a major role in developing policy. It does this directly through policy-making units, such as the Crime Reduction and Community Safety Group, the Respect Task Force and the Office for Security and Counter Terrorism, and by sponsoring non-departmental public bodies (NDPB), which make policy in their own right. An NDPB is an organisation funded by government but whose day-to-day operations are independent of it. NDPBs relevant to policy-making for criminal investigations are:

- *Her Majesty's Inspector of Constabulary (HMIC).* The Chief HMIC is the Home Secretary's senior professional advisor on policing. The principle role of the HMIC is to carry out inspections of police forces to ensure that they efficiently and effectively discharge their policing functions. They make reports to the Home Secretary based on their inspection, and these may be published.

- *National Policing Improvement Agency (NPIA)*. The NPIA was established under the Police and Justice Act 2006 to streamline the number of organisations that had previously provided support to the police at a national level. It has statutory objectives under the Act, and these are:

(a) developing good practice in policing
(b) providing expert support to the police service
(c) carrying out a national threat assessment for police forces
(d) sharing international understanding of policing issues
(e) providing national IT, procurement and training support.

NPIA staff are drawn from police organisations, industry, government departments and the education sector. The main focus of the NPIA's work is policing improvement in England and Wales, but it has officers on secondment from forces in Scotland and Northern Ireland and collaborates with relevent bodies in those countries on some initiatives.

- *The Independent Police Complaints Commission (IPCC)*. The IPCC investigates complaints against the police and sets standards by which the police themselves investigate some types of complaints.

In addition to the above, the Home Office leads the National Policing Board. The Home Secretary is the chair of this board, and other members are the Minister for Policing, Security and Community Safety, and representatives of relevant Home Office departments, ACPO, the Association of Police Authorities (APA), HMIC and NPIA. The main functions of the Board are as follows:

- To agree the Home Secretary's annual national strategic priorities for policing and key priorities for the National Policing Improvement Agency.

- The set agreed priorities for the police reform programme.

- To enable Ministers, the professional leaders of the police service and police authorities to monitor progress in implementing the reform programme and identify and overcome barriers to delivery.

- To provide a regular forum for debate and three-way communication between the tripartite partners on the opportunities and challenges facing policing.

A Policing Reference Group made up of police staff associations, unions and other bodies representing groups in the police service, enables other stakeholders to have an input into the work of National Policing Board.

Association of Chief Police Officers (ACPO)

The Association of Chief Police Officers of England, Wales and Northern Ireland (ACPO) is the representative body of chief officer ranks. The chief officer ranks are as follows:

Constabularies	City of London Police	Metropolitan Police
Chief Constable	Commissioner	Commissioner
Deputy Chief Constable	Assistant Commissioner	Deputy Commissioner
Assistant Chief Constable	Deputy Commissioner	Assistant Commissioner
		Deputy Assistant Commissioner
		Commander

ACPO has no statutory function and membership is voluntary. Notwithstanding this apparent informal basis, it has become highly influential in developing policy that aims to co-ordinate policing activity. ACPO policy is developed by a number of business areas, each of which is led by a chief constable. Each business area is divided into a number of portfolios which are led by an officer of ACPO rank and made up of practitioners with relevant expertise. The ACPO business areas and portfolios are as follows:

Business area	Portfolios
Citizen focus	• Standards and quality • Visibility and the wider police family • Neighbourhood policing • Responsiveness policing • Citizen journey
Crime	• Forensic science • Organised crime • Intelligence • Drugs • Firearms • Violent crime

Business area	Portfolios
	• Acquisitive crime • Standards, competencies and training • Technology • Economic crime
Criminal justice	• Pre-trial • Trial • Integration • Victims and witnesses • Disposal/enforcement • New/revised CJ legislation • CJIT • Performance monitoring • Youth justice • CJS professional development • Confidence in the CJS • PNLD
Finance and resources	• Procurement • Police Expenditure Forecasting Group/ Spending Review • CIPFA/Statistics • Activity-based costing • Property Services Managers' Group • Police Efficiency Group • Sponsorship and income generation • Charging methodology • Mutual aid • Directors of Finance National Meetings • Fleet management transport • Pensions
Information management	• Communications • Police National Computer • Information Assurance • Data protection and freedom of information • Futures • In-service systems • Emerging systems • CJIT

Business area	Portfolios
Performance management	• Performance measurement (development) • Inspection regime • Crime statistics • National contact management portfolio • Performance management (training) • NMIS (National Management Info System) • Business area head's portfolio
Race and diversity	• Hate crime • Asylum and immigration • Sexual orientation • Faith and community tension • Gender (internal) • Gender (external) • Independent advisory groups • Gypsies and travellers • Mental health and disability • Performance management • Progression • Race equality • Training • Age
Terrorism and allied matters	• Operational • Technical • International liaison • Legislation • Training
Uniformed operations	• Operational issues • Conflict management • Emergency procedures • Road policing
Workforce development	• Personnel management • Reward and recognition • Learning development • Safer and healthier policing • Leadership • Workforce modernisation • HR modernisation

Each portfolio holder is responsible for policy and practice in their respective area. How they do this varies, but many subdivide the portfolio into a number of working groups looking at a relevant area. For example, the Violence Portfolio in the Crime Business Area is subdivided into groups, one of which is the Homicide Working Group (HWG). The HWG develops policy and practice in relation to homicide and major incident investigation. It is led by a chief constable and the vice chair is usually of assistant chief constable rank. Other members of the group are senior detectives, usually heads of CID, representing each region. There are also representatives from the Home Office, NPIA, the Special Investigation Branch of the Royal Military Police, the Health and Safety Executive (who are often involved in the investigation of fatal incidents relating to industrial or transport accidents), SOCA, and a forensic science practitioner. Individual members are responsible for monitoring developments in specific areas of business relevant to the investigation of homicide and major incidents, and these include, among others, pathology, training and forensic science. Specific pieces of work are also commissioned and individual members are responsible for progressing these. The HWG meets once every quarter to review new developments and to progress the work it has initiated, and their individual policy or practice papers are distributed to forces, either as hard copies sent to chief constables or published on the ACPO website or in the *Journal of Homicide and Major Incident Investigation*, the official publication of the HWG. The main practice documents that the HWG publish are the ACPO *Murder Investigation Manual*, which provides advice to senior investigation officers on the strategies and tactics involved in homicide investigation, and the ACPO *Guidance on Major Incident Room Standardised Administration Procedures (MIRSAP)*, which sets standards for the management of a major incident room.

A large number of similar groups within ACPO have the potential to develop policy in relation to criminal investigation. To control the flow of this material to the service, a Policy Unit co-ordinates the work of them all and a committee of chief officers approves all policy before it is distributed.

Police forces

Although it is common to hear people talk of the police service, the reality is that there is no single organisation that fits that description. Each of the individual police forces in the UK is a wholly independent organisation that, in theory at least, is able to define its own structures, policy and procedures. Policing organisations include those that have a broad policing remit over a particular geographical area, for example Cambridgeshire Constabulary or the Greater Manchester Police. Police forces have a complex policy framework simply because they are responsible for a wide range of strategic issues, from responding to emergencies through to neighbourhood security. Criminal investigation is one of their key strategic objectives and a great deal of their policy is aimed at setting and achieving objectives in relation to it. Much of this will be shaped by national policy from the Home Office, ACPO or ACPOS but some will be aimed at dealing with local issues such as force objectives or the relationship between the force and other criminal justice and relevant agencies.

Force objectives tend to be set annually. Some are derived from the National Policing Plan set by the Home Secretary while others are set locally following consultation with the Police Authority, the community and partner agencies. These objectives will very often define particular types of crime or behaviour that the force will focus its efforts on during the coming year. Policy in relation to how the force will work with local agencies is also influenced by national policy but will be tailored to that area. For example, national policy encourages co-operation between police forces, local authorities and health authorities in relation to the investigation of child abuse. How this co-operation is achieved in any one location is a matter for local negotiation. It will be included within a force policy that guides investigators on the steps they need to take to ensure that there is effective co-operation in such investigations.

Types of policy

Policy in relation to the investigation of crime tends to be written to influence one of the following objectives.

The achievement of national or local political objectives
The law cannot determine which crimes will be investigated, the resources that will be made available to the investigation or the way in which they will be used. Such issues are often dealt with by policy. For example, the Police Reform Act 2002 requires the Home Secretary to produce an annual National Policing Plan, which sets out the strategic policing priorities for each year. The plans cover a three-year rolling period and the first was published in 2002. The 2005–2008 plan contained the following chapters:

1 *The Home Secretary's key priorities*, which were to:

   (a) Reduce overall crime – including violent and drug-related crime – in line with the government's Public Service Agreements (PSAs).

   (b) Provide a citizen-focused police service which responds to the needs of communities and individuals, especially victims and witnesses, and inspires public confidence in the police, particularly among minority ethnic communities.

   (c) Take action with partners to increase sanction detection rates and target prolific and other priority offenders.

   (d) Reduce people's concerns about crime, and anti-social behaviour and disorder.

   (e) Combat serious and organised crime, within and across force boundaries.

2 *Contexts*, which relates the key priorities to wider government objectives and the national strategic assessment of what crimes are likely to impact on communities during the coming years.

3 *Delivering the key priorities*, which sets out the way that forces should approach the five key priorities while taking into account local circumstances.

4 *Performance management*, which explains how progress towards achieving the five key priorities will be measured.

5 *Resources*, which describes the government's approach to providing the resources required to deliver policing in general, and the five key priorities in particular.

Although there is a statutory basis for the National Policing Plan, there is no statutory basis for its content. The key priorities, how they are to be measured and the resources that are made available for achieving them are wholly determined by government policy. Because the government's five key priorities are all concerned with crime, the National Policing Plan is highly influential in determining what gets investigated and the resources that are available to do it. The priorities are incorporated into each police force's own objectives and they form the basis of various inspection and reporting regimes that are designed to ensure that they are delivered. This influences the way in which police forces and other relevant agencies respond to crime.

Achieving common national standards

Because police forces are all independent and make policy in their own right, there are a great many things that they do differently. There are benefits to this in that it enables them to tailor their service to meet local needs and conditions. However, in doing things differently it is natural that there will be inconsistencies between forces. In some cases this is undesirable and national policy seeks to ensure that forces have national standards in some areas of operation. One of these is the way in which they record crimes reported to them. A common standard is important in this case because if all forces recorded crimes differently it would be impossible to form an accurate national picture of crime. The National Crime Recording Standards were introduced by the Home Office in 2002 to bring consistency to the way in which the police record crime throughout the country, and are issued to forces in the *Home Office Counting Rules for Recorded Crime*. The standards provide guidance on when and how to record crime, the categories to record it under, when a crime can be counted as detected and rules for sending this information to the Home Office to be collated nationally.

The promotion of good practice

With the police service's acceptance of the importance of good investigative practice has come an increased use of manuals that seek to promote its use. They generally focus on a particular investigative technique or the investigation of a particular type of crime. Where this guidance is produced by the Home Office or ACPO it has the force of policy, in that it reflects authorised practice in a particular area. One of the earliest manuals of this type was the ACPO *Murder Investigation Manual*, which was first published in September 1998 and has been updated regularly since. It was compiled by a group of experienced senior investigating officers (SIOs) who were supported by experts and other professionals working in the criminal justice system. They carried out extensive consultation within the police service and beyond to identify good practice, and the manual brought together the vast array of issues involved in homicide investigation. It provides a reference point for the investigation of all types of major crime and underpins training and development of SIOs. Because it is an authoritative guide to practice in this area it also forms the basis of inspections, audits and reviews of homicide investigation.

Good practice is also promoted through training, continuous professional development conferences, websites such as the NPIA Genesis site, which has a variety of resources for practitioners and through journals and magazines such as *Police Review* and *Police Professional*.

Improvements in customer service

Victim and witness care together with community reassurance are key objectives of the criminal investigation but are rarely covered by the criminal law. Policy fills this gap. An example is the *Code of Practice for Victims of Crime*, issued by the Office for Criminal Justice Reform in 2005, which provides guidance to organisations in the criminal justice sector on the services they should be providing to victims of crime. These include:

- A right to information about their crime within certain time limits and the right to be notified of any arrests that are made together with any court cases.
- A family liaison police officer for bereaved relatives.
- Information from the Criminal Injuries Compensation Authority (CICA).
- Information about Victim Support.
- Enhanced services for vulnerable or intimidated victims.
- An option to opt out of receiving services if they are not wanted.

The code acts as a minimum standard against which the services provided to victims of crime can be measured. Where victims feel that they have not received the level of service they expect they can use the code to complain to the police or to the Parliamentary Ombudsman. The code also requires the police and the CPS to form joint Witness Care Units to ensure that the interests of victims are considered during the prosecution process.

By providing minimum standards, a complaints procedure and a model for Witness Care Units, the code has been highly influential on investigative practice in the area of victim and witness care.

Resource management

Police officers and police staff are by far the single most important resource that the police service has. Policy is often aimed at providing guidance to chief constables about the way in which this resource should be managed. An example is the ACPO *Practice Advice on*

the Resources and the People Assets of the National Intelligence Model
(2007). This describes the roles that are required to make NIM work
effectively in a police force, the training people should receive in order
to be able to perform those roles, and the management structures
that should be put into place to support them. Policies such as this
ensure that there is national consistency in the way in which police
forces manage their resources and it also means that development of
the processes and procedures involved can be done centrally, rather
than every force having to develop them individually.

The management of inter-agency co-operation

Many investigations require co-operation between a number of
agencies and policy can be used to ensure that all of those involved
understand how this co-operation is to be managed and the role
that each agency takes in the investigation. For example, a protocol
exists between ACPO and the Ministry of Defence on the way in
which deaths that occur on land owned by the Ministry of Defence
will be investigated. Such a protocol is needed because a number of
police agencies may have jurisdiction on such land: the Ministry of
Defence Police, the Royal Military Police and the local constabulary.
The protocol provides guidance to all concerned on who has primacy,
how information is to be shared between the police forces involved
and how investigations are to be co-ordinated. Although it does not
deal with any strategic issues, the protocol is highly influential in
individual investigations in these circumstances.

It can be seen from the above that policy has a number of sources
and seeks to achieve a wide range of objectives. It is therefore
more difficult for investigators to access than the law, which is well
documented for them. Policy is nonetheless influential in shaping
how investigations are carried out. It influences the objectives that
are being sought, the resources that are available to achieve them and
the processes by which they are to be achieved.

Conclusion

The law provides a framework for investigators by defining in
concrete terms the type of behaviour that constitutes a criminal
offence, by defining the powers that investigators have to gather
information about a criminal offence, and by setting the standards
for the type, quality and volume of information that are required

before someone can be prosecuted. The police are not obliged to investigate any particular case or use any particular statute. They have a broad crime control mandate and can exercise discretion in how they achieve their objectives. These objectives are not derived from the law, but from a complex policy framework which has at its head the Home Secretary, followed by ACPO and individual chief constables. The objectives they set, and the principles they wish them to be achieved by, determine which crimes get investigated, to what degree and by whom. Thus it can be argued that criminal law is used by the police as a resource for achieving organisational objectives and they certainly don't seek to enforce all laws all the time. Given the range of human behaviour that has been deemed to be criminal and the extent to which people engage in it, it would be impossible for them to do so.

Investigative practice determines the way in which investigators put the law and policy to use in individual cases. In some cases this involves following routine procedures that have been designed to ensure compliance with the relevant legislation. In others it involves complex problem-solving that requires a high level of knowledge, skill and understanding across the full range of issues involved in investigative practice. In either case, investigators need a thorough grasp of the legislation and policy and how these are applied in practice by the courts and police forces.

Further reading

There is a wealth of material on the criminal law and its practice and most libraries provide ready access to reports of individual cases. The Ministry of Justice website is a good source of material (www. justice.gov.uk) and the Office of Public Sector Information (www. opsi.gov.uk) publishes Acts of Parliament online. P. Roberts and A. Zuckerman, *Criminal Evidence* (Oxford: Oxford University Press, 2004) provides in-depth critical analysis of the way in which criminal law is made and practised. P. Connor, G. Hutton, G. McKinnon and D. Johnston, *Blackstone's Police Investigators' Manual 2008* (Oxford: Oxford University Press, 2008) provides investigators with a guide to the criminal law that is tailored specifically to their needs. S. Calligan *Points to Prove* (6th edn, Goole: New Police Bookshop, 2006) is also aimed at practitioners and shows how investigators break down legislation into specific elements and the type of information they seek to gather in order to prove each one.

P. Ozin, H. Horton and P. Spivey, *PACE: A Practical Guide to the Police and Criminal Evidence Act 1984* (Oxford: Oxford University Press, 2006) is written for practitioners and provides a guide to the legislation that underpins virtually all investigative practice. C. Harfield and K. Harfield, *Covert Investigation: A Practical Guide for Investigators* (Oxford: Oxford University Press, 2005) is written by practitioners and provides a guide to the relevant legislation and how it is used in operational situations. V. Williams, *Surveillance and Intelligence Law Handbook* (Oxford: Oxford University Press, 2006) is a comprehensive source of material on the legal aspects of all surveillance techniques.

M. Tonry, *Confronting Crime: Crime Control Policy under New Labour* (Cullompton: Willan Publishing, 2003) examines the political thinking that underpins many of the changes to the criminal law and criminal justice system during the recent past. A different perspective on the political debate about the causes of crime and the most appropriate policy response to it is provided in P. Hitchens, *A Brief History of Crime: The Decline of Order, Justice and Liberty in England* (London: Atlantic Books, 2003).

Policing policy debates tend not to produce a significant literature of their own. They are generally played out between the various stakeholders and in the media. A good source for current issues is the Home Office website (www.homeoffice.gov.uk). This site also provides links to Her Majesty's Inspector of Constabulary (www.homeoffice.gov.uk/hmic/), from where reports that underpin policy developments can be downloaded, for example, HMIC, *Closing the Gap: A Review of the Fitness for Purpose of the Current Structure of Policing in England and Wales* (London: HMIC, 2005), which led to an intense debate about whether the amalgamation of forces would lead to improved services, including criminal investigation. This debate was extensively reported in the media and was eventually resolved in favour of not going ahead with amalgamations. Police authorities were highly influential in this debate and each has a website where policy is often published. ACPO has their own website (www.acpo.police.uk) where many of their policies are available to download.

Chapter 4

Information

Introduction

The law defines the type of behaviour and mental states that must be proved if someone is to be found guilty of a criminal offence. It also shapes the process by which investigators go about the task of locating and gathering the evidence needed to do this. The rules of evidence mean that courts can hear any information that is both relevant to the case and admissible in law. The test of relevance and admissibility are sufficiently wide to mean that under the right circumstances almost any type of information can be presented to a court as evidence. As a consequence, the range of information that is of interest to investigators as potential evidence is very wide. Furthermore, the problems of investigation are not limited to evidence-gathering. Information that would fail the test of relevance and admissibility if it was presented to a court as evidence can still be used by the police to make progress in an investigation by increasing their knowledge of an offence or an offender. For example, an anonymous telephone call to the effect that a person has controlled drugs in their home falls well short of the standards that would enable it to be used in evidence against that person. It may, however, lead the police to locate the drugs and charge the person with an offence based on evidence of possession. The anonymous information is therefore of very high value to the investigation even though it is of no evidential value.

Information in all its forms is therefore central to criminal investigation and the process of investigation principally involves the gathering, interpretation and presentation of information (Maguire 2003: 370). This chapter considers the characteristics of information, how it is generated during the commission of a criminal offence, why there is attrition between the information generated by a criminal offence and the amount that is eventually used in the criminal justice system, how information is transmitted to the police and how it can become distorted in the process.

Information

From an investigator's point of view, two types of information are important. The first is information as *knowledge*. This most often means the first-hand knowledge that victims, witnesses and offenders have about a crime and which they can relate directly to investigators and to courts as testimony. Occasionally it can include information from those with no first-hand knowledge of a crime, such as informants or opinion from experts. The second type is information as *data*, most often in the form of objects, documents, images, recordings and scientific samples from which investigators and courts can infer facts about the case. Both types of information can be used in evidence, but they have different characteristics, as discussed below.

Information as knowledge

A key objective for investigators is to locate those with knowledge of the crime and manage the transfer of that knowledge to the investigation in ways that enable it to be used by investigators and subsequently in court. This involves the use of techniques to locate victims, witnesses and offenders as well as the techniques of recruiting informants and working with experts. This is almost wholly an issue of human communication. There are some technical and procedural issues around locating people in the first place, but obtaining access to their knowledge of the crime depends almost entirely on their willingness to communicate it and the investigator's ability to receive it. The technique for doing this is called investigative interviewing and is examined in more detail in Chapter 5. Those who have knowledge about a crime that may be of use to investigators include the following:

Witnesses and victims

The term 'witness' covers a wide range of people, including victims, who have seen or heard some act related to the crime. They may have seen the crime committed, in which case they are usually referred to as eyewitnesses, although this term has no special status under the law. They may have witnessed some significant act before the crime was committed, such as offenders threatening victims or making preparations to commit the crime. Acts witnessed after a crime can include offenders being in possession of stolen property, or bloodstained clothing, disposing of evidence or leaving scenes. In some cases, offenders tell others what they have done and they then become witnesses. Investigators themselves can become witnesses in a case if they locate data that incriminates an offender, if an offender makes incriminating statements to them during interviews, or if they carry out surveillance that leads them to witness something that is relevant to the case.

Even where victims have no knowledge that could link an offender to a crime, they will usually be able to give sufficient information to prove that an offence has taken place, and information useful to the investigation, such as the time, date and place where the offence occurred, details of the method used to commit it, and in property crimes descriptions of stolen items. Victims often know who the offender is and so may be able to identify them to the police and provide useful information about their previous behaviour and where they can be located. Where they do not know them, they may be able to provide descriptions and other useful information such as the details of vehicles they used.

Offenders

Naturally, offenders are the best source of information about the crimes they have committed. Sometimes they choose to communicate this to others, including investigators. Many of them communicate this knowledge to family, friends and associates, who then become witnesses to the case (Stelfox 2006: 79). A high proportion of offenders (60 per cent) make some form of admission to investigators when they are arrested and interviewed about the offence (Gudjonsson 2007: 476).

Informants

This term is used to describe the wide range of people who may have information relevant to a crime without being a victim, witness or offender. They include those described under Section 26(8) of the Regulation of Investigatory Powers Act 2000 (RIPA) as 'covert human intelligence sources' (CHIS), that is, a person who establishes or maintains a relationship with someone for the purpose of obtaining information that is disclosed covertly to investigators. A CHIS may spontaneously volunteer information to investigators or may be recruited specifically with the intention of gathering information about a particular person or type of crime. The type of information provided, and its usefulness, varies enormously and includes details about criminals such as where they are living, the vehicles they are using, locations of stolen or other types of property or plans for future criminal activity. Because of their proximity to criminals there is always the potential for CHISs to become witnesses, although most do not simply because the information they have is often third-hand and so is not admissible as evidence.

The *Covert Human Intelligence Sources (CHIS) Code of Practice* issued by the Home Office under RIPA makes it clear that the provisions of the Act are not intended to cover circumstances where members of the public volunteer information to investigators as part of their civic duty or to situations where people provide information through telephone hotlines such as Crimestoppers. The term 'community informant' is often used to describe those who are not in the type of relationships to criminals covered by RIPA but have information about a local crime or an offender that they are willing to share with investigators. As with CHISs, this information is very varied and can cover the type of crime that is being committed in an area, those thought to be responsible, community reaction to it, the identities of possible witnesses or other sources of information, and the identification of locations where crime is believed to take place.

Expert advisors

As a general rule, courts are reluctant to hear evidence of a person's opinion. An exception to this is someone who the court recognises as an expert witness, whose training or experience enables them to offer an opinion to a court on a particular matter. For example, a forensic scientist may be allowed to give an expert opinion that the pattern made by the distribution of blood on a wall indicates that the victim was standing in a particular place when struck in a particular manner by the suspect. In giving this opinion the scientist will draw upon the literature of blood distribution and their general scientific knowledge and will be able to explain objectively why they hold that opinion. Opinion of this type is often provided to courts by experts from areas such as medicine, forensic sciences, engineering and psychology, where there is a recognised literature that can support the opinions given.

Whereas courts require experts to give opinion in relation to information that has already been submitted to them as evidence, investigators often need expert opinion in order to locate or interpret the information in the first place. This may involve the same type of experts as those used by courts, but this is not always the case. For example, where a body is located in a river, investigators may consult local fishermen or sailors to establish the likely point at which the body entered the water. In providing this opinion, these people will be drawing on their own experience but are unlikely to be able to point to a body of literature or experimentation of a type that would enable a court to use them as expert witnesses. Their information is nonetheless useful to investigators if it enables them to identify a crime scene.

Even where there is a body of literature, opinion given to the police will not always be admitted as evidence. Behavioural investigative advisors (BIA), often called offender profilers, are able to draw on a body of literature and research to provide investigators with an opinion as to the characteristics of offenders based on what is known of the offence. However, courts are unlikely to allow this to be used as evidence because it will be seen as being prejudicial to the case, suggesting as it does that the offender has characteristics shared by the accused. There is then a wide range of opinion that investigators can access that is unlikely to find its way into the evidence seen by courts, but is nonetheless extremely useful to them in locating and interpreting other information.

Cognition and knowledge

What people think they know about any subject and their ability to recover it and communicate it to others as a memory depends on a number of factors. How well they perceived an event in the first place is an obvious starting point. We experience the world through our five senses. Sight and hearing are the two most relevant to criminal investigation, although taste, smell and touch occasionally play a role. As our brain receives this sensory information it tries to interpret what it means and to store it for future use. The interpretation of sensory information is highly dependent on what we already know of the world: for example, knowing the difference between a gunshot and a door slamming. But the context in which we have the experience can be equally important. For example, a loud bang in the middle of a forest may be interpreted as a gunshot rather than a door slamming because the context makes the former more likely. Of course, people with different experiences of the world and in different contexts may interpret a loud bang as resulting from a car backfiring or a bottle of champagne being opened.

All of this illustrates that from the point at which we first start to acquire our knowledge of an event, things can go wrong due to our failure to interpret the sensory input correctly. This is understandable given the vast amount of sensory input we receive during our waking hours. We cope with this by paying more attention to those inputs that we consider important to us and less to those we believe will not be as useful. This is illustrated by the commonly reported phenomenon of 'weapon focus', where the victims of violent crime are often able to describe the weapons used in great detail but are less clear on other features of the event, the reason being that what was of most importance to them during the incident was the weapon, and so that is what they focused on (Williamson 2007: 77).

The level of attention paid to an event can be problematic in those cases where witnesses do not realise that what they are witnessing may be connected to a crime. They may pay great attention to the description of someone they see climbing into a neighbour's house through a window, but a great deal less to someone who is apparently innocently walking down the street. If it later transpires that the person walking down the street was involved in a crime, witnesses' descriptions may be vague due to their limited attention to what they thought was an insignificant event.

Sensory information is first stored in a sensory store, where it is retained for periods of up to a few seconds. We are not conscious of all of this information and if it is not being used it is quickly lost. If the information is being attended to it goes into the short-term, or working, memory. This is information that we are conscious of, and although it can be lost over about 20 seconds it can be retained by passing into the long-term memory. Our long-term memories appear to have an unlimited capacity but memories decay over time and a great deal can be lost in the first few hours. It is information in the long-term memory of witnesses that constitutes their knowledge of a crime.

However, these memories are not simply recordings of the events that can be replayed accurately at will. As was seen above, the memory itself is unlikely to represent the total sensory information about an event that was received by the witness. In addition, the way they interpreted it may be inaccurate, which is a problem that can be compounded by drug use, physical or emotional states and level of intelligence. But once in the long-term memory, knowledge of an event can become distorted by a range of factors such as discussions witnesses have with others about the event, things they read or hear in the media, the way that questions are put to them by investigators or their mental landscape, which may impose prejudices, assumptions or hypotheses about people and situations on to their memory of the event. These factors mean that witnesses can unintentionally add or subtract detail from their memories, but will still experience the memory as though it were real and may therefore provide a convincing, but inaccurate, account of events to investigators.

The cognitive processes described above can affect witnesses' memories across the full spectrum of knowledge that investigators are interested in, from their descriptions of what they saw or hear through to their identification of suspects on identification parades or from images. But this does not mean that witnesses are always, or even often, wrong. Mistakes are more likely to occur in relation to the fine detail than to the central information about what took place (Williamson 2007: 79). In many investigations it would be difficult to imagine how witnesses could be mistaken about this central information; for example, a victim of domestic violence is hardly likely to be mistaken about the fact that her husband beat her, although she may have some difficulty recollecting exactly how many blows there were.

Information as data

Whereas information as knowledge can only come from human beings, information as data can be derived from a range of sources, such as fingerprints, CCTV, documents, items left at or taken from a scene, and DNA. This data enables investigators and courts to infer facts from it, and thereby increase their knowledge of the crime. Information as data is often very simple to use. For example, an article stolen during a burglary and found hidden in a suspect's home is data. It cannot tell investigators how it got there or who was responsible for the burglary, but it can be used along with other information to make inferences about how it got there and who was responsible for the burglary.

Other types of data require more complex techniques to identify it, gather it and use it. Fingerprints provide a useful example. The configuration of the ridges on people's fingers is thought to be unique to each individual. In the late nineteenth century, fingerprints began to be used for the bureaucratic purpose of ensuring that a person was who they said they were, and this was done by taking a print of their fingertip and comparing it to one that was already on record. It was quickly realised that this technique had an application in crime investigation because when offenders touch an object during the course of a crime they may leave a print of their finger on its surface. If a technique could be developed for locating and gathering such prints, it would enable offenders to be identified. Over time a number of techniques have been developed for locating and gathering fingerprints from a wide range of surfaces and it is now a widely used method of investigation. It is standard practice to keep a record of the fingerprints of known criminals to compare against those found at crime scenes. Even where a fingerprint cannot be matched to someone already known to the police, it is still a very useful way of connecting someone to the scene of a crime once they have been identified as a suspect by other methods.

It can be seen, however, that fingerprints left at the scenes of crimes are not knowledge. They are inert and can tell us nothing until they have been subject to a process that turns them into knowledge. They are data. The same is true of a great deal of the information that is of interest to investigators. CCTV images and sound recordings are data, records of someone's phone use or financial transactions are data, DNA is data, and there are many more examples. What is of significance to investigators is that each type of data generally requires its own technique to locate it, gather it and use it in an investigation: that is, to turn it into knowledge. The data left on the handle of a knife in the form of a fingerprint can only become knowledge for the investigator when it is recovered in a format that enables it to be tested against the national fingerprint database or against suspects. It is convenient to divide data into three categories.

1 *Trace material*. This term refers to any material that results from contact between two things. It is derived from Locard's exchange principle, which holds that every contact between two things leaves a trace. In many cases this material is very small and easily damaged or destroyed and it requires specialist crime scene investigation or other scientific techniques to identify and recover it. It could include fingerprints, bodily fluids, hair, fibres, chemicals or physical marks.

2 *Electronic data*. Electronic data sources include CCTV systems, telephone systems, computers, electronic surveillance equipment such as listening devices and other types of electronic recording systems.

3 *Articles*. Articles covers a wide range of data from things taken from scenes of crime, such as stolen property, weapons used in a crime, vehicles and documents written by offenders.

Investigators are therefore looking for two types of information. They are looking for those with knowledge about the crime that can be transferred to the investigation and they are looking for data from which knowledge can be derived. The distinction between these two types of knowledge is an important one because it underlines the two main sets of skills required by investigators: the ability to communicate effectively with a wide range of people to gain access to what they know about a crime and manage its transfer to the investigation, and the mastery of a wide range of techniques aimed at locating, gathering and using data from which facts about the case can be inferred. In relation to some types of data, these techniques are highly specialised and require the participation of those with the necessary technical expertise such as crime scene investigators or forensic scientists, but even where this is the case, investigators need sufficient knowledge to identify the potential for such material to be present and to task a specialist to look for it and examine it. Table 4.1 lists the type of information that is generated by a crime.

Classifying information

Once investigators have gathered information, it is common to hear them discuss it in relation to three classes: information, intelligence and evidence. These terms are often used with little precision and with local variation. In practice this may not matter provided everyone involved in the investigation, prosecution and defence understands the way in which terms are being used in that case. However, they have specific, and different, meanings, which can be important for investigators, as explored below.

Information

The characteristics of information that are of interest to investigators have already been discussed. In relation to its classification, information is a cover-all term used to describe anything gathered by the police that does not fall into either of the following classes.

93

Table 4.1 The types of information generated by a crime

Type of information	How generated
Knowledge	
Victim and witness accounts	Victims and witnesses may see or hear something of relevance before, during or after the incident. This could include those investigators who have witnessed some relevant fact as a consequence of interviewing suspects, or by carrying out searches or surveillance.
Offender accounts	Offenders may tell others of their involvement in the crime or may make incriminating statements to the police during an investigation.
Informant accounts	Informants learn of information relevant to a crime without having witnessed the events themselves.
Police intelligence	The police may have intelligence from their own records, from partner agencies or from the community that is relevant to an investigation.
Information as data	
Trace material	Offenders leave forensic evidence at the scene in the form of fingerprints, DNA, hair, fibres, impressions, or take forensic material from the scene.
Artefacts	Offenders may take items from the scene of a crime or may leave items there that connect them to the offence. In some cases offenders may be caught in possession of illegal articles or substances, such as controlled drugs, forged money, abusive images of children and suchlike.
Passive data	Offenders may be caught on CCTV cameras or other surveillance systems. Offenders may leave an audit trail of incriminating financial records, or create electronic records of computer use.

Intelligence

Within the police service, intelligence generally has two primary uses. It can be used to make business decisions, such as setting organisational priorities, patrol patterns and suchlike. When used in this way it tends to include information such as crime figures, victim surveys, opinion polls and performance statistics. It is also used to make operational decisions, such as who to investigate, the best time to search a particular premises or where to locate a suspect for arrest. Used in this way it is called operational intelligence and generally includes information about where people live, their lifestyle, associates, and criminal activity, all of which can assist investigators to decide how best to gather more information about them if they become suspects in a crime.

Most intelligence used by the police is what is known as 'open source', which means that it is publicly available. Open source material includes a wide range of information that is created by public and private bodies, such as electoral registers, Driver and Vehicle Licensing Centre (DVLC) records, and credit and business data. In contrast, closed source intelligence comes from sources that are not publicly available, such as informers or police databases such as the PNC or fingerprint databases, which the police wish to keep confidential. The term intelligence is therefore most often used by investigators to describe information from a confidential or sensitive source or from a police database that keeps information about individuals. The term is, however, applied indiscriminately to a wide range of information. From the point of view of an investigator, this does not really make any difference because it is the quality of the information in terms of the knowledge it gives them that is of value, not how it is described. It differs little from information in general and is perhaps more appropriately thought of as being institutionalised information in that it is kept on databases or developed by intelligence systems but its value is no more or less than other information that may become available to investigators. It is significant to note in this respect that the term intelligence is not recognised in the criminal law.

Evidence

Within the criminal justice system not all information has the same status. Ultimately, the police are seeking information that can be converted into evidence (Innes 2003: 56, Maguire 2003: 370), but the rules of evidence mean that not all of the information gathered during an investigation can be used in this way.

95

There is no single definition by which information can be judged to be evidence. At its simplest, evidence is anything that a court allows the prosecution or defence to put before it in order to prove or disprove the facts at issue. Evidence has two main characteristics: *relevance* and *admissibility*.

Information is relevant if its effect is to make guilt or innocence more or less probable. This means that any information relating to the act that constitutes the offence, the offender's state of mind at the time of the offence or even the overall circumstances or story of the crime (called the *res gestae*) is relevant. Thus, for example, the fact that an accused was found in possession of stolen goods, that he admitted to the police that he knew they were stolen and that he had earlier visited a pub where he bought them from a man he did not know (a not infrequent story) are all relevant pieces of information at a trial for handling stolen goods.

Second, evidence must be admissible, and not all information that is relevant is admissible. As a general (but not exclusive) rule, the following types of information are not admissible:

- Hearsay evidence
- Evidence of opinion (except where a court decides to hear expert opinion)
- Evidence of an accused's character
- Information that is privileged
- Evidence that the court excludes because of fairness or for clarity.

There are many exceptions and variations to the above. As a consequence, a body of knowledge has developed in the form of case law and statute, sometimes referred to as 'the rules of evidence', that assists courts to determine what information they will or will not admit as evidence in individual cases. Some of these rules are complex and their interpretation is often a contested area within a trial, so it is not always easy to predict what information will or will not be accepted as evidence in a particular trial. The difficulty of this should not be overstated, however. Investigators soon learn what is likely to be allowed and what disallowed. In any event, it is the lawyers presenting the case to the court who have the responsibility for selecting the information they wish to present as being relevant to the case and admissible. It is the job of investigators to gather material in ways that maximise the chances of it being admitted as evidence by a court. However, it is self-evident that if investigators have not gathered the information in the first place, it is unlikely to be available to present to the court. Investigators must, therefore, have a good working knowledge of the rules of evidence in order to identify information that has the potential to become evidence.

Whether something is labelled information, intelligence or evidence is due entirely to the use to which it is being put by investigators. ACPO *Core Investigation Doctrine* illustrates this by using the example of a CCTV image. It may be information when it informs the police that an incident is occurring at a particular time; it may be termed intelligence when it is used with other information to suggest the identities of those involved; and it may be evidence when it is used in a prosecution file against an accused (ACPO 2005b: 46).

Material

Investigators gather information within the specific context of the criminal law with the intention of bringing offenders to justice. This means that they are not simply increasing their personal knowledge of the incident, as would be the case if they were carrying out private study; at some point they must transmit this knowledge to others. They may do this internally, for example when communicating progress in the case to managers, or externally, for example when providing victims with updates. Ultimately, they may pass this knowledge to others in the criminal justice system who use the information to prosecute and defend a case. The information that investigators gather must therefore be contained in a form that enables it to be transmitted, in order for others to examine and interpret it. The term used in the CPIA 1996 and defined in the Code of Practice written under Part II of the Act to describe the many forms that information comes in is 'material'.

> Material is material of any kind, including information and objects, which is obtained in the course of a criminal investigation and which may be relevant to the investigation.; Material may be relevant to an investigation if it appears to an investigator, or to the officer in charge of an investigation, or to the disclosure officer, that it has some bearing on any offence under investigation or any person being investigated, or on the surrounding circumstances of the case, unless it is incapable of having any impact on the case.

This comprehensive definition is intended to include anything that investigators could potentially gather during an investigation.

Material can be thought of as the form in which information is recorded for the purposes of an investigation. Some material is available in its original form, for example large articles such as tools and stolen property, or documents. Some is recorded in the form of photographs of crime scenes or statements of witness accounts. Some, for example witness accounts, may be recorded in several ways: there may be a tape recording of the phone call the witness made to the police reporting the incident; the officer who first attended may have recorded brief details of what the witness said in a notebook; an investigator may later have interviewed the witness in more depth and taken notes of that interview; finally, a formal witness statement will have been taken for use by lawyers and court. The tape, the notebook, the rough notes and the formal written statement are all material recording the account of the witness. In the case of accounts, however, what courts are ultimately interested in is hearing the witness personally in court under oath. Commonly, forms of material include:

- Statements
- Documents
- Reports
- Physical exhibits such as weapons, clothing, stolen goods and biological or chemical material
- Fingerprints
- Images
- Audio or video recordings.

Thus, from the point of view of investigators, information always has a tangible form in that it is contained in material of one sort or another. It is the location and collection of this material that is at the heart of the investigation process.

Information profiles

When people engage in behaviour that has been deemed to be criminal they generate information in a number of ways. They may be observed by witnesses doing or saying something relevant to the crime; they may take articles from the crime scene or leave things there that can link them to the offence; their presence in a particular place may be recorded on a surveillance system; their interaction with various electronic systems, such as banking facilities, creates records that can link them to the crime; and their interaction with the physical environment can generate forensic evidence such as fingerprints, fibres and DNA, which can be used to identify them as the offender.

The total information generated by the commission of a particular offence can be thought of as its information profile and it is this information that investigators seek to gather. Because offenders commit crime in different ways and in different types of environments, they generate different types and volumes of information. This information is also distributed to different degrees among scenes, witnesses and electronic systems. As a consequence of these differences, the information profile of each offence is likely to be in some ways unique. A homicide committed in the course of a burglary provides a good example of how an information profile is generated during the course of an incident and how it could easily be different. In this case, the offender committed a burglary in the early hours of the morning by forcing a ground-floor kitchen window and climbing into the house. The victim, who was alone in the house, awoke and confronted the offender. The offender stabbed the victim before fleeing through the same kitchen window by which he had entered.

The physical evidence that this incident generated was the offender's fingerprints; some of these were in the victim's blood, thus linking him to the attack. The victim's blood also spilled on to the offender's shoes and he carried it away from the scene with him. The accounts generated by this incident were that of the victim himself, who survived the attack for some while and was able to describe to the police what had happened, and that of a next-door neighbour who had heard the attack and looked out of a window, from where he saw the offender running away from the victim's home. These accounts gave the police an accurate timing of the offence, information on the type of incident they were dealing with and a description of the offender. The fingerprint and the blood on the shoe were later to link the offender to this crime.

The information in this case arose from the unique dynamics of that incident and it can easily be imagined how slight changes to the circumstances of the incident could have changed the level of information. Leaving aside the obvious point that had the victim slept through the burglary the homicide might never have occurred in the first place, other changes such as the offender wearing gloves, the victim dying during the attack, the neighbour not hearing the attack or not going to a window from where he could see the offender fleeing, would all have changed the level of information that was available for the police to collect in this case.

This example shows how the circumstances in which individual crimes are committed produce a unique information profile, varying by volume, type and distribution. Measuring the amount of information generated by offences is impossible and investigators can never predict for certain how much information there is to gather and where it is distributed. However, because some types of offence are committed in ways that are very similar, they generate information profiles that are typical of that offence type.

For example, those who commit burglaries of homes tend to force an entry through a door or window and search rooms for valuables. This means that the information profile of burglary will often contain marks and fibres at the point of entry where physical force has been used to gain access. Fingerprints may be found in those areas that have been searched and footwear marks may be left as offenders make their way around the building. There are unlikely to be witnesses to the burglary itself because offenders are able to control the time and place at which they break in, but neighbours may have seen the burglar in the area immediately before or after the offence and there may be witnesses who later see the offender with the stolen goods. There will also generally be a list of items stolen from the house together with their description, and possession of this property could subsequently connect offenders to the crime.

Naturally there will be differences between individual burglaries because every home is different, not all burglars will use the same method, and some burglars will be more skilled than others at reducing the information they generate during the course of the crime. Even so, the information profiles of burglaries committed in homes are likely to be broadly similar because of the way in which such offences are committed. In contrast, the information profile of a fraud is more likely to consist of falsified documents, diverted monies or goods and the misrepresentation of facts. There is unlikely to be a single crime scene of the type found in burglaries and witnesses are more likely to be found among those who work with offenders or who have business dealings with them. Banking and other financial information is also likely to be generated. As with burglaries, the information profile of frauds will vary between individual offences, but all frauds are likely to have a broadly similar profile.

The differences in the information profiles between offence types arise from the way in which each type of offence is characteristically committed. Table 4.2 shows the differences between the information profiles of a typical burglary and a typical fraud.

The techniques of investigation (which are discussed in Chapter 5) are generally designed to locate and gather particular types of information from particular sources. For example, where investigators believe that the witnesses to a crime may live or work in a particular location they will generally visit all premises in the area to identify them. This involves using a technique commonly known as 'house to house', which is described in detail in the ACPO *Practice Advice on House to House Enquiries* (2006). If, on the other hand, they believe that the witnesses are likely to be found amongst those who were in a particular place at the time of the offence, for example witnesses to an assault in a bar, they will most likely question those they know were present with a view to finding out what they saw of the incident, but also what they know of others who were also present at the same time. This technique is known as 'snowballing' because the investigation gathers more witnesses as it rolls along. The relationship between information types and the techniques investigators use to locate and gather it means that the investigation of different types of crime use characteristic menus of techniques. For example, the techniques of crime scene examination are used far more often in the investigation of burglary than they are in fraud because of the differences in the information profiles of the two crime types.

An understanding of the type of information that is generated by a criminal offence, its volume and the way it is distributed between scenes and among witnesses, together with an insight into the type of variation that exists between crimes, is essential for investigators because they must know what type of information they are looking for and where it might be found. If they do not have this knowledge they would find it difficult to choose the correct techniques to deploy in any given situation.

The problem from an investigator's point of view is that at the outset of an investigation they rarely know what the information profile of a case is with any degree of certainty. When a crime is first reported, they may have very little information from the person reporting it, and may not even know if the behaviour complained of is a crime. The action they take will be determined by their understanding of the type of crime and its typical information profile. In the case of burglary they will generally assume that physical evidence may be found at the scene, and will therefore arrange for a crime scene investigator to attend. In the case of an assault they may want to gather evidence of the injuries and any physical evidence that has transferred from

Table 4.2 Comparison of information profiles between burglary and fraud

	Burglary	Fraud
Crime Scene	Points of entry: • Tool marks • Shoe marks • Fingerprints • Fibres from the offender's clothing • DNA if offenders cut themselves, spit or leave other bodily fluids. Areas searched: • Very similar to the point of entry.	May be difficult to identify a significant scene. Where one does exist: • Latent impressions in surfaces and documents may indicate forgery/alteration of documents. • Fingerprints and DNA may prove the unauthorised presence of someone in scene.
Witnesses	• Unlikely to have seen the burglary but may be located among those living and working nearby who may have seen offenders going to or leaving the house. • There may be eyewitnesses to offender's possession of stolen articles • Offenders may confide their guilt in someone.	• Unlikely to have seen the fraud but may be located among those who work with offenders or for companies and institutions doing business with them. • Offenders may confide their guilt in others.
The proceeds of crime	• Offenders may be found in possession of identifiable stolen items. • Offenders may be found in possession of money or goods exchanged for stolen items.	• The proceeds are unlikely to be identifiable goods. • Offenders may be found in possession of money or goods derived from the fraud.

Passive data   CCTV may provide images of offenders:

- Prior to the offence
- During the offence
- After the offence.

Financial records may provide material about offenders profiting from the offence.

CCTV may provide images of offenders:

- Prior to the offence
- During the offence
- After the offence.

Financial records may provide material about offenders profiting from the offence.

Financial records may provide material relating to fraudulent transactions.

Procurement, invoicing and delivery systems may provide material relating to fraudulent transactions.

the offender to the victim, and will arrange an examination by a forensic medical examiner. In the case of fraud, they may carry out a preliminary examination of the alleged offender's financial records to identify any income that corresponds to the alleged offence. The point is that all these techniques are used on the assumption that certain types of information may have been generated because of the type of crime that is involved. The type of information gathered as the result of these preliminary investigations will determine the way in which the investigation unfolds thereafter.

The attrition of information

There is generally a great deal of attrition between the volume of information contained in the information profile of an offence, the volume of material that is gathered during an investigation and, if a suspect is charged with an offence, the volume of evidence presented to a court. The point is illustrated in Figure 4.1.

This attrition occurs for a number of reasons. Information as data, particularly the type of information collected for forensic examination such as body fluids, fibres and impressions, is very fragile and may degrade before it can be recovered. Data that is recorded automatically, such as CCTV images, may be wiped clean or recorded over before anyone realises its value to the investigation. Information as knowledge can be lost due to the cognitive processes described above or may not come to the attention of investigators because of the choices made by victims, witnesses and offenders. Lastly, investigators may make decisions that mean they fail to identify information or may misinterpret it once they have located it. All these issues are discussed in more detail in Chapter 8, where the question of how crimes come to be solved is considered. For the present, it is sufficient to note that one of the main aims of an

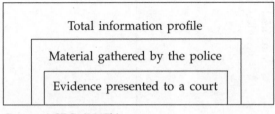

Source: ACPO (2005b)

Figure 4.1 Attrition of information

investigation is to ensure that the attrition between the information profile of crime and the evidence presented to courts is as small as possible.

Conclusion

Information is central to the task of criminal investigation. The information that is of interest to investigators is of two types: information as knowledge and information as data. This distinction is an important one because each of these types has different characteristics, which means that the techniques used to locate, gather and use them are different. Information as knowledge requires investigators to identify those who know something about the offence and to manage the transfer of that knowledge to the investigation. This requires investigators to understand some of the cognitive processes involved in creating what people know about any event and knowing how to communicate effectively to ensure that they pass it to the investigation effectively. Communication skills are the key to success here and they form the basis of the techniques of investigative interviewing, which is discussed more fully in Chapter 5. In relation to information as data, the issues are a great deal different. Here, the difficulties facing investigators are mainly technical ones concerned with the legality of gaining access to premises where data may be found or access to data that is owned by others, such as financial records. The range of data that is of interest is also very wide and investigators must know its characteristics if they are to successfully locate it, recover it and use it.

The amount of information generated by the offence, or its information profile, will be a significant factor in determining the outcome of an investigation. Where offenders have, through planning or good luck, generated small information profiles, it may be impossible for investigators to make progress in the case. In other cases the information profile will be large and so there is a greater chance of identifying and gathering individual items of information. But whatever the size of the information profile, the behaviour after the event of offenders, witnesses and communities can significantly affect the chances that investigators will locate the material they need to bring the case to a successful conclusion. Investigators can maximise their chances of locating and gathering the material in the information profile through the skilled use of the techniques of criminal investigation, which are discussed in the next chapter.

Further reading

The subject of information as knowledge is generally dealt with in the psychological literature. A good introduction is provided in P.B. Ainsworth, *Psychology, Law and Eyewitness Testimony* (Chichester: Wiley, 2001) and by A. Memon, A. Vrij and R. Bull, *Psychology and Law: Truthfulness, Accuracy and Credibility* (2nd edn, Chichester: John Wiley, 2003). A short account of the main issues of information as knowledge is provided in T. Williamson, 'Psychology and Criminal Investigation' in T. Newburn, T. Williamson and A. Wright, *Handbook of Criminal Investigation* (Cullompton: Willan Publishing, 2007).

With the exception of trace material, which is included in the extensive literature on forensic science, information as data has received a great deal less attention by researchers than information as knowledge. Good sources for information about trace materials are A.R.W. Jackson and J.M. Jackson, *Forensic Science* (2nd edn, Harlow: Pearson Educational, 2008), which has good sections on individual types of trace material.

The relationship between types of crime and the information profiles they give rise to has not been explored by researchers and this is an area that has a great deal of potential for practitioner researchers.

Chapter 5

The techniques of investigation

Introduction

Previous chapters have examined how the criminal law is used to define certain types of behaviour as being criminal and how, when people behave in these ways, they create an information profile. This chapter examines the techniques that are available to investigators to locate, gather and use the information in that profile. Although there is a limited number of these techniques, the range of circumstances in which criminal offences are committed and the many ways in which the various players behave afterwards means that these techniques are used in a wide variety of ways. Proficiency in applying them across the full spectrum of situations where they will be required is a key skill for investigators.

To a large extent, the techniques of criminal investigation correspond to the types of information discussed in Chapter 4. Table 5.1 shows this relationship, together with key sub-techniques and the types of material that the techniques characteristically produce.

The basics of these practical skills can be taught, but competence in their use can only really be developed by using them in operational settings. As investigators become more experienced and progress to more complex investigations they should become more skilled in applying the techniques in more difficult circumstances.

Table 5.1 The techniques of criminal investigation

Information type	Technique	Key sub-technique	Material
Knowledge	Investigative interviewing	Victims and witnesses	Witness statements, officers' notes, audio tapes, video tapes, any notes the victim or witness made themselves prior to police interview.
		Suspects	Taped interviews, officers' notes, written statements made by the suspect.
		Community informants	Officers' notes, intelligence reports.
		Covert Human Intelligence Sources (CHIS)	Intelligence reports.
	Surveillance	Human surveillance	Surveillance logs, officers' notes, officers' statements, photographic or video images.
		Technical surveillance	Photographic or video images, audio recordings.
	Witness canvassing	Media appeals	} Copies of media products, records of calls from the public, contact details for potential witnesses.
		House-to-house enquiries	
		Anniversary and road checks	
		Snowballing	
	Intelligence management and analysis		Database information, intelligence reports.

Data		
Search		Found articles, officers' notes, witness statements from those involved in the search.
Crime scene investigation		Found trace material, photographic and video images, officers' notes, witness statements from those involved in the examination.
Forensic examination	Science, Pathology, Medical examination, Accountancy	Trace material, scientists' notes, witness statements describing the process, its findings and the significance they have for the investigation.
CCTV		CCTV images, officers' notes, witness statements from those involved in managing CCTV systems and those involved in finding and analysing images.
Financial		Financial transaction data (including bank and credit card details), officers' notes, witness statements from those involved in managing financial records and those involved in finding and investigating them.
Telephone data		Telephone billing data, cell site analysis, officers' notes, witness statements from those involved in managing the data and those involved in locating it and investigating it.
Computer records		Computer data, officers' notes, witness statements from those involved in making the computer records and those involved in locating and investigating them.
Elimination enquiries	Can involve all of the above	Officers' notes, witness statement.

Knowledge

The key focus of a criminal investigation is to acquire knowledge about the offence under investigation. This can come from a variety of sources:

- Those with direct knowledge of the offence: victims, witnesses and offenders. In some circumstances, investigators may acquire direct knowledge through the use of interview, surveillance, search or forensic techniques.

- Those with indirect knowledge of the offence or information relevant to it: community informants, and covert human intelligence sources (CHIS).

These sources become known to investigators in various ways. Some come forward spontaneously, often while initial investigations are being carried out at scenes or as the result of techniques specifically designed to locate them such as media appeals or house-to-house enquiries. Some are identified through other techniques of investigation such as the examination of CCTV images, financial records or telephone analysis. Less often, they are identified as a result of forensic techniques, for example when DNA at the scene of an assault is found to be from someone who was present but was not the offender. This section will deal primarily with the two techniques that are specifically associated with the location of witnesses: media appeals and house-to-house enquiries. Other techniques will be dealt with later in the chapter.

Locating witnesses

Media appeals
Most investigators view the media as a mixed blessing. There is no doubt that media appeals do lead to the identification of witnesses and the generation of useful material. How often this happens is unknown, although anecdotally it is rare. Most media outlets – newspapers, radio and television – are primarily interested in acquiring material to provide interesting stories. Crime is high on their list of interesting stories and so they are always willing to cover it. This provides investigators with an opportunity to publicise crimes and appeal for witnesses. Finding witnesses will not be a reporter's principal interest. Developing a good story is their objective and so investigators often find themselves in a position where they must

provide information about a crime in the hope that the media will include an appeal for witnesses. Most often the media view this as a fair trade-off and are happy to oblige, particularly local media which has an interest in maintaining a good working relationship with investigators in their area. There is no guarantee that a story will be reported in ways that are favourable to the investigation. Most investigators sooner or later experience situations where a crime is reported in a way that is unhelpful, simply because it makes a better story, or it is not reported at all because it is considered too mundane.

Major crime investigations and high-profile incidents always attract media interest and investigators are usually able to deploy specialist resources from their force media department in these cases. Trained staff are able to advise on a media strategy that maximises the chance of the crime being reported in ways that support the investigation. This often includes strategies for keeping the story in the news even when interest in it is waning. Smaller, local investigations rarely receive this type of professional support and, depending on a force's policies, investigators are often left to formulate and implement their own media strategy.

The first step in gaining publicity for an individual crime is to ensure that the victim is willing to have the details publicised. Strictly speaking, the police are able to publicise crime without the consent of victims, in which case they would seek to ensure anonymity for them, but this is only likely to happen in the case of serious offences where the public interest overrides the wishes of individuals. In the case of less serious crime, with which the vast majority of investigations are concerned, it makes sense to seek publicity for those crimes only where the victim is happy to co-operate. Most local media have a system of ringing the police in their area regularly to be updated on crimes that may be of interest to them and this is the usual way in which investigators bring crimes to their attention. In using the media, a balance has to be struck between the needs of an investigation and causing unnecessary fear amongst local communities. There is always the danger that crime stories will be sensationalised in ways that misrepresent the real level of threat of crime within a community, without producing any useful material for the investigation.

House-to-house enquiries (HtoH)

House-to-house enquiries is the name given to the techniques that can be used for two purposes:

- To identify suspects by establishing who lives or works in a particular location and obtaining an account of their movements during relevant times.
- To canvass for witnesses in areas relevant to the crime.

In most cases investigators will seek to achieve both these objectives. The ACPO *Murder Investigation Manual* (2006a: 189) identifies a third, ancillary, objective of providing reassurance and advice to the community following a crime.

HtoH is most often used in residential locations but can be deployed in any area where people are associated with premises, for example business parks, shopping centres or industrial estates. Although they are often associated with homicide or other serious crime, HtoH is a technique that can be used in any type of investigation. At its simplest HtoH can involve nothing more than visiting premises adjacent to the crime scene or along a route thought to have been used by an offender to identify witnesses. This is probably the most common use of this technique. In homicide or major incident investigations it can be resource-intensive and can generate a large volume of material that must be processed and may lead to a great many subsequent enquiries.

Clarity and timing are the key features of HtoH. Investigators need to have a clear idea of what information they are seeking and in complex cases may develop a questionnaire to ensure that all the information they require is collected in a structured way. In more straightforward cases they will simply be trying to assess if the occupants saw anything of value and will in all probability simply ask that question. Timing can be a significant factor because it is important that investigators know enough about the crime to decide on the best area in which to conduct enquiries and to frame sensible questions. For this reason investigators sometimes wait for more information to become available before embarking on large-scale HtoH, although there is obviously a tension between this and the need to gather information as quickly as possible.

Overall, HtoH is a very basic investigative technique that can be undertaken by anyone. Despite its simplicity, it is potentially one of the most fruitful in that it has the potential to quickly identify witnesses who may, if not approached directly in this way, take some time to be discovered by other means.

Snowballing

Snowballing is a technique often used to identify witnesses and simply involves asking those interviewed if they know of anyone else who may be a witness. Like a snowball gathering more snow as it rolls down a hill, this technique gathers more witnesses as investigators work their way through those they already know of. Although this is an obvious thing to do, it can be highly effective in identifying those who were present during an incident. Snowballing can also draw on other investigative techniques, such as CCTV viewing and the analysis of communications data. By identifying one person in an image, or in a sequence of phone calls, investigators can often use this simple technique to identify everyone else who was present.

Anniversary appeals and stop checks

Most of us have some form of routine to our lives and visit the same locations on a regular basis. The frequency with which we do so obviously varies depending on the type of activity involved. We may visit the same newspaper shop each morning, the same supermarket each week, the same barber each month and the same hotel each year. If a crime occurs in virtually any location, there will be those whose routine takes them to or near the scene, and they may be potential witnesses. They may leave the scene without realising that something they saw was significant, or believing that other witnesses will come forward and their account would add little of value. They may also wish not to become involved with the investigation. Whatever the reason, such people can often be located by investigators making enquiries in the area at times when regular visitors are likely to be identified.

Anniversary appeals are a way of doing this. The exact method used will vary depending on the venue and the number of people involved. If the venue is small and there are only a few visitors, then approaching each one and interviewing them is a viable option, but as the size of the venue and the number of people grows, this becomes more difficult. In these circumstances investigators often use police mobile offices or even officers standing with notices drawing attention to the incident as a way of canvassing for witnesses. This is obviously a less satisfactory method as it requires witnesses to volunteer, but it is sometimes the only viable option. Some venues, such as motorways and main roads, make it almost impossible to carry out this type of activity and in these case notices at the side of the carriageway are used to appeal for witnesses.

In the investigation of very serious crimes, the police have the power to stop and question pedestrians and motorists to establish if they are witnesses. The procedure in these cases is the same as for carrying out small-scale anniversary checks where each individual is spoken to.

Investigative interviewing

Investigative interviewing is the pre-eminent technique of criminal investigation. Without effective interviewing, no other technique is likely to be effective and most investigations would not get beyond the initial report. Investigators have to use investigative interviewing techniques to get initial accounts from victims and witnesses that enable them to identify both the type of situation they are dealing with and the other techniques that may be of value in gathering further material. Interview techniques are also valuable in gathering material throughout the investigation, particularly when interviewing suspects, during which the products of all other techniques are brought together. Because investigative interviewing is a technique that can be mastered by every investigator, it is also one that is readily deployed when the situation requires. There is no need to task specialists or await results. Interviews can be done quickly and cheaply and the results are instantly available. For this reason, all investigators need to be proficient in investigative interviewing.

The model of investigative interviewing adopted in England, Wales and Northern Ireland was developed in response to widespread criticism of techniques the police used to interview suspects until the 1990s. These were focused almost exclusively on obtaining a confession, rather than on generating material in general. In 1992, the PEACE model of investigative interviewing was introduced.

Preparation and planning
Engage and explain
Account
Closure
Evaluation

The model aims at legal and ethical compliance as well as maximising the material generated during the interview. The model was intended to be applied to both witness and suspect interviews, but there is little doubt that it has been more influential in the latter.

Victims and witnesses
The law provides investigators with a great deal of freedom when speaking to people during the course of an investigation. As a basic

starting point they can speak to anyone who is willing to speak to them. They can if they wish, record what is said in writing and, although they cannot repeat this to a court – that would be hearsay evidence – they could state to a court that the person had relevant information and the court could summons the person to appear to give evidence. The courts have a number of coercive powers to make people give evidence, although they are very reluctant to use them on the grounds that evidence obtained by coercion is considered unsound.

Although circumstances vary enormously, the general pattern is for investigators to obtain an initial account of what victims and witnesses know when they first encounter them, and then follow this up with a formal interview during which a written statement is taken. The reason for this two-stage process is simply that many victim and witnesses will be at the scene of the crime as the investigators arrive in response to a call for assistance. Investigators need to gain information about the nature of the incident and the role played by those present, so they must ask some preliminary questions. There is often little opportunity to plan such encounters or to record the answers with any degree of accuracy. It may also be that victims or witnesses are injured, or that the situation is potentially dangerous, and so investigators' first priorities will be to provide medical assistance or to make the situation safe rather than to gather material that is useful to the investigation. These first encounters are therefore inherently difficult to manage from a material-gathering point of view. It is usually only when investigators have dealt with immediate problems of injuries or safety, and have enough information to understand what has occurred and the roles played by those present, that purposeful interviewing and recording can begin. At this stage often only the salient points of what victims and witnesses say are recorded, with a view to a more thorough interview at a later stage when a statement can be obtained, either written or on tape.

When responding to reports of major crimes a large number of people may be spoken to as potential witnesses and individual officers may not have sufficient information themselves to know if they are witnesses or not. In such cases they submit initial accounts to the major incident room, which arranges to have written statements taken if necessary.

The PEACE model is still relevant to the taking of an initial account, but clearly has to be modified to the situation in which investigators find themselves. With practice investigators develop a method for approaching such situations, and planning in this context often involves nothing more than having a structured way of obtaining the information from those present. Some forces have experimented with hand-held tape recorders and even mobile video cameras, and these have the potential to overcome this problem entirely, although there is presently no information available on how practical investigators have found them to be.

During this initial contact, investigators must also determine the status of the victim or witness in relation to various statutory and procedural provisions aimed at providing enhanced safeguards for children, and vulnerable and intimidated witnesses.

Initial accounts are followed as soon as possible by the recording of the victim's or witness's statement, which will be either written, or in audio or video format, according to local practice and the legal and procedural requirements relating to the case. There are different procedures relating to each of these methods of recording. Whichever method is used, the principal challenge facing investigators is to ensure that they gather the fullest account possible in ways that maintain the integrity of the information. As was seen in Chapter 4, an individual's account of what they saw or heard can become distorted in a number of ways, and investigators must ensure, as far as they are able, that they do not inadvertently contribute to this problem.

Written statements

Most witness accounts are recorded in written statements. A written statement is an account of a witness's evidence, prepared for use in court. It is not necessarily everything that the witness said to investigators. It is obvious that it could not be. A great deal of the conversation between investigators and witnesses is incidental to their account. Investigators will try to put witnesses at ease, will explain the process to them and may try to build a rapport by discussing issues that are not relevant to the investigation. In other words, investigators will have conversations with witnesses about a whole array of issues that will not be included in the statement. Even when they are discussing issues that are central to a witness's account, there will be repetition, witnesses may digress, pass comments that are irrelevant or ask the investigator questions about process or procedure. They may even discuss things that investigators know will not be allowed by the court. Investigators are forced to make choices about how much of this to include and so no witness statement taken by an investigator can be considered to reflect everything that was said during the interview, nor are they expected to. The witness statement is supposed to be an accurate reflection of what the witness knows of the crime which enables those involved in the investigation, the defence, the prosecution or trial to see what the witness will say if called to give evidence at a trial. It is open to either the defence or the prosecution to call any witness to give oral evidence and it is this, not the contents of their written statement, that constitutes their testimony in the case. On many occasions, all the parties to a trial will agree that the statement is an accurate reflection of a witness's testimony and in such cases they agree not to call the witness to give oral evidence, and their statement is used instead.

The danger with witness statements is that by leaving out much of what is said, it is possible to omit information that could be useful to an investigator, prosecutor or defence solicitor. Lawyers also sometimes fear that a statement made in this way is subject to manipulation by investigators who may, knowingly or not, steer witnesses towards presenting their accounts in ways that are favourable to the case they are building. Despite these shortcomings, written statements remain the most common way for witness accounts to be recorded.

Audio and video recordings

Audio and video recordings are increasingly used to capture witness accounts. There are two main reasons for this.

First, a recording can overcome some of the shortcomings of written statements discussed above. An audio or video recording makes everything that was said during an interview available to those who need it. This enables a more detailed examination of the witness's account to be carried out and so provides a much richer source of material than is available in a written statement. From the point of view of the quality of material produced, recording of this sort is far preferable to written statements. The main drawback is that facilities for carrying out witness interviews at police stations are limited and so may not always be readily available when they are needed. Audio and video recordings also give rise to a far greater volume of material that may need to be transcribed for court purposes. It seems likely, however, that the benefits of recording witness interviews in this way will mean that these difficulties will eventually be overcome.

Second, witness accounts may be recorded in order to minimise the number of times witnesses have to recount their evidence. This happens most often in the case of child victims of abuse. The police, social workers and medical staff may all need information about what happened and to reduce the number of times the child has to recount the events a joint interview is carried out and then shared with those who have legitimate need of it.

As with written statements, if the parties agree, the video or extracts or transcripts from it can be used in court to avoid the witness giving evidence in person.

Community informants and covert human intelligence sources (CHIS)

The principles of investigative interviewing that are applied to witnesses apply equally to community informants and CHISs. A number of legal steps under the Regulation of Investigatory Powers Act 2000 (RIPA) are required to be taken before a CHIS can be tasked with gathering information on behalf of investigators. No such constraints apply, however, to community informants, who generally provide more general information about crime and community issues in an area. Interviews with both these types of informants need to be as rigorous as those with victims or witnesses, because although there may be an expectation that the material they provide is unlikely to become evidence, it can be extremely useful to the investigation and so its quality is important. Furthermore, both community informants and CHISs can in some circumstances become witnesses in court and so it is important that they have been treated in accordance with the principles of investigative interviewing from the outset.

Suspects

The interviewing of suspects is potentially one of the most difficult techniques investigators have to carry out. Suspects may choose to exercise their right not to speak to investigators during interview, some may lie about their involvement in the crime, some may lie about some aspects of it while being truthful in others, some will provide a frank and honest account, and some may have only a sketchy idea of the crime because of intoxication, drug misuse or for other reasons which have impaired their ability to recall. Some of those interviewed as suspects will undoubtedly be innocent of the crime. Some will be articulate, some will have great difficulty in making themselves understood, some will be clever, others less so. Some will be vulnerable to making false confessions of their involvement.

The key to dealing with this mass of potential responses from interviewees is to understand that it is not the interviewer's role to arrive at the truth. That is the role of the courts. Far less is it an investigator's role to obtain a confession, although until the introduction of the PEACE model that was the understanding of many investigators, and it is still the basis of interviewing techniques in some countries. In the UK, the role of the interviewer is to get a suspect's account of their involvement in the offence in a way that provides the maximum confidence from the courts that it has been obtained fairly and that facilitates its corroboration or refutation by other material. This actually takes a great deal of skill and requires the investigator to have a thorough knowledge of the points that need to be proved for the offence being investigated, the relevant case law, and the way in which the material gathered during the investigation implicates the suspect. In particular, the investigator needs to understand any gaps, anomalies or uncertainties in the material and how these might be explored during interview.

For example, in a burglary case the only evidence may be a suspect's fingerprint found at the scene. Enquiries with the victim may have established that the suspect is not known to them and this has led to the inference that the suspect is the offender. There are, of course, other potential explanations. The suspect may have had legitimate access to the house which the victim has forgotten about or was unaware of. As far as possible these will have been investigated prior to the interview but it is likely that the investigator has some gaps in their knowledge about how the suspect's fingerprint came to be in the house. The obvious way of filling this gap is to ask the suspect. If there is an innocent explanation, all well and good, but if the suspect is the offender, revealing the existence of a fingerprint too early may provide the suspect with the opportunity to improvise an explanation that leads to them escaping justice. In this situation many investigators would not reveal the presence of the fingerprint to the suspect but would question them about their work and lifestyle with a focus on whether they go into people's houses. This will be followed by questions about their acquaintances to establish if they know the victim or anyone associated with them. Further questions may be put to them about the occasions when they have visited that area or that street. They will then be asked if they have had legitimate access to the house in question. If the answer is 'no', they will be invited to explain the presence of their fingerprint. If they say 'yes' they will be asked questions to verify that fact, such as when, who with and for what purpose. If they are lying it is highly unlikely that they will be able to sustain a series of answers that are consistent across the full range of these questions. If they are telling the truth, they will have provided a rich amount of detail that will enable investigators to corroborate their answers.

Questioning in this manner is not designed to obtain a confession, although that is still a possibility. It is designed to obtain an account that can be tested in ways that enable courts to use it to determine guilt or innocence.

Surveillance

Surveillance techniques are used to enable investigators to obtain knowledge of offenders directly, rather than through witnesses or informants. They are used to keep observations on locations, for example a shopping area where street robberies are taking place, or people such as a suspected drug-dealer. They are particularly useful in situations where an offence may take place and investigators want to be on hand to observe it themselves and make an arrest, and in situations where it is unlikely that there will be other witnesses who will come forward.

Surveillance techniques can be divided into two basic types: human surveillance, which seeks to put investigators into positions where they can directly witness the actions of offenders, and technical surveillance, where devices such as cameras or microphones are placed in locations where they will record the actions or speech of offenders.

Human surveillance can be further divided into *static*, where officers use an observation post to carry out surveillance of a location associated with an offender or an offence, and *mobile*, where investigators follow offenders with the intention of recording their movements, contacts and behaviour. Static surveillance can be carried out by any investigator. The level of expertise required to remain undetected depends on the level of criminal experience of the offender and the circumstances in which the surveillance is being carried out. For example, it is common for investigators to keep high-crime locations under surveillance with the object of identifying offenders. Such an operation may involve little more than observing the area from a nearby building and alerting other officers to stop suspicious people and vehicles. Finding observation posts overlooking the area and occupying them in ways that will not alert offenders is likely to be relatively easy and the observations themselves to be straightforward. Such operations are very common and present few difficulties. On the other hand, keeping the home of a drug-dealer under observation in this way is likely to be a great deal harder because residential areas generally present fewer suitable observation posts and the offender may be sufficiently cautious to avoid committing incriminating acts in sight of them or to check them out before doing so. The operational difficulty of carrying out a static observation in this type of case will usually call for experienced and well-trained investigators.

Mobile surveillance is inherently difficult and those who carry it out have received specialist training in the relevant techniques. This is to avoid situations where offenders continually identify that they are subject of surveillance and, over time, develop counter-surveillance techniques of their own. Mobile surveillance usually calls for a large team of trained investigators who have specialist equipment that enables them to keep in communication with each other.

Technical surveillance involves placing listening or viewing devices in locations where they are likely to capture useful material. CCTV cameras deployed in public and private spaces are a form of surveillance of this type but it is usually used overtly in such situations. The essence of technical surveillance in the sense used here is that it is covert. Specialist technicians are required to install and maintain the equipment and so investigators wishing to use this type of surveillance have to liaise with specialist units in order to deploy this technique.

Covert[1] surveillance encroaches on Article 8 of the Human Rights Act 1998, which deals with the right to respect for private and family life. As a consequence, both human and technical surveillance are regulated by RIPA, which provides a legal basis for this encroachment provided it is authorised. There are various levels of authorisation depending on the severity of the encroachment. In all instances, investigators must make out a written case for carrying out the surveillance against particular individuals or locations.

The first challenge faced by investigators carrying out surveillance is to remain covert and the techniques by which this is achieved are the subject of various training courses. The second is to ensure the credibility of the material that is gathered. This is less of a problem where technical surveillance is used because the product can be recorded for use in court, although the circumstances in which devices are used sometimes means that the quality of the product is low. Where human surveillance is used, investigators will maintain logs of what they have observed and, where these observations are used in evidence, they will give direct testimony of what they have seen. Clearly, this leaves them open to challenge that they have either not seen the events they report or that they have misinterpreted them. To improve the credibility of the evidence, investigators often try to ensure that there is more than one person involved in the observation or that it is recorded on camera or video.

Not all the material gathered by surveillance is used as evidence. However, it may be useful to the investigation in many other ways by identifying associates of suspects, their movements, future intentions, locations they frequent, the vehicles they use and so on. Because of its value in doing this, it is often thought of simply as an intelligence technique, but this is a mistake. Like all the other techniques of criminal investigation, surveillance is primarily concerned with gathering material, much of which can be used as evidence if the correct procedures are followed.

Intelligence management

In most cases, investigators will want to identify any intelligence that has already been collected that may be relevant to their enquiry. This involves accessing intelligence databases managed by the police and partner agencies such as SOCA, Interpol, the Royal Military Police or foreign police agencies. Intelligence from these sources will have been subject to data-processing rules that are designed to test its veracity and reliability and investigators can therefore use it to increase their knowledge of a crime, a type of offending, a location or an individual.

Intelligence databases

The following is a sample of the intelligence databases that investigators routinely have access to:

- *Force intelligence systems*, which vary from force to force but all hold details which are submitted in a standard way using what is known as a 5x5x5 information/intelligence form. This form enables a standard assessment to be made of the source, the intelligence and the way in which it should be handled. Each of these is given a score out of five, hence the name. They are also linked to other data systems in the force and partner agencies, such as the crime recording system, and so they can often provide statistical data.

- *Police National Computer (PNC)*, which holds details of convicted people, details of stolen vehicles and some vehicle and driver information.

- *Open source information*, which forces often subscribe to such as voter records and credit-rating agencies, which can provide information about where people live and with whom.

Intelligence management requires investigators to identify the way in which intelligence databases can contribute to their investigation and then either to access it directly themselves or task an intelligence specialist to acquire the information. The format in which intelligence is made available to investigators depends to a large extent on the system from which it is acquired and ranges from a computer print-out to an analyst's report. Analytical reports are the result of tasking an analyst with a specific question. The analyst will then access various sources of information and intelligence to provide a report tailored to the investigators' needs.

The knowledge provided by intelligence has a wide range of uses within an investigation and it is impossible to describe them all. However, here are two examples of the types of ways in which investigators can use intelligence.

Example 1. During the investigation of an assault on a housing estate a witness describes the offender and says that they do not know his identity but have seen him in the area regularly and that he drives a red car. They think his first name may be Johnny. The force intelligence system is used to identify a John Smith who lives two streets away from the scene who has previous convictions for violence and fits the description of the offender. A check with the PNC shows that he owns a red car. None of this has any value as evidence against John Smith but it provides investigators with the opportunity of carrying out further enquiries to establish if he was the offender.

Example 2. During the investigation of an allegation that John Smith raped his estranged girlfriend, a search of the crime recording system shows that he has been the subject of two previous allegations of rape. Both previous victims were ex-girlfriends of Smith and the same method was used. On each occasion, Smith admitted having sex with the women but claimed that it was consensual. In both of these previous cases, the CPS were unable to prosecute Smith because of a lack of corroborating evidence. This intelligence can influence the interview strategy and may even lead to the re-interview of the previous victims with a view to gathering more material about the crimes committed against them. Under certain circumstances it may even be used as evidence of Smith's bad character.

Covert techniques

It is not uncommon to hear the term 'covert techniques' used as a collective description for the techniques of surveillance, CHIS management, undercover deployments, witness protection and intelligence management. The range of techniques described in this way varies from force to force. There is some logic in lumping these techniques together in this way as they all require a degree of confidentiality and sensitivity in how they are tasked and implemented and in how the material gathered by their use is managed. The use of some of these techniques also requires applications to be made under RIPA legislation.

The use of these covert techniques was once the preserve of specialist units targeting organised criminals and the procedures for managing them tended to centre on these squads. Although the knowledge, skills and understanding required to apply each of the techniques was different, common to them all was that they were deployed covertly and this led to them being described under that heading. But the knowledge, skills and understanding needed to apply each of the techniques differs so greatly that each has to be considered as an independent technique in its own right. For example, the practice required to recruit and manage a CHIS has little in common with that required to keep a suspect under surveillance. Both require practitioners to know how to deploy them covertly, but individually the techniques involve completely different sets of knowledge, skills and understanding. Furthermore, some, such as CHIS management, actually have more in common with other techniques such as investigative interviewing. Bundling these very different practices under the heading of 'covert techniques' risks suggesting a degree of commonality that in reality does not exist. As a consequence, the approach taken in this book is to deal with them separately, or, as in the case of CHIS management, under the technique to which they are most closely associated. Undercover techniques and witness protection are advanced techniques that are beyond the scope of this book and so are not dealt with here.

Readers working within police forces will find that some have specialist posts to ensure that covert techniques are managed with rigour. The post holders provide valuable sources of advice on how they can be used in individual cases.

Data

In Chapter 4, data was categorised as trace material, artefacts and electronic data. All the techniques shown in Table 5.1 above could be used in relation to almost anything falling within these categories. For example, a weapon is an artefact that may be found during the search of a crime scene, but it is then likely that it will be subject to a number of techniques to identify trace material that enables it to be linked to an offender. Similarly, a phone is an artefact that contains electronic data and so may be subject to search and forensic techniques.

A particular type of data is passive data. This is a term used to describe the product of automatic data-gathering systems such as many CCTV and financial systems. Although it usually falls within the category of electronic data, it is treated separately here because such systems are generally not owned by the police and so there are a number of legal and technical issues involved in gathering and using it that do not apply to electronic data gathered by the police themselves, for example in the form of covert listening devices.

Artefacts and trace material

As noted in Chapter 4, artefacts can be almost anything of a tangible nature, including stolen property, clothing, weapons or items used in the commission of a crime. Trace material is any type of organic or physical material that results from the contact between two things (Locard's exchange principle). The search for artefacts and trace material is a key part of most criminal investigations and involves two related techniques, search and crime scene management.

Search

The technique associated with artefacts is that of search. It is a very commonly used technique and, like HtoH, is extremely easy to deploy by investigators. In the context of a criminal investigation, a search has been defined as: 'the application and management of systematic procedures and appropriate detection equipment to locate specified targets' (ACPO 2005: 14).

Searches can be carried out by individual officers applying common sense to the search of crime scenes or a suspect's home or vehicle. For largescale or complex searches, investigators have access to specially trained search officers, known as Police Search Advisors (PolSA) and can call on trained dogs, underwater search units, air support and an array of technical equipment designed to locate specific types of artefacts.

There are legal constraints on searching private premises. Generally, investigators require either the owner's permission to carry out such a searche or a search warrant granted by a magistrate that gives them the legal power to search even if the owner does not agree to it. There is no legal barrier to searching public places. There are also a number of restrictions on the type of material that investigators can search for, as in the case of legally privileged material as defined by Section 10 of PACE.

The degree of difficulty of searching is determined by the location being searched, the nature and size of the item being searched for, the effort, if any, that has gone into concealing it and the amount of information investigators have about its location. If, following an assault, the offender drops a weapon at the scene without making any effort to conceal it, the first investigator to arrive is likely to find it during a routine search of the area. If, on the other hand, it is thrown into an unspecified part of a reservoir, divers will be required to carry out the search and the size and nature of the area involved means it will be difficult to locate the weapon without more specific information.

Crime scene management

The examination of crime scenes can provide investigators with a range of possibilities for furthering an investigation, and these fall into two categories:

- Interpretation of the circumstances in which the offence has occurred, which will assist in determining the possible type and location of material in the information profile.
- The recovery of material that assists in the above interpretation or that can be used to implicate a suspect.

As a consequence of its portrayal in the news and entertainment media, crime scene investigation is often associated with the specialist techniques used to recover trace material from the scene of a crime. Even within the police service, crime scene investigation is often held to be synonymous with the work of crime scene investigators (CSI) who are specialist in these techniques. While their work in the identification and recovery of material that may be invisible to the naked eye or is easily destroyed or contaminated is invaluable, much of what needs to be done in relation to crime scene examination can be done by any competent investigator.

The first decision investigators are likely to have to make in relation to any location is whether or not it is a crime scene. The term 'crime scene' is used to describe any location in which a significant activity relating to a crime takes place. It is not confined to the location where the crime took place. A crime scene could be any of the following (ACPO 2006A: 134):

- Places used to plan the crime;
- Places where encounters between a victim and offender took place;
- Places where the offender attacked a victim;
- Places where the offender detained a victim;
- Vehicles or other forms of conveyance used in the crime;
- Body deposition site, in the case of homicide;
- Weapons;
- Weapon deposition sites;
- Places used to clean or discard material used in or obtained during the offence;
- Routes to and from any scene(s);
- People who have come into contact with a suspect or a scene, including witnesses, victims, suspects and their homes, workplaces and vehicles.

Having confirmed that a location, person, vehicle or article is a crime scene, the key decision to be made is of its potential to produce material. This will determine the type of examination that will be required. This is a wider question than simply deciding that it may reveal trace material. The interpretation of a scene will include assessing how the victim and offender, together with any witnesses, got to and from the scene and the nature of the activity that took place there. The assessment will also include finding any CCTV or other passive data that may have recorded the scene and the routes to or from it, or transactions or activity that occurred there, for example the withdrawal of cash from an ATM. This is also likely to indicate where witnesses may be found among premises overlooking these sites or people who routinely use them.

Some characteristics of the offender may also be inferred from an examination of a crime scene, for example the use of a distinctive method to break into premises.

A visual search of the scene may also reveal things left by an offender. In the case of a spontaneous fight in a pub, an offender may leave a beer glass or a bottle to join the fight. An examination of the scene may locate them so that they can be analysed for fingerprints and DNA.

Identifying crime scenes and assessing what they reveal about the offence and their potential to reveal trace material are usually essential before a crime scene investigator is tasked with examining the scene. Crime scene investigators have been trained in a range of techniques that enable them to preserve scenes that are vulnerable to contamination or decay and to locate and recover trace material. In some cases, such as burglary in a house, their use may be more or less automatic because the investigation of such crimes is usually a priority and they generally provide the types of scene that can yield useful trace material. Similarly, in major crime enquiries such as homicide and serious wounding, CSIs are likely to be routinely used because of the seriousness of the offence. In most other cases, however, it is the responsibility of the investigator to assess the potential of the scene to yield trace material and then task a CSI to carry out an examination. Where trace material is located it is generally subject to a forensic investigation, which is discussed in detail below.

Passive data management

Passive data is the term used to describe the wide range of data collected by systems designed primarily for purposes other than criminal investigation, but which under certain circumstances may be of value to an investigation. Such systems include those that collect financial information, retail transactions, telephone data, internet traffic, security surveillance systems, GPS navigation systems, clocking in and out systems, health records and many, many more. The type of data collected varies widely, as do the technical systems by which it is captured and stored. In many cases there are legal restrictions on how the data can be used by those who collect it, on the degree of access that investigators have to it and what they can use it for.

Collecting and retaining this type of data can be expensive for its owners and they may only keep it for a relatively short period of time. The first task for investigators is therefore to quickly identify if there is any passive data that may assist the investigation and to secure it before it is lost. This is particularly important in the case of some CCTV systems which retain data for only 24 hours before recording over it. The second task is to identify the legal restrictions on its use and the types of authority that are required to gain access to it. The data and the systems that contain it will generally be privately owned and so at the very least the police require consensual access to it or a power to seize it as evidence. In many cases, the data will be subject to further legal protection, above and beyond that given to all private property that the police may want to seize as potential evidence. This is particularly so in the case of communications data which is covered by the provisions of RIPA (see Chapter 3). The third issue that investigators are likely to face is the technical question of how to recover the data in a form that does not corrupt it in any way and enables it to be analysed, stored and presented as evidence if required. The fourth task is to analyse the data. This may or may not be difficult depending on the volume and type of analysis required. It is, therefore, important that the person carrying out the analysis has a good knowledge of the type of data, how it was generated and stored by the original owner, what it means and how it can be integrated with other information gathered during the investigation.

Because of the wide variety of types of passive data, the technical skills required to collect and analyse it are equally varied. In some cases this requires specialist training, such as that available for financial investigators and those analysing computer data. However, often investigators must improvise methods once they have located the passive data and satisfied any legal requirements about its use. This generally involves finding someone with the necessary technical skills and working out a solution with them.

The main use to which passive data is put is undoubtedly establishing identities from CCTV images. This can connect a suspect to an incident or put them in the vicinity at a relevant time. Images are also often used to locate potential witnesses to incidents. Other uses of passive data include verification of witness accounts and suspects' alibis. This can be done in a variety of ways, such as, by timing purchases from shops, withdrawals from cash machines or telephone calls. The use of data of this type is considered routine by investigators and they quickly acquire the knowledge and skills they need to use it in this way. Sources of passive data include:

- *CCTV surveillance systems in public places, business and private premises.* It has been estimated that there are some five million CCTV systems in the UK and that the average Londoner will have their image captured by CCTV about 300 times a day. Given that a great deal of crime is spontaneous, this level of coverage means that many crimes are captured on CCTV and it is an extremely valuable source of material for investigations.

- *Financial data.* Investigators have always made use of financial records in the investigation of crime, but this was traditionally at the more complex end of the spectrum, involving cases of fraud, money-laundering and so on. The shift from paper records of transactions to digital records together with new measures under the Proceeds of Crime Act 2002 designed to deny criminals the proceeds of their crimes, has made using financial data a great deal easier. In addition to enabling investigators to know what money has passed through someone's accounts, financial data also facilities identification of their associates, by tracking who the suspect has received payments from and made them to. Their presence in particular locations at certain times can be established by the use of credit and debit cards, as well as withdrawals they make from ATMs. Their ownership of homes, vehicles, boats and other facilities can be established from the payments they make in relation to them. Unless someone leads an entirely cash-based life (and some still do) it is virtually impossible to do anything without leaving a financial footprint that investigators can use.

- *Telecom data*. This data includes information about the time, duration and origin or destination of calls to or from a particular telephone (usually known as 'billing information') as well as analysis of the location of a particular mobile phone within the network of transmitters used by the telephone company (usually known as 'cell site analysis'). This means that if someone's telephone number is known, then who they phone, when and from where can generally be established. Alternatively, if a crime occurs in a particular location, use of cell site analysis can often identify who may have been nearby at the time.

Other sources of passive data are loyalty cards, membership cards and lists, security entry systems, vehicle diagnostic systems, GPS navigation systems, personal computers, clocking on and flexi-time records, and many, many more.

The analysis of passive data often requires specialist training and equipment. Some of this is available within the service – most forces have the necessary equipment and personnel to examine CCTV material – but some requires the application of forensic techniques that cannot be provided by a force. In these cases, specialist services are generally bought in from independent companies, as with forensic image analysis and forensic telecommunications analysis.

Forensic investigation

The term 'forensic' means relating to courts or to the law. In relation to criminal investigation, it was originally applied to the techniques of biological or physical science that were used during a criminal investigation or in the interpretation of evidence. These became collectively known as 'forensic science'. The term is now used to describe a wider range of techniques and processes that provide equally valuable services to criminal investigation and can logically be thought of as being 'forensic'. One difficulty is setting a boundary around them. Almost any academic discipline or professional technique can be described as being forensic if it is used during the course of a criminal investigation or to interpret evidence during a trial. Of most interest to investigators are those disciplines and techniques that have been specifically developed to be applied to the problem of criminal investigation or the interpretation of evidence, rather than those that can become incidentally involved on rare occasions. Even using this limited definition, the number of disciplines is large and includes forensic medical examination, forensic accountancy, forensic psychology, forensic pathology, forensic image analysis, forensic archaeology, forensic podiatry, forensic psychiatry, forensic telecommunications, and many more. The Council for the Registration of Forensic Practitioners (CRFP) lists 26 subject areas and many of these have significant sub-specialities.

The Council for the Registration of Forensic Practitioners (CRFP)

The CRFP was established in 1999 to promote public confidence in forensic practice. This followed a number of miscarriages of justice arising from poor forensic evidence. The CRFP was sponsored by the Home Office but intends to become a self-funding organisation. It maintains a register of practitioners in 26 areas of specialisation, many of which have a number of sub-specialisations. Practitioners pay a fee to be on the register and must provide evidence that they meet the standards for their specialisation before being registered. Registration is voluntary and so not all forensic practitioners are registered with the CRFP.

Forensic disciplines vary in relation to the scientific, technological or procedural knowledge and processes that underpin them and the way in which they can be applied in individual cases. However, all have the same objective: to locate, gather and interpret material for an investigation. The ability of forensic disciplines to locate material differs and some are more useful than others in this respect. Forensic science, for example, has a range of techniques that can be applied to a crime scene to locate material that would not otherwise be found; forensic pathology and forensic medical examination have the same potential with human bodies. Other disciplines are more interpretive; forensic podiatry interprets the way suspects walk and relates that to images of an offender to determine if they are the same person. In doing this, the discipline is entirely interpretive of material that has already been located and gathered. Therefore, the degree to which forensic disciplines can assist at any particular point of an investigation varies. Despite this variation, they all present investigators with essentially the same problem:

- Knowing which discipline can contribute to an investigation.
- Formulating a specific task that can be accomplished by the particular discipline.
- Interpreting the findings and integrating them into the knowledge with the other material gathered.
- Quality controlling processes that are outside the investigator's knowledge.

Because forensic disciplines have tended to develop independently of each other, there is no single approach to any of these problems. The following presents a summary of the main issues.

Knowing which discipline can contribute to an investigation

Investigators need to identify the opportunities to use forensic investigation in any particular case but they also need knowledge of which techniques are available and what they can contribute. The traditional approach has been to try and provide investigators with some knowledge about all the disciplines they may require. As the number of disciplines and the techniques they use grows, this becomes increasingly difficult and while investigators will naturally get to know the ones they use often, they may have less insight into less well-known disciplines or new techniques. Because forensic disciplines have developed independently of each other and are linked to different academic disciplines and areas of practice within a force, there is no single source of information available to investigators. In relation to forensic science, forces usually employ scientific services managers (SSM) to co-ordinate the force's relationship with forensic science providers and they are able to advise on the services available. Crime scene investigators receive training in the forensic techniques relevant to their role and are in frequent contact with forensic services and so they provide another useful point of contact. In relation to other forensic disciplines information is less readily available and so investigators rely on informal contacts in areas of practice which may have knowledge of relevant forensic disciplines, for example, fraud squads for forensic accountants, intelligence units for forensic telecoms analysis, and so on.

Irrespective of the forensic discipline, the objective is likely to centre on locating material, and gathering it or interpreting it. This may give rise to new material, it may identify new lines of enquiry, or it may help investigators to better understand what has occurred or the *modus operandi* used. Very often the objective will be to determine if a particular suspect is connected with the offence. This is most often through comparisons with DNA or fingerprints associated with the offence, but can also include a range of other comparisons such as footwear, documents, fibres and images. DNA and fingerprints are particularly useful because samples recovered during an investigation can be compared to the National DNA Database or to IDENT1, which can match them to known individuals.

The National DNA Database

The National DNA Database was established in 1995. Until 2001, profiles were only stored for those convicted of an offence but since then the profiles of all those arrested for an offence have been stored. The database now holds over 3.5 million DNA profiles which the government believes represents the majority of the known active offender population (www.homeoffice.gov. uk).

A sample recovered by a crime scene investigator from a scene or otherwise associated with an offence can be searched against this database to identify a match. When a match is found, it is identified to the relevant investigators as a probability of the sample originating from the named individual. Where no match is found, investigators can request that the sample remains on the database to be compared with DNA profiles of those newly convicted or arrested.

IDENT1

IDENT1 is a database holding the fingerprint records of those convicted of an offence. Fingerprints found at the scene of a crime can be compared to these records to identify suspects and,

---

as with the National DNA Database, where no match is found the prints can remain on the system to be compared with new additions. The database holds over 7 million fingerprint records and matches an average of 6,500 fingerprints to people every month.

Formulating a specific task

Having identified that a particular forensic discipline may be able to contribute something to an investigation, investigators must formulate a meaningful task that it can carry out. The TV cliché of 'doing a full forensic examination' on a scene is simply not an option. Without a clear understanding of what is already known about an offence and the objective that an investigator is seeking to achieve, a forensic practitioner would end up applying random techniques in the hope that one of them turned up something useful. This is not only time-consuming and expensive, it risks swamping the investigation with irrelevant material. What is required by all forensic disciplines is a clear objective and an understanding of how it is to be achieved. This requires a dialogue between the investigators and the forensic practitioner, thus enabling the latter to apply their specialist knowledge to the problem and identify the most appropriate techniques to achieve the objective. It is not necessary that the investigator understands the technique, so long as they set a clear objective and know what type of result can be expected.

A typical objective may be to find out if a particular gun fired a bullet recovered from a scene. The investigator may have very little knowledge about the techniques used to determine this, but may simply know that this is the type of question that forensic ballistics can answer. They will know that the answer will be yes or no and that it will be supported by photographs of a test fired bullet and the recovered one, together with a statement from a ballistics expert comparing the marks made on them by the gun.

Interpreting and integrating findings

In the above example, interpreting the findings of the examination is not difficult. There are well-established practices that are not difficult to understand and result in a clear-cut answer. Even where results are more complex than in this example, one of the skills of forensic practitioners should be explaining their findings in ways that are easily understood. A key skill for investigators is integrating these findings into the investigation. How valuable it is to know that the gun fired the bullet will depend on a great many other factors, particularly whether investigators know whose finger was on the trigger at the time.

A similar problem is often encountered in forensic telephone analysis, which may show that phone A rang phone B at a relevant time, but knowing whose hands they were in can be an entirely different problem. So meeting the objective of the examination may be useful but may not progress a case very much by itself. Doing this will often require the information to be integrated with other material, such as intelligence from a CHIS about whose finger was on the trigger, material from CCTV that puts them at the scene, and fingerprints on cartridge cases recovered from the scene that connect them to the incident. It is the job of the investigator to integrate all this material into what is already known about the crime in order to make sense of it.

The same material may also be subject to analysis by several forensic practitioners. Where this happens, investigators must integrate the various approaches taken. In a fraud enquiry, a document may require a forensic accountant to be tasked with examining what it says about how a financial transaction was carried out, a forensic scientist may be tasked with identifying whether it is genuine in relation to paper and ink type together with the printer or pen used, another forensic scientist may be tasked with establishing if a suspect's DNA is on the document, and a fingerprint expert may be tasked with establishing whose fingerprints it bears. All these forensic experts will provide information to the investigator and be able to interpret what their findings mean from the point of view of their discipline. It is the investigator's role to synthesise the whole of this information into what is already known of the investigation. They must therefore understand the meaning that each of the disciplines attributes to their own findings and how this can be related to the findings of the other disciplines, and what is already known.

Quality control

The quality control of forensic processes is difficult for individual investigators, who do not generally possess the scientific or technical knowledge required to check if the correct procedures have been followed by forensic practitioners or to validate the conclusions they have reached. There have been some notable failures by forensic practitioners. In the investigation of the murder of Damilola Taylor in London in 2000, for example, forensic scientists failed to detect his blood on shoes and a sweatshirt belonging to a suspect. It was only during a reinvestigation of the case that further tests were carried out, which uncovered the material that had been missed. Investigators are almost entirely reliant on the quality assurance processes of those involved but they can at least satisfy themselves that those processes exist and are being applied.

Forensic disciplines

As noted above, forensic disciplines are an open-ended category, but listed below are the ones that investigators will come across most often.

Forensic science

The underlying rationale of forensic science was explained by the French forensic scientist Edmond Locard in what has become known as Locard's exchange principle. This holds that where there is contact between two items, there will be an exchange of material. Forensic science is the application of science and technology to identify, recover and interpret this material. The material may be biological or physical in origin. Biological material can include bodily fluids (blood, urine, semen, saliva), hair and cells. Physical material includes glass, fibres, paints and impressions left on material such as writing, footwear marks, tool marks and fingerprints. Although it is relatively straightforward to describe forensic science in this way, the reality is that it comprises a wide spectrum of specialisations, knowledge and techniques, all of which can be used singly or in combination.

Applying these techniques requires specialist training and equipment and is carried out by forensic scientists and technicians, most of whom specialise in a particular sub-discipline. Individual police forces employ some forensic scientists, but it is more common to buy in forensic science services from a private company when they are required. This is usually done under a contract with one of the large forensic science providers, and these services are managed by a force's scientific services manager (SSM). Fingerprint examination is usually an exception to this arrangement. Because it predates the development of many of the forensic science techniques now in use, it is generally managed within each police force and fingerprints are shared on the IDENT1 database (see above).

Forensic scientists do not routinely turn out to crime scenes and because most work for private agencies they are not immediately available to consult. As noted above, SSMs and crime scene investigators are the most readily available sources of information about forensic science issues for investigators. They are often supplemented by a consultancy service made available by the forensic science provider used by a force and at a national level by forensic science advice available from the Specialist Operations Centre of the NPIA.

Forensic medical examination

Forensic medical examiners (FME), sometimes also known as police surgeons, are doctors or nurses who specialise in the examination of victims or suspects to gather material. This may involve the interpretation of injuries, the taking of samples such as urine, saliva, blood or hair for analysis, or the recovery of trace material. FMEs also offer medical care, which is particularly useful in the examination of victims of sexual assault. FMEs can play a therapeutic role at the same time as gathering material and interpreting injuries. This avoids the need for victims to undergo separate examinations.

Most FMEs are self-employed and provide general services to a particular BCU. They will turn out to scenes of sudden deaths to pronounce life extinct, take samples of blood or urine from drivers suspected of being intoxicated, advise on the medical condition of those taken into custody, and examine victims and suspects of minor assaults. Some FMEs specialise in the examination of child victims or the victims of sexual assault. Where a force has a sexual assaults referral centre, such as the St Mary's Centre in Manchester or the Haven in the Metropolitan Police area, a panel of specialist FMEs will generally be employed to provide services at the centre.

Forensic pathology

Forensic pathology is used in the investigation of suspicious deaths. Its principal focus is the body of the victim and samples taken from it, although pathologists can also often assist in examining and interpreting the scene of a death. They can locate, gather and analyse material that helps to interpret what occurred at a scene, the time and cause of a victim's death and the type of weapon used in an attack. Forensic pathologists can also collect trace material from bodies that is sent for examination by forensic scientists.

Forensic pathologists are qualified pathologists who have undertaken additional medico-legal training and are registered with the Home Office, hence the often-heard term Home Office pathologist. Each police force has a contract with a number of Home Office pathologists, who are usually in a single practice which enables them to provide round-the-clock cover and to peer review each other's work.

Forensic psychology

Forensic psychology applies the theories and processes of the discipline of psychology to criminal investigation. At one time this was largely confined to offender profiling, where the characteristics of the offender are inferred from the material gathered during an investigation. While this is still an important part of forensic psychology, practitioners are now known as behavioural investigative advisors, a title that emphasises the wider range of services they now offer to investigators, which include:

- Offender profiling
- Geographical analysis, which infers the relationship between an offender and the geographic aspects of a crime
- Advising on media statements
- Informing interview strategies
- Developing linkage criteria in serial cases
- Assessing the veracity of witness and suspect accounts.

Forensic image analysis

Forensic image analysis provides investigators with a range of services relating to images recovered from CCTV systems, cameras, mobile phones, computers or other sources. FIA services include:

- Enhancing poor-quality or damaged images to make their content clearer.
- Comparing images to identify features that are of interest, usually matching suspects to images of offenders.
- Converting scene photography to 3D digital models, which enables events to be reconstructed and accounts compared.

Some forces have the facilities to carry out routine work of this sort themselves, but more complex work is generally done by outside specialists.

Forensic telecoms examination

Forensic telecoms examination is concerned with the retrieval of telecoms data from communications systems such as mobile and wired telephone networks, telephones, faxes and pagers, its examination and its interpretation. This information can be used to identify when calls were made, the equipment employed and its location at the time of the call. This can be extremely useful in analysing criminal networks or identifying where individuals were at significant times and who they were communicating with.

Elimination enquiries

Elimination enquiries enable investigators to make progress in those cases where other techniques have not identified a suspect. They do this by identifying groups of people who share a common characteristic, which may also be shared by the offender. Examples might be all the males in a bar at the time of an assault, all a victim's relatives, and all those with previous convictions for a particular type of offending in an area. Individuals in the group are traced and systematically eliminated from the group by using a common criterion. Those who cannot be eliminated in this way can then be the subject of more focused enquiries to see if they are suspects for the crime. Elimination enquiries are often referred to as TIE enquiries, particularly when used in major crime investigations.

Elimination enquiries have been included here at the end of the list of techniques of investigation because they generally use some aspects of all other techniques. They are not used in every investigation. Where the identity of the suspect is known from the outset or is quickly discovered by the application of one of the techniques discussed above, it is unlikely that the investigation will need to use elimination enquiries. In volume crime enquiries of the type carried out by PIP Level 1 investigators, it is highly unlikely that the resources required to carry out elimination enquiries will be available. It is therefore mainly used by PIP Level 2 and 3 investigators in those cases where no immediate suspect has been identified.

TIE

This term comes from the HOLMES system used in major investigations. It denotes the instruction given to investigating officers to 'trace, interview and eliminate' a particular subject. There is some variation in the terminology used to describe this technique; some investigators prefer the term trace/implicate/eliminate. Irrespective of the terminology, the technique is used in the same way nationally.

TIE categories

A TIE category is a group of people, sharing a common characteristic, that is likely to include the offender. The common characteristic of the group will depend on the unique circumstances of the crime being investigated. Typically they include:

- Those with access to the scene at the time of the offence.
- Those living in, or associated with, a certain geographical area.
- Those associated with the victim.
- Those with previous convictions for similar offences (usually known as MO suspects).
- Those with physical characteristics similar to the offender.
- Those with access to certain types of vehicle.

The more investigators know about a crime, the greater the chance of constructing an accurate TIE category.

Populating TIE categories

It is important that the population falling within each category is accurately identified. This is easier in some cases than in others. Where investigators have access to accurate records, such as membership lists or employee records, it is usually fairly easy to identify those who should be included in the group. Where such information is not available it may be difficult to identify those in some groups. The following are useful ways of populating TIE categories:

- Official records, such as membership lists, payrolls, electoral registers
- Police intelligence databases
- Media appeals
- Snowballing (the technique of interviewing known members of a TIE category to identify other members of the group).

The police generally call those within a particular group 'TIE subjects'.

Setting priorities for TIE subjects

The number of TIE subjects in a category can be very large. Therefore investigators will start enquiries with those who are most likely to be the offender. They prioritise by applying a number of filters, such as:

- Proximity to the scene.
- Date of last conviction of MO suspects.
- Age (or where the age of the offender is not known, those who fall within the most likely age range of offenders for that category of crime).
- Sex (or where the sex of the offender is not known, those who are of the sex most likely to have committed the crime).

Setting suspect parameters

Suspect parameters are the known characteristics of the offender that can be used to implicate or eliminate those in a TIE category, including:

- Sex
- Age
- Physical characteristics
- Fingerprints
- Forensic characteristics such as DNA, fibres, footmarks
- Ownership of a particular make or colour of vehicle
- Ownership of particular clothing.

The value of these characteristics differs in the elimination of TIE subjects from the group. A fingerprint or DNA sample is likely to eliminate all those other than the offender, whereas knowing only the sex of the offender is of less value.

Setting time parameters

Knowing the times within which a crime was committed enables parameters to be set that are useful in eliminating people from a TIE category, simply by showing that the subject was elsewhere when the crime was committed. As with suspect parameters, it is often difficult for investigators to know exactly when a crime occurred, and therefore time parameters are generally set between the earliest time and the latest time at which the crime could have been committed. It is obviously desirable that the time parameters are set as narrowly as possible, as this will enable a greater number of people to be eliminated.

Choosing elimination criteria

It is important that a consistent criterion is used to eliminate TIE subjects from the category. The HOLMES database, which is used in major incident and homicide investigation, uses a six-point scale to do this:

1 Forensic elimination, e.g. DNA, footwear, fingerprint
2 Description (suspect parameters)
3 Independent witness (alibi)
4 Associate or relative (alibi)
5 Spouse or common law relationship (alibi)
6 Not eliminated.

Although HOLMES is unlikely to be used in most investigations, this scale provides a useful framework for setting elimination criteria that has been tried and tested in many thousands of major investigations. The list is hierarchical, with 1 being the most certain type of elimination and 5 being the least certain. Investigators must decide which level of elimination they will apply in each case. This will depend on the material available to them, the unique circumstances of the offence and the characteristics of the TIE category. For example, forensic material is not always available and there may be no description of the offender, in which case investigators will have little option but to use alibi as a criteria; that is, the subject can show that they were elsewhere during the time parameters and so not available to commit the offence. In these cases, an independent witness who can verify a TIE subject's alibi is considered to be more reliable than an associate, who is considered to be more reliable than a spouse. These are, of course, general rules that need to be applied intelligently in each case.

An important principle of TIE enquiries is that elimination is always provisional and should be rigorously tested against the material to hand and to any new material that later becomes available. It is good practice to regard TIE subjects as being eliminated from the TIE category, not as being eliminated as the offender. For example, someone who has been eliminated against criterion 5, an alibi supported by a spouse, can always be re-examined if new material comes to light that allows a forensic elimination criteria to be set.

Conducting TIE enquiries

When carrying out TIE enquiries investigators keep in mind that TIE subjects may also be witnesses, particularly if they were present at the scene, or if they are in a group who may know the victim or offender. Each subject of the TIE category is interviewed using the

PEACE model of investigative interviewing to gather the information that enables the criteria to be applied. Where the elimination criterion is an alibi, investigators must thoroughly check this with those who can verify it. Where the criteria are based on forensic material or fingerprints, these should be obtained and tested.

Where forensic evidence or other compelling material links a TIE subject to the offence, or if their alibi is shown to be false, it is likely that they will be treated as a suspect. There are, however, circumstances when it is impossible to verify an alibi, for example if someone says they were at home alone watching TV. In such cases, the subject is unlikely to be considered a suspect until further enquiries have been carried out to gather material that may implicate or eliminate them from the investigation.

Worked example of a TIE strategy

An investigation into the section 18 assault of a man in a busy town-centre bar has failed to identify the suspect and the investigator decides to use a TIE strategy.

The suspect parameters are based on witness accounts and are set as:

White male, 20 to 30 years, 5'10" to 6'2" tall, short dark hair, wearing a gold earring in his left ear. These details are an amalgam of the descriptions given by several witnesses. No clothing is included because some witnesses were unsure of what the offender was wearing. The time parameters are between 22:15 hrs and 22:30 hrs. Again, these are based on the accounts of several witnesses.

The TIE category is all males in the bar at the time of the offence.

Populating the TIE category is clearly difficult because it is not known who was in the bar or even how many people were there. The investigator adopts a snowballing technique starting with the witnesses who are already known. By this method 20 people are identified and four fit the suspect parameters. Three of these were with others who provide credible alibis, to the effect that although they were in the bar at the time they were not involved in the assault. The fourth states that he did not visit the bar that evening and was alone at home at the time of the assault. This generates further enquiries to test the sighting of him in the bar at the time of the assault and whether he can be identified as the offender. (ACPO 2005b: 96)

Conclusion

The techniques of criminal investigation are varied in terms of the knowledge, skills and understanding that investigators need in order to use them. Many can be applied directly by investigators themselves whie others require specialist skills or equipment. The basic level of skill and knowledge required is not necessarily high, and in relation to PIP Level 1 at least, can be acquired by all investigators. What is more difficult is knowing what techniques to apply in any given situation, being skilled in adapting them to the unique circumstances of the case and being competent in using the material generated. In order to do this, investigators must have a clear understanding of what can be achieved by each technique, when it is appropriate to use it, the legal provisions relating to its use, the resource requirements to use it effectively and the outcomes that are likely to be achieved.

Given the wide range of circumstances in which crimes occur and the varied behaviour of those involved, it is impossible to teach how techniques can be used in every case. This is why investigators traditionally value experience so highly. Experience means that they have the opportunity of applying the techniques in a variety of situations, learning what difficulties may be encountered and how they can be overcome. Experience also better equips investigators to address novel situations because they will be able to draw on their knowledge of previous applications of a technique and adapt it to the present situation.

In theory, the more experience they have, the better they will be at doing this. But experience is expensive and time-consuming to gain and it is impossible for investigators to encounter every variation of criminal behaviour, so even the most experienced will have gaps in their knowledge. For this reason investigative practice seeks to identify the underlying principles of criminal investigation that can be taught, to give investigators a better understanding of how the techniques of investigation can be applied. Investigative practice is not a short cut to experience, but it does provide a solid foundation on which investigators can build.

Further reading

Some techniques of criminal investigation have been well documented in the academic literature, but the available material is patchy and many techniques have not been the subject of practitioner-focused research. Practitioners should also be aware that material produced for practitioners in one jurisdiction may not be applicable to their own. For example, some of the techniques in the US literature on investigative interviewing focus on persuading people to admit their guilt, which would not be considered good practice in the UK for reasons already outlined in this book.

There is no specific literature on the techniques of witness canvassing, but A. Fiest, *The Effective Use of the Media in Serious Crime Investigations.* Policing and Reducing Crime Unit Paper 120 (London: Home Office, 1999) examines some of the issues involved in using the media.

Investigative interviewing is an area that has received a lot of attention from psychologists, and as a consequence there is an accessible literature on it. R. Milne and R. Bull, *Investigative Interviewing: Psychology and Practice* (Chichester: John Wiley, 1999) is written by two academics who have been highly influential in the development in police interviewing techniques in England and Wales and describes the underlying rationale for them. T. Williamson (ed.), *Investigative Interviewing: Rights, Research, Regulation* (Cullompton: Willan Publishing, 2005) provides an overview of the contemporary issues in investigative interviewing with contributions from practitioners as well as academics.

There is no publically available material for practitioners on the range of surveillance techniques currently used by police forces in England and Wales. D. Clark, 'Covert Surveillance and Informer Handling', in T. Newburn, T. Williamson and A. Wright (eds), *Handbook of Criminal Investigation* (Cullompton: Willan Publishing, 2007) provides an accessible introduction to policy, practice and law in this area. The social science literature treats surveillance in its wider governmental and social context and so provides practitioners with a wider view of the issues involved. S. Hier and J. Greenberg, *The Surveillance Studies Reader* (Maidenhead: Open University Press, 2007) provides a good introduction to this literature. In the field of intelligence management, C. Harfield and K. Harfield, *Intelligence, Community and Partnership* (Oxford: Oxford University Press, 2008) is written by practitioners and provides a guide to the use of intelligence across a wide range of policing functions. J. Ratcliffe, *Intelligence-led Policing* (Cullompton: Willan Publishing, 2008) surveys the origin and development of the concept of intelligence-led policing from both UK and US perspectives.

There is no publically available literature on search techniques for investigators. Crime scene investigation is, however, better served.

I. Pepper, *Crime Scene Investigation: Methods and Procedures* (Maidenhead: Open University Press, 2004) is aimed primarily at student crime scene investigators but provides investigators with a good introduction to the subject.

Passive data management techniques have not been well documented, although the social science and legal literature on surveillance in general noted above is often relevant in relation to the wider use of such material and the issues this gives rise to. An issue of the *Journal of Homicide and Major Incident Investigation* (Vol. 3, Issue 2, Autumn 2007), contains papers written by practitioners on the use of many of the techniques involved in using passive data for criminal investigation.

The literature on the many forensic disciplines that may be used during a criminal investigation is large, but is almost exclusively aimed at practitioners and students within each field. Surprisingly little has been written for investigators about how these techniques are integrated into a criminal investigation. This possibly reflects the wide range of disciplines involved and the absence of a common methodology. Introductions to some of the forensic disciplines mentioned in this chapter can be found in the following.

For forensic science, A.R.W. Jackson and J.M. Jackson, *Forensic Science* (2nd edn, Harlow: Pearson Educational, 2008), For forensic pathology, T. Cook and A. Tattersall, *Blackstone's Senior Investigating Officers Handbook* (Oxford: Oxford University Press, 2008). Chapter 12 covers the role of forensic pathology in the investigation of homicide. For forensic psychology, L. Alison, *The Forensic Psychologist's Case Book* (Cullompton: Willan Publishing, 2005) has contributions from many who have been instrumental in integrating psychology into criminal investigation, and provides insights into the many areas where this has occurred. G. Davies, C. Hollin and R. Bull, *Forensic Psychology* (Chichester: John Wiley, 2008) examines current psychological insights across crime, its investigation, the trial process and sentencing.

No literature has been found that can be recommended to investigators for forensic medical examination, forensic image analysis or forensic telecoms examinations.

Note

1 Covert investigations are 'investigations of which the suspect is assumed to be unaware and which infringes upon the private life of the suspect' (Harfield and Harfield 2005: 2).

Chapter 6

The investigation process and investigative decision-making

Introduction

Criminal investigation is an information-processing activity that relies heavily on the decision-making abilities of investigators. Where investigations remain undetected or miscarriages of justice occur, it is often through flawed decision-making (see, for example, the Byford Report 1982, the Macpherson Report 1999, the Shipman Inquiry Third Report 2003, and Nicol *et al.* 2004). Failures of decision-making are not confined to major investigations or difficult cases. A study carried out in 1992 for the Royal Commission on Criminal Justice found that the most common type of error in crime investigation in general was that of decision-making (Irvine and Dunningham 1993: 37). Investigators are increasingly required to document their decision-making, for example, in decision logs and on applications to the surveillance commissioners under the Regulation of Investigatory Procedures Act 2000. While this makes it easier to hold investigators to account for what they do, there has been little research aimed at helping them to make better decisions (Barrett 2005: 47). This chapter examines the type of decisions that investigators have to make, the investigative process within which those decisions are made and then some of the key factors that are relevant to decision-making in criminal investigation.

The investigation process

The reactive and proactive models

It is often said that there are two approaches to criminal investigation: the reactive approach, which focuses on the investigation of individual crimes reported to the police, and the proactive approach, which focuses on investigating those who are suspected of committing crimes. The distinction between these two types of investigation lies both in the starting point and in the techniques used to gather the material. Reactive investigations typically start with the report or discovery of a crime. Thereafter, the investigation focuses on identifying material from crime scenes, victims, witnesses and other sources to identify suspects and gather sufficient evidence to bring them to justice. Proactive investigations typically start with the identification through intelligence analysis of those who investigators believe are committing offences. These are usually offences associated with organised crime such as drug-dealing, people-trafficking and money-laundering, but can include other types of crime, particularly where investigators are focusing on persistent or serious offenders. These investigations focus on gathering evidence to connect suspects to the criminal activity, usually through covert techniques such as surveillance.

From the investigator's point of view, the distinction between reactive and proactive investigation can be small. Many of the techniques are similar, and once a suspect has been arrested the techniques used are exactly the same. There is also no difference in terms of the types of decisions that need to be made and the way that material is handled. As a consequence, the two approaches have much more in common than they have differences. Some types of investigative units within police forces may make the strategic decision to rely more on one or other of these approaches, but this is essentially a strategic decision that follows from the type of crime they are most often investigating. There is very little difference between the two approaches when it comes to the investigation process or the decisions that need making within that process.

The ACPO model

Despite the fact that all crimes are to some degree unique and require the techniques of investigation to be applied in a wide variety of situations, most go through a series of standard stages. These stages are shown in the model of the investigation process used in ACPO's *Core Investigative Doctrine*, shown in Figure 6.1.

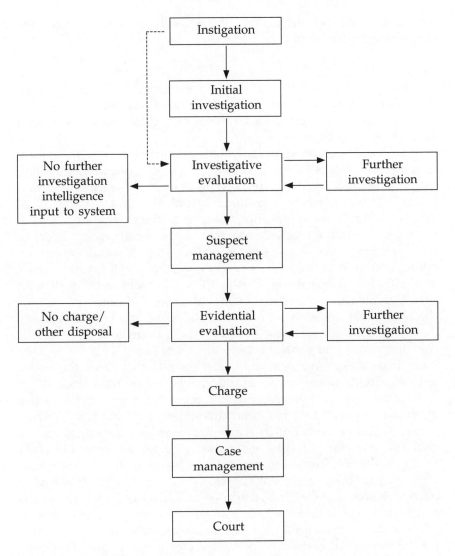

Figure 6.1 The stages of criminal investigations

The phases in the model tend to be sequential. The only exception occurs when a suspect is arrested straight away and so investigators may have to carry out the instigation or initial response while undertaking some elements of suspect management. Even where this does happen, investigators will generally try to complete the instigation and the initial response phases first because the material they gather during those two phases will inevitably inform the suspect management phase.

Instigation

The instigation phase of a criminal investigation is the point when the police become aware that an offence may have been committed and their obligations under the Criminal Procedure and Investigations Act 1996 (CPIA) begin.

Most reactive criminal investigations are instigated when members of the public report to the police that a crime has been committed. In the overwhelming majority of cases these calls are received at a police call centre where a member of police staff takes the initial details. Other forms of reporting are to patrolling officers or to force websites. The police receive many thousands of calls each day, all of which require action of one sort or another. Not all of these are about crimes and most police forces operate a system of call grading aimed at identifying the most urgent calls to enable them to be dealt with first. In some cases, forces may deal with reports of minor crime over the phone and not send an officer to the scene at all. In these cases the police seek to gain enough information to create a crime report over the phone and further investigative action will only be taken if more information comes to light later. In all other cases the police tend to allocate the report to an officer who attend the scene.

Another means of instigation is a report of crime to the police by another agency that has been investigating an incident. A wide range of agencies other than the police carry out investigations for civil and criminal purposes and these cases are sometimes referred to the police for further investigation. This typically occurs where the investigation of a civil matter uncovers criminal conduct that is outside the remit of the original agency, or in the case of social services or medical professionals where routine work uncovers evidence of criminal activity. In general, there are well-established mechanisms for the transfer of cases from other agencies to the police; these lead to the allocation of the case to an investigator who will liaise with a representative of the original agency.

Proactive investigations are instigated by the identification of a person or group as being involved in criminal behaviour. This is generally done by analysis of crime intelligence. Each BCU and those investigative units with a remit to target particular types of crime regularly hold Tasking and Co-ordinating Group meetings where the progress of ongoing investigations is monitored and new trends identified within their area of responsibility. Where they believe they have identified a person or group that may be the subject of a future operation they will instigate a criminal investigation. At this stage, this is often aimed at collating what is already known about the person or group, together with preliminary activities such as surveillance or financial investigation, in order to develop a 'target profile'. This enables a decision to be made as to whether or not to deploy further resources to the investigation and the type of activity that will be required.

One problem for investigators is that the instigation of a criminal investigation generally takes place within a call centre or a tasking and co-ordinating group meeting, and they are not involved in the process. There is a danger that material that is of potential value to the investigation is lost. ACPO *Core Investigative Doctrine* advises investigators to pay particular attention to understanding how such material is created during the instigation phase of investigations and how it can be recovered.

The initial response

The initial response to a report of crime generally involves sending an investigator, usually a uniformed patrol officer, to the scene of the crime or to the person reporting it with the intention of securing evidence and conducting initial enquiries. In many cases, the response will be to a crime that has just occurred, which may involve public disorder or traumatised victims and witnesses. The first officer on the scene will need to attend to these issues before they can start an investigation.

Investigators generally seek to locate material from three sources during the initial response: the scene, victims and witnesses. The scene of the crime, together with the routes offenders took to and from it, may contain physical material or be covered by CCTV cameras or other automatic recording systems which could provide useful material. Identifying scenes is therefore usually a priority for the initial investigator, and where there is a danger that material could be lost, for example if the scene is outside or is being used by people who may inadvertently damage material, they will take action to secure the scene and preserve the material.

Those making the initial response may search the scene themselves or call in specialist crime scene investigators (CSI), who are trained to search for trace material. They will also carry out initial interviews with victims and witnesses and arrest suspects where their identities are known and if they can be traced immediately. The main thrust of the initial response is on ensuring that everything is done to identify and gather the available material before it is lost, thus making it available for later phases in the process. The key decision-making involved is interpreting the information that investigators are presented with and selecting the most appropriate technique to gather more material. In so doing, those involved will be applying the 'golden hour' principle and using 'fast track actions'.

The 'golden hour' and 'fast track action'

As was seen in Chapter 4, the information profile of a crime consists of the total material generated by its commission. This material is usually most abundant during the period immediately following the commission of the crime. Trace material may not have been disturbed or deteriorated, witnesses may still be nearby and their recollections of events will be fresh. CCTV systems often only retain images for a short time but these are likely to be still available. Suspects may still be in the immediate vicinity, and it may be possible to identify and arrest them. As time passes, it is likely that these sources of material will become more difficult to locate; in the case of trace material it may deteriorate altogether. While, it is rare for investigators to be at the scene of a crime during the period immediately following its commission, the 'golden hour' describes a principle whereby investigators seek to ensure that as soon as they become aware of a crime, effective action is taken so that the material that is available is identified and secured. This is not simply a matter of speed; it is also important that the correct action is taken. The ACPO *Core Investigative Doctrine* notes that the first opportunity to gather material may be the last; so it is important that good decisions are taken during the early stages of an investigation to ensure that all potential sources of material are explored properly before being lost or contaminated.

The term 'fast track action' is closely linked to the golden hour and describes 'Any investigative actions which, if pursued immediately are likely to establish important facts, preserve evidence or lead to the early resolution of the investigation' (ACPO *Murder Investigation Manual* 2006a: 41). Fast track actions will most often be taken during the initial response phase as investigators react to the material that becomes available to them, but opportunities for fast track actions can occur at any stage of the investigation. They are particularly useful when investigators are responding to incidents that are still ongoing or have only recently happened. Material in the form of witnesses, trace material and articles associated with the crime may be readily available at the scenes of these incidents if investigators take prompt action to gather them.

The golden hour and fast track actions are important elements in the criminal investigation process. Success is often dependent on investigators recognising opportunities to secure material and taking decisive action to ensure that it is done effectively. It would not be an overstatement to say that in the majority of cases, the final outcome of an investigation is determined by the action taken during the initial response by the first officer to get to the scene. If they make sound decisions and act on them, the amount of material that is secured at the point where it is most readily available and in its most pristine form will be maximised. If they do not, it is highly unlikely that those who carry out investigative activity later in the process can compensate for these lost opportunities.

Investigative evaluation

At the end of the initial investigation an evaluation has to be carried out to assess the material that has been gathered and decide what it means for the investigation. This evaluation determines the choices that investigators make during the rest of the enquiry. In particular, the evaluation will decide on the techniques that are used to gather further material. The ACPO *Core Investigative Doctrine* (2005b: 64) describes this process as enabling investigators to 'step back' from the rush of investigative action and to consider the investigation in 'slow time'. Investigators are encouraged to carry out evaluations in every case, even those that appear to be straightforward.

In some cases the investigative evaluation may be carried out by a crime evaluator, who will determine whether further investigation is required. Where a large amount of material has been gathered investigators may task analysts to assist. For the most part, however, evaluations are carried out by the investigators themselves. They are essential at the end of the initial response, but can also be carried out periodically throughout the investigation to ensure that the material gathered has been correctly interpreted and that no opportunities to take action have been missed. An investigation is usually an iterative process that involves taking action to gather material, evaluating what it means and deciding what further action can be taken, taking that action and then evaluating the outcome. This process can continue over many cycles until sufficient material has been gathered to bring an offender to justice or until a decision is taken to file the case as unsolved (see Figure 6.2).

The evaluation phase provides investigators with a structured approach to decision-making and a number of disciplines that are designed to minimise the difficulties of making good decisions on the

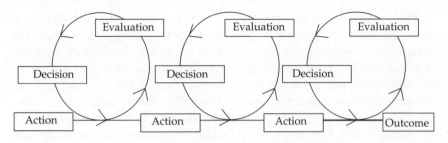

Figure 6.2 The interative nature of the investigation process

type of limited material that is often available during an investigation. For example, investigators are encouraged to set clear objectives for the evaluation and to use the 5WH formula (Who – What – When – Where – Why – How) to give structure to the material they have gathered:

- *Who* is relevant to the investigation, victim(s), witnesses, and suspect(s)?

- *Where* did the offence take place? Are there other locations that are relevant?

- *What* has occurred? This may be immediately obvious, but in some cases the investigator will have to piece together the available material by locating witnesses, interviewing victims and suspects, developing intelligence or building reasonable hypotheses.

- *When* did the offence and other significant events take place?

- *Why* was this offence committed in this location against this victim at this time?

- *How* was the offence committed?

Decision-making and the difficulties it can present during criminal investigation are discussed in more detail later in this chapter.

Further investigation
Further investigation involves the selection of the most appropriate investigative techniques to gather the material required to fill the gaps identified during the evaluation. In probably the majority of cases, the problem is one of moving forward from the first evaluation. The material gathered during the initial response leaves too large a gap to

be filled and it is difficult to identify a technique that could be used with any hope of success. For example, in the case of a domestic burglary, an effective initial response may have included a crime scene investigation, house-to-house enquiries, viewing of local CCTV systems and circulating descriptions of the property stolen. Within the intelligence office, the MO of the offence may have been compared to others in the area to see if the offence was part of a pattern that identified a likely suspect. If all these enquiries have failed to gather material that identified a suspect, the gap between what investigators know about the offence and what they need to enable them to use an investigative technique to make progress is very large indeed.

Depending on the area where the offence took place, it may be worthwhile to publicise it to encourage more witnesses to come forward or to interview informants in the hope of identifying a suspect. But such measures may not succeed if the information profile of the crime is very low. The most that investigators can hope to do is to provide a thorough record of the action they have taken and the material that has been gathered. This will support the analysis of wider trends that may later provide intelligence opportunities, and leave a good basis for reopening the investigation if additional material becomes available. Where there is sufficient material to indicate a way forward investigators will use one of the investigative techniques described in Chapter 5 to gather further material.

Where further action is possible, investigators often use the term 'line of enquiry' to refer to a number of actions that have a particular focus, for example tracing a person described as being at the scene of a crime. In small investigations there are likely to be relatively few lines of enquiry; in a major investigation such as homicide there may be a great number. The 'main line of enquiry' is usually a series of actions that appears to have the potential to lead to the suspect, this is, therefore, given a higher priority than others (ACPO 2006a: 59). Identifying lines of enquiry is a key skill for investigators. It involves carrying out a good evaluation of the material, and matching that to their knowledge of investigative techniques and their applicability in any given circumstance.

Suspect management

Once a suspect has been identified a range of techniques become available to investigators that enable them to either implicate the suspect in the offence or eliminate them from the investigation. These include search and forensic examinations of the suspect and any premises and vehicle they are associated with, the use of identification procedures if there is an eyewitness to the crime and, most importantly, the interview of the suspect to gather their account of their involvement in the crime. The iterative nature of the process described above is equally apparent during this phase of the investigation. Evaluations of the material will be carried out to identify what it means for the investigation, what further material is required and what action needs to be taken to acquire it.

Evidential evaluation

The decision to charge a suspect with an offence is the responsibility of the CPS. However, in deciding whether or not to send a case to them for consideration investigators must make a preliminary decision as to the sufficiency of the evidence they have collected. In doing this they must apply essentially the same test to the material as will the CPS lawyer. This is, that the evidence gathered in the case provides a realistic prospect of a conviction (Section 5.2 of the Code for Crown Prosecutors) and that it is in the public interest to proceed with the case (Section 5.6).

The key difference between investigative and evidential evaluation is that during an investigative evaluation, investigators are free to use all available material even though it may not be evidentially admissible. When carrying out an evidential evaluation, investigators need to assess the strength of the case taking into account only the evidentially admissible material. If a case is to go to charge, further work may arise out of the Crown Prosecutor's review of the material. This may identify additional lines of enquiry that need to be pursued.

Case management

Even when someone is charged with an offence there is still a great deal of work for investigators to do. Any lines of enquiry that are not yet complete need to be finalised. All the material to be used in the prosecution needs to be in an evidential format. Any material they have gathered that is not to be used in the prosecution needs to be correctly recorded and passed to the CPS, who have a duty to review it and disclose to the defence anything that may be relevant to their case. In preparing the case for court, prosecutors may require additional enquiries to be made and the defence may provide information that leads to further investigation. While all of this is taking place, victims and witnesses need to be managed through the court process and all exhibits have to be properly labelled and stored. In more high-profile cases, investigators may be involved in media management before and during the trial.

After the trial, witness care is still sometimes required, exhibits need to be disposed of and intelligence generated by the case needs to be disseminated, although most of this will have been done as the intelligence is generated during the investigation.

Summary

Because the key information needs of all criminal investigations are broadly similar, the stages through which each investigation progresses are the same. This means that despite wide variations in the type, volume and distribution of information associated with different crimes, and variations in the way in which offenders, victims and witnesses behave after a crime, investigators have a stable process that they can apply to most situations they are presented with. This process supports the use of a range of information-gathering techniques that investigators deploy according to their judgement about what is required in the unique circumstances of each case.

Investigative decision-making

The investigation process discussed above shows the type of decisions that have to be made by investigators and the sequence in which they are made. This section examines how those decisions are made and the way in which practitioners use the material gathered during an investigation to develop lines of enquiry. The ethical aspects of decision-making are also examined.

The three key decision areas

Although many decisions have to be made during the course of an investigation, there are generally three key ones to be taken during any evaluation of material:

1 Is the behaviour under consideration a criminal offence?
2 Who might be a suspect?
3 What further material needs to be gathered?

Although each of these decision-making areas appears to follow each other sequentially, in practice they do not. It is often the case that investigators have a clear idea of who was responsible for a particular behaviour, but do not know whether the behaviour itself was a criminal offence. Likewise, there may be evidence at the scene in the

157

form of DNA or fingerprints that would provide conclusive evidence of an individual's involvement, but there are no suspects to compare it against. As a consequence, investigators may work on the three areas simultaneously, and each is considered individually below.

Is the behaviour under consideration a criminal offence?

In Chapter 2 the way in which the law defines some behaviours as criminal was examined. The police provide a mechanism by which those who believe that a criminal offence has been committed can report it for investigation. Police forces also carry out analysis to identify criminal offending that has not been reported. In both cases, investigators need to decide if the behaviour reported to them, or uncovered as a result of analysis, amounts to a criminal offence. If it is a crime it is recorded as such in line with the *Home Office Counting Rules*. Making such decisions causes very little difficulty in the majority of cases. Although people may use non-legal terminology when describing the behaviour they believe may be criminal, their meaning is generally clear. Colloquialisms such as 'beaten up', 'mugged', 'ripped off', 'interfered with' (in a sexual context), are not difficult to place in the appropriate legal category once sufficient detail is known. However, occasionally a behaviour that is thought to be criminal will either be difficult to place in a particular criminal category or will be found not to be a crime.

A difficulty sometimes arises where the circumstances presented to investigators are capable of both an innocent explanation and a guilty one. Homicide investigators are often faced with this problem during the early stages of a case. Many deaths are reported to the police and most are from natural causes, but officers attending the scenes of these reports may occasionally be faced with badly decomposed bodies, apparent suicides, or circumstances that could be interpreted as being suspicious, such as an old person dead within an insecure house. The question is often one of 'Did he fall or was he pushed?' and a great deal of work may have to be carried out simply to establish whether or not the circumstances amount to an offence. Such cases are relatively infrequent and for the most part decisions of this type cause little difficulty.

Who might be a suspect?

The term 'suspect' is used to denote those whom investigators believe could be the offender, but against whom there is as yet insufficient evidence to recommend a prosecution. Although the law does not use the word 'suspect' it does stipulate that investigators must caution anyone before they ask them questions if there are grounds to suspect them of committing an offence (Section 10.1, Code of Practice C, PACE 1984). A *de facto* definition of a suspect is thus someone whom investigators believe may be the offender and who they would be obliged to caution if they wished to interview them. They are not obliged to interview them and in some cases may not do so until they have gathered more material.

It is important to remember that there is a big difference between a suspect and an offender. In identifying suspects, investigators are doing nothing more than establishing a reason to believe that an individual could be an offender. This is a preliminary first step towards gathering evidence that is sufficient to either eliminate them from the enquiry or to implicate them to the extent that they are prosecuted. But investigators need to be careful not to confuse the two, and this area is dealt with in more detail below.

There are generally two ways in which suspects are generated: *allegations* and *inferences*. Allegations occur when someone informs investigators both that a crime has been committed and that they think they know the identity of the person who committed it. Given that a great deal of crime occurs between people who know each other, allegations are a very frequent source of suspect generation, and are particularly likely in sexual and physical assaults, thefts in the workplace and frauds. However, any type of crime committed spontaneously and in front of witnesses may give rise to an allegation.

From an investigator's point of view, allegations have the advantage that they often provide sufficient information to determine that a crime has occurred, together with witness accounts that are easily converted into evidence. Allegations can also be made by informants, and while these do not have the advantage of being able to be turned into evidence quite so easily as those from victims and witnesses, they do, depending on how reliable the information is judged to be, provide investigators with a clear starting point for their enquiries.

Where no allegations are made as to the identity of the suspect, investigators must gather sufficient material to enable them to make inferences about their likely identity. A wide range of material is used to do this and the way it is identified and gathered depends to a large extent on the unique circumstances of each case. Inferences are mainly of the following types:

1 *Forensic inference.* Both fingerprints and DNA provide material that uniquely identifies individuals and this can be used to infer that

someone is a suspect if it can be matched to an individual. Matching can occur because the individual's name is already on a database against which the material can be searched, or by using sampling techniques that identify the originator of the fingerprints or DNA from a particular population. These techniques are discussed in more detail in Chapter 5.

2 *Characteristic inference.* Even where victims and witnesses do not know the identity of an offender, they are often able to give investigators information about some characteristic that may be of use in identifying them. A physical characteristic such as a tattoo, an item of clothing, a type of vehicle they were using, or even their accent or the words they used may on occasions help investigators identify suspects.

3 *Modus operandi characteristic.* Some offenders are known to commit certain types of crime or to use particular methods and these can sometimes be used by investigators to generate suspects.

4 *Uniquely linking features.* Sometimes a unique link between the crime and certain individuals enables the police to infer that they are suspects. Investigations are occasionally heard of where officers follow trails of blood or footsteps in the snow from a crime scene to an offender's front door. Sometimes offenders leave a coat or jacket with their address in at a crime scene, or they ring home from the scene enabling them to be traced. Footwear marks at scenes are also used to provide unique links between offenders and the crime.

5 *Passive data inferences.* Passive data is dealt with in Chapter 5. The most common form of passive data is CCTV images, which can be used to infer the identity of suspects, as can financial records and other methods by which people leave an electronic footprint at a scene.

What further material needs to be gathered?

Once suspects are identified, investigators can gather material to decide whether or not a case against them can be made. This is not the same as identifying whether or not they are the offender. That is the role of the court. The role of investigators is to identify as many sources of material as possible and to gather the maximum amount of material from each. This material is then evaluated to establish if it contains sufficient evidence to mount a prosecution. If it does, the file is passed to the CPS, who decides if a prosecution is justified, and if it is, what charges should be used to prosecute the suspect.

Gathering evidence is often considered the most difficult problem within an investigation, but in reality, if investigators have already solved the first two problems they are a long way along the road to having the evidence they need to send the file to the CPS. This is because the material that led to someone being identified as a suspect can often be used as evidence in a prosecution. This is particularly so where an allegation is made by a victim or witness who is able to provide first-hand evidence of the suspect's involvement, which may be sufficient in itself to prove the offence. The same is often true where suspects have been identified through fingerprints, DNA or other types of inference that are readily converted into evidence. In many cases, however, the material that leads to someone being identified as a suspect is not sufficient to support a prosecution and so investigators must decide what type of additional material is required and where it might be located.

It often happens that further investigations provide additional material that leads investigators to eliminate suspects from the investigation. A fingerprint found at the scene of a crime may be from someone who was there legitimately at the time the offence was committed. Sometimes investigators believe that they have identified a suspect with some degree of certainty, but they cannot locate sufficient material to mount a prosecution. Naturally, this is an area that requires great care on the part of the investigator, because one of the reasons they are unable to find evidence may be that the suspect is not the offender.

Investigators may be presented with numerous problems that are unique to the circumstances of the particular investigation. However, most will fall within one or other of the three key decision areas, and the primary function of the investigation process is to gather enough material to enable these decisions to be made. In doing this, investigators follow a structured approach that enables them to deal with each investigation in a systematic way.

The nature of investigative decision-making

What little research has been carried out into investigative decision-making suggests that investigators rely on a set of rules that they develop from their own experiences of conducting investigations or that they learn from colleagues (Adhami and Browne 1996; Smith and Flannigan 2000; Saunders 2001). These heuristics enable investigators to make sense of the situations they are faced with and provide a framework that helps them to understand the material they gather. They are an efficient means of decision-making and are common to many occupational groups. But the strong tradition in the police service of 'learning on the job' means that the repertoire of working rules that investigators have access to is highly dependent on their personal experience. As a consequence, even apparently experienced investigators may have gaps in their repertoire when they are faced with situations they have not encountered before. An investigator's ability to make decisions may therefore be limited by the extent of their past experience and the degree to which they are able to adapt it to any new situation.

In addition to the limitations of investigators' heuristics can be added the common and well-documented problems of human cognition, which are as likely to affect investigators as everyone else (Stelfox and Pease 2005: 192). These working rules can become so familiar to investigators that they are not always aware that they are using them. This may lead to difficulties in describing how a particular decision was reached. Investigators may refer to these decisions as being based on hunches, gut reaction or intuition, and are unable to explain the rationale behind them, making it difficult for others to understand the decision-making process. In principle there may be nothing wrong in following hunches or gut reactions, but investigators are expected to account for their decisions to others and so they must have a good understanding of how they have arrived at them. The following are all factors that influence their decisions.

Personal bias
Decisions can be unconsciously affected by personal perceptions of people, places and situations. Racism, sexism and homophobia are all well-known biases that can influence the thought process without the individual realising the effect that they are having. But personal bias can affect decision-making at a more mundane level. For example, an investigator attending the scene of a burglary may decide not to conduct house-to-house enquiries in the vicinity because of an assumption that no one will tell them anything worthwhile. In this situation, the opportunity to gather information from the immediate neighbours is missed and this may have a detrimental effect on the investigation.

Verification bias
If investigators develop a fixed view as to what has occurred or

who is responsible for a crime, there is a danger that they focus on the material that supports that view. This will lead to a situation where they only gather material that reinforces their original view. They will ignore alternative lines of enquiry or sources of material. Investigators should avoid taking too firm a view on any point until they have gathered the maximum amount of material.

Availability error

There is a danger that investigators will base their decisions about the investigation on material that is vivid and memorable, dramatic, emotionally charged or easy to visualise. Such material might be psychologically compelling, because it appears familiar or is linked to a memory, but it may not necessarily reflect all the material at the investigator's disposal. Investigators should maintain an open and objective approach to gathering material and be prepared to challenge their own reasoning behind a decision.

Other factors affecting decision-making

There are a number of other factors that may adversely affect the quality of decision-making. While no one can rid their mind of all of these, they can understand the effect they have and so compensate for them. Factors that may affect decision-making include:

- Sweeping statements that overgeneralise and ignore contradictory evidence.

- Oversimplifying the facts by assuming clearly defined boundaries when it is not possible to do so.

- Making inferences from the particular to the general, e.g. assuming that because some are, all are.

- Begging the question, e.g. taking things for granted that have not yet been proven.

- Special pleading, e.g. stressing only one viewpoint and ignoring other more relevant or plausible opinions because they conflict (the arrogance of experience).

- Potted thinking, i.e. using simplistic assertions in an unwarrantable fashion, e.g. using slogans or catchphrases in arguments.

- Early assumptions about material or a source of material that can potentially misdirect the focus of an investigation and cause relevant material to be overlooked.

- Building unlikely hypotheses that do not reflect the known facts, ultimately causing the investigation to become misdirected, or an opportunity to be overlooked.

There are dangers in overstating the extent to which the use of investigators' working rules for decision-making are problematic. All occupational groups develop and use such rules and in reality there is no effective alternative. Investigators must, however, be aware of the potential pitfalls, and actively challenge their personal perceptions and understanding.

The investigative mindset

To a large extent, good decision-making is about adopting an attitude of mind towards the investigation, what the ACPO *Core Investigative Doctrine* (2005b: 60) calls an 'Investigative Mindset'. This enables investigators to bring some order to the way in which they examine material and make decisions. It is a state of mind that involves applying a set of principles to the investigation process. This enables investigators to take a disciplined approach to decision-making which can be explained to others. The investigative mindset can be broken down into the five principles:

- Understanding the sources of material
- Planning and preparation
- Examination
- Recording and collation
- Evaluation.

Understanding sources of material

An understanding of the provenance and characteristics of the source of material is essential in order to conduct an effective examination of it. This enables investigators to identify any characteristics particular to the source that may determine the way it is examined. Understanding the nature of the source will assist investigators to determine what it can contribute to the investigation and to explain its characteristics to others.

When investigators are carrying out a formal evaluation of material they also need to ensure that they have a complete understanding of its relevance, reliability and, if they are seeking to use it as evidence, its admissibility.

The CPIA Code of Practice states that:

Material may be relevant to an investigation if it appears to an investigator, the officer in charge of an investigation, or to the disclosure officer, that it has some bearing on any offence under investigation or any person being investigated, or on the surrounding circumstances of the case, unless it is incapable of having an impact on the case.

This provides a broad definition of what may be relevant and encourages investigators to use as much material as possible in the evaluation process. This is particularly true during the early stages of an investigation when it may be impossible to determine what will eventually be relevant and what will not. In practice, investigators only exclude material as irrelevant only after careful consideration and if they are absolutely sure that it cannot provide anything of use to the investigation.

It is in the nature of criminal investigations that it is not always easy for investigators to come to a view about the reliability of the material they have gathered. Where the material consists of the accounts of victims, witnesses, suspects or informants, they have to be viewed in light of the cognitive processes described in Chapter 4. If the source is physical material, investigators need to check that the inferences drawn from it are reasonable and cover all the possible interpretations. It is a mistake to accept the first or the most obvious inference. These may often turn out to be correct, but it is not always so. A clear understanding of the reliability of the material enables investigators to determine the weight they should give to it in the evaluation. The following factors need to be considered.

• Where the source of the material is a person, factors such as their level of intoxication, the use of prescription or illegal drugs, their opportunity to witness or know the facts in their account, their relationship to key players in the investigation and their motivations to be involved in the investigation are all easily checked and may impact on the degree of reliability given to their material. Investigators are advised in *Core Investigative Doctrine* to avoid making judgements about the reliability of material based on factors such as lifestyle, previous offending history or associates, as these may not be relevant to the investigation in hand. However, where the material is to be used as evidence, such factors may be raised in court to undermine the credibility of the witness and so they may need to be thoroughly looked into to enable courts to make a judgement.

- Material that can be corroborated by an independent source will generally have higher reliability than material that cannot be corroborated.

- Corroboration by a person such as a spouse, a relative or someone else associated with the source, or one of the key players in the investigation, will generally be viewed as being less objective than independent corroboration.

- Material that cannot be corroborated or that conflicts with other material may be thought of as being less reliable.

- Material as data that does not have a complete audit trail leading from its creation to its recovery by investigators is always treated with caution. For example, a fingerprint found on a knife used in a wounding a year ago may be of less value to the investigation if it is not known with some degree of certainty who handled the knife in the intervening period. On the other hand, if it is known that it never left the possession of the suspect or was concealed near the scene it will be of far more value.

Planning and preparation

Usually the first opportunity to examine a source of material is the only opportunity. The process of scene examination will invariably alter a scene and it is, therefore, important to get it right first time. The recollection that victims and witnesses have of events will fade or become contaminated by versions of events they later hear from others and so it is essential that all the material they can provide is obtained as early as possible. The same principle applies for many other sources of material. Careful planning is required to ensure that the examination reveals all the available material that the source can provide.

Examination

Examination can be divided into three separate processes, and the extent to which any of these is relevant to a particular examination is determined by the source and its characteristics. The three elements are as follows:

- *Account*. In interview situations, victims, witnesses and suspects are encouraged to provide an account of their knowledge of, or involvement in, the incident. When examining other sources of material, the account will be interpreted by the person carrying out the examination. For example, an investigator may infer that the offender entered the scene of a burglary through the window because it has been forced open from the outside, or that a person seen in a CCTV image may be the offender because they are wearing a distinctive item of clothing as described by a witness. Those carrying out such examinations should be in a position to explain their findings or interpretations to others. They should also consider alternative explanations. The degree of difficulty involved in inferring an account from a source largely depends on the nature of the source, any legal or procedural considerations relating to how the material must be treated, and the level of material that investigators already have. The more material investigators have about a crime, the easier it will be to draw inferences about the contribution a source can make to the investigation.

- *Clarification.* Having obtained an account from the source, investigators should clarify any inconsistencies or ambiguities that it contains. This may involve testing it against other material already gathered or identifying actions to acquire further material to clarify it. For example, when viewing a CCTV image, the events shown may, on first consideration, appear to verify a witness account of an incident. However, the time shown on the image may be inconsistent with the time of the incident given by witnesses. Testing the accuracy of the clock on the CCTV system that generated the image would lead to material that either confirms or casts doubt on the witness's reliability.

- *Challenge.* Experience shows that even those sources of material that at first appear to be of unquestionable reliability can be wrong, and that material that appears to indicate one thing can later be found to support a totally different interpretation. Investigators should, therefore, continually challenge both the meaning and the reliability of any material they gather. Investigators should treat all material as possibly being wrong and regard all sources of material as potentially misleading. This is summed up by the ABC approach:

  Assume nothing;
  Believe nothing;
  Challenge everything.

Every account should be checked for inconsistency or conflict with other material. Investigators are most likely to be misled because they have not paid attention to detail. *Prima facie* assumptions should never be made and material should never be accepted without question. Investigators should constantly search for corroboration.

Recording and collation

Before closing the examination of a source of material, investigators should consider the following:

- The records that need to be made of the examination.
- If required, how the source is to be stored.
- The security of the source.
- Access arrangements to the source if it is under third party control.

Where the source is to remain in the control of a third party they should be informed of their responsibilities in relation to the CPIA.

Evaluation

Evaluation as discussed here is less formal than that in the ACPO model earlier in the chapter and is intended to identify any immediate actions that need to be taken in relation to the source, or the material that was gathered from it. These include actions to test the reliability of the source or the material gathered from it, or any fast track actions that may be needed to secure other material. Applying the investigative mindset to the examination of all sources of material will ensure that:

- The maximum amount of material is gathered.
- Its reliability is tested at the earliest opportunity.
- Immediate action is taken in relation to it.
- Relevant records are made.
- The material is appropriately stored.

Applying the investigative mindset

Applying the investigative mindset should assist investigators to guard against being influenced by their first impression of the material. This is particularly important in relation to material gathered from victims, witnesses and suspects in the early stages of an investigation when they may still be traumatised or under stress caused by the commission of the offence. Those who appear to be reluctant to assist, or even hostile, may have useful material which if dealt with correctly they will share with investigators. Conversely, those who appear compliant or willing may be presenting self-serving versions of events. The mindset helps investigators to keep an open mind and to be receptive to alternative views or explanations, and prevents them from rushing to premature judgements about the meaning of any material or the reliability of its source. By not accepting material at face value they avoid the risk of overlooking alternative sources of material or alternative interpretations. The application of the investigative mindset from the outset assists investigators in identifying areas that require development or challenge through further investigative action. It also helps them to make structured and auditable decisions.

Record-keeping and decision-making

Record-keeping is an important part of the decision-making process for investigators. There are two main reasons why accurate records are kept. First, it ensures the integrity of the material gathered. The importance of keeping accurate records in relation to the gathering of victim and witness accounts and when interviewing suspects has already been referred to in earlier chapters. The same is true of material relating to information as data, where record-keeping is often referred to as 'exhibits management'. The object of exhibits management is to create a record of the material itself, how it was acquired by the investigation, what tests, if any, were undertaken in relation to it, how it was stored and who has had access to it prior to it being introduced into evidence at court: in other words, an audit trail of everything that has occurred in relation to the material from the time it was acquired by the investigation. There are a number of reasons for this. Where the material is subject to scientific or technical examination, such records provide courts with an assurance that the material has not been contaminated or altered in ways that may influence test results or their interpretation. Where the material is used to prove a unique link to the accused, for example an item of clothing found at a scene that has been matched to the offender, it is obviously important that the coat produced to the court for examination is the same one found at the scene. Courts expect investigators to be able to provide an audit trail to prove the integrity of all material used as evidence and so good record-keeping of this type is essential.

As with all types of material, there is no way of knowing how it will be used at the time it is acquired, and so accurate records

Criminal Investigation

must be kept from the outset on the assumption that all material is potentially evidence in a trial or will be disclosed to the defence for their use.

The second reason for keeping records is as an aid to decision-making and recall. There is no common policy for the level of records that investigators should keep, although as a general rule, the more complex the enquiry, the more important it is to keep accurate records of decisions because of the increased volume of material that has to be managed and the greater range of decisions that have to be made. In homicide and other major crime enquiries, it is standard practice for the SIO to keep a record of all key decisions, which may relate to issues such as:

- Defining what the scenes are and their parameters, which will influence the areas searched.
- Decisions about the strategies that are to be adopted for the crime scene searches, forensic examinations and other types of searches.
- The suspect parameters, that is, those characteristics of the suspects that are known with sufficient confidence to enable comparisons to be made between individuals.
- The time parameters, that is, the times between which it is thought the offence occurred.
- The interpretation they have put on material and why.
- The lines of enquiry that are to be followed and the techniques that are to be used.
- The grounds for using legal powers, for example the arrest of a suspect.

The above are simply examples; in practice, investigators should keep a record of anything they believe may be useful to them or to others, or anything they may have to explain to others at a later stage.

Good record-keeping is essential in those cases where it is likely that the investigation will be passed to others to continue. They will need to know what investigative activity has already been carried out and the reasons why action has not yet been taken in relation to something that could or should have been done. Records will be required of victim and witness care, intelligence that has been passed to others and the work that is being undertaken by others such as forensic scientists where results are still awaited.

The keeping of records should not be thought of simply as the creation of an audit trail of exhibit management or the key decisions made during the investigation. Many investigators find that the

170

discipline of record-keeping is an aid to decision-making. The routine of sitting down to write up how they have interpreted material or the results of evaluations, and the decisions they have taken as a consequence, forces them to take time to think through the issues before writing them down. Not all investigations require a high level of record-keeping, but the skill of good record-keeping is one that all investigators should develop.

Methods of record-keeping vary from force to force and so there is no common system that can be described. As a general minimum all police officers use pocket notebooks, which, as their name suggests, are designed to be small enough to be carried around by patrol officers. Their size limits their usefulness for recording large amounts of information, and so specialist investigators may keep records in what are variously referred to as day books or diaries. These are often officially issued by forces and are simply a larger format than the pocket notebook. SIOs generally record their decisions in such books. The crime recording systems used by many forces enable records of investigative activity to be kept, although this is often at a much lower level of detail than is possible in pocket books or day diaries.

Ethics and decision-making

Decision-making is not simply a question of processing information and making choices about the course of action that is most likely to be effective in getting the job done. How those choices are made and the types of outcomes they may lead to for individuals, communities and society as a whole are held by most people to be of some importance. As a result, most professional practice includes a code of ethics that seeks to guide decision-making.

The police are often required to take action on limited, incomplete or contested information where the outcomes can have significant implications for the liberty and well-being of individuals and the wider social good. In the UK, the importance of ethics to guide the choices that the police make have been the subject of some interest (Neyroud and Beckley 2001), while ACPO provides, in the *Police Service Statement of Common Purpose*, a number of principles that seek to set a broad ethical framework for policing. In addition, some police forces, such as, the Police Service of Northern Ireland (PSNI) have developed a code of ethics that lays down the standards of behaviour expected of officers and provides an ethical framework within which decisions and actions should be taken. The *Core Investigative Doctrine* seeks to contribute to the ethical framework of criminal investigation by proposing a number of principles that are 'designed to ensure that investigations are conducted in ways which are ethical and encourage community support'. These principles are (NCPE 2005: 20):

- When a crime is reported, or it is suspected that one may have been committed, investigators should conduct an effective investigation.

- The exercise of legal powers should not be oppressive and should be proportionate to the crime under investigation.

- As far as operationally practical and having due regard to an individual's right to confidentiality, investigations should be carried out as transparently as possible, in particular, victims, witnesses and suspects should be kept updated with developments in the case.

- Investigators should take all reasonable steps to understand the particular needs of individuals including their culture, religious beliefs, ethnic origin, sexuality, disability or lifestyle.

- Investigators should have particular regard for vulnerable adults and children.

- Investigators should respect the professional ethics of others. This is particularly important when working with those whose role it is to support suspects.

Truth and falsity

Finally in this chapter we consider the concept that causes a great deal of difficulty in decision-making during the investigative process: truth and falsity. It seems to be common sense that investigators are seeking to uncover the truth about what occurred when a crime was committed and in doing so they will use their judgement to decide what to believe and what not to believe about the material they gather. For many years this is exactly what investigators were taught to do, and 'discovering the truth' was put forward as being the objective of a criminal investigation. However, the concepts of truth, and its opposite, falsity, have been found to be problematic in the context of a criminal investigation. This is because investigators rarely have enough material to reconstruct exactly what occurred during a crime and so their knowledge is always in some way incomplete. This leaves open the possibility that they will revise their view if new material becomes available. To think in terms of truth or falsity tends to close off this possibility because, as was discussed above, once we believe that we understand the truth of something we tend to stop looking at other possibilities.

Furthermore, there is no requirement for investigators to come to any final view on the truth or falsity of any issue, because that is the role of the court. An investigator is required to maximise the amount of material that is available to a court to do this. This requires investigators to make many judgements about the validity of material, its meaning and its reliability. It also requires them to come to conclusions about the likelihood of individuals being the offender. What it does not require them to do is to form any firm opinion about whether or not any particular individual is telling the truth or that any piece of evidence proves that a suspect is guilty. They are required only to come to a decision about the likelihood of a court finding material relevant and admissible, and the likelihood that if they do so they will conclude that a particular individual is guilty of the offence.

What is known from long experience is that such judgements are contingent and can easily be revised in the light of new material becoming available. It is also known that the verdict of a court is sometimes not the final version of events and that new material or new interpretations of old material will force a revision of earlier findings. It is therefore of little value for investigators to think in terms of truth or falsity. It is far better for them to think in terms of the relevance and admissibility of material and how it could be corroborated or disconfirmed. This leaves them far more open to the possibilities of additional material and of new interpretations of material they already have.

It may be argued that adopting a more neutral stance on the question of what is true will leave investigators open to the interpretations that others put on material and will thus make it easier for liars to get away with crime. This is not so. Good liars succeed simply because they get others to accept their version of events as true. By rejecting the notion that they are able to uncover the truth and focusing instead on questioning every account and seeking confirmation of all facts, investigators are far more likely to expose liars than they would otherwise be. They are also far more likely to avoid the sort of errors discussed earlier in this chapter.

These are difficult ideas to put into practice, simply because investigators constantly deal with people who use the concepts of truth and falsity in relation to their knowledge of a crime. This is particularly so of victims, who naturally resent any suggestion that their account of their experience is anything other than correct. This is always a difficult area for investigators to negotiate. In particular, many victims of interpersonal crime such as assault and sexual offences are reluctant to report them to the police because they do not feel that they will be believed. Good investigative interview skills and a sympathetic approach enable investigators to negotiate this difficult ground but it should be remembered that even in those cases where the needs of victims require a great deal of understanding and sympathy, they do not override the needs of justice for investigators to keep an open mind on the question of truth and falsity.

Conclusion

Good investigative practice depends on good decision-making. The process of criminal investigation provides a structure that enables the activities and decisions involved to be organised and implemented in a systematic way in all cases, even though there is a wide variation between each one. Each phase of the process requires decisions to be made about the meaning of the material that is available, its reliability and how it can be used to identify further investigative opportunities and, ultimately, its evidential value. But there are many obstacles to good decision-making during the criminal investigation process. The most obvious one is that the material needed to make a good decision may simply not be available. Offenders and witnesses can sometimes effectively control the transmission of information to investigators, material can degrade over time because of environmental factors or because the systems on which it is recorded keep it for only a limited time. It is entirely possible to make good decisions on limited material, but it requires an acute awareness of the many difficulties involved and the ways in which investigators biases and assumptions can lead to wrong inferences being drawn. Good investigative practice can minimise these dangers by providing investigators with a systematic way of approaching the task of decision-making and by providing them with the knowledge of the law and human behaviour that they need in order to inform the judgements they make. Developing effective and ethical decision-making practice for investigators is far from complete but the ACPO *Core Investigative*

Doctrine has at least put the issue on the agenda so that further work can be done.

Further reading

There are few books written about the process of criminal investigation for practitioners that are available outside of the police service. For those with access to them, ACPO, *Practice Advice on Core Investigative Doctrine* (2006) and ACPO, *Guidance on the National Intelligence Mode* (2005) are key texts. Both are published by the NPIA on behalf of ACPO and are available to those with access to the Genesis database on the Criminal Justice Extranet.

T. Newburn, T. Williamson and A. Wright (eds), *Handbook of Criminal Investigation* (Cullompton: Willan Publishing, 2007) provides a great deal of material that is relevant to practitioners, and T. Newburn, *Handbook of Policing* (Cullompton: Willan Publishing, 2003) does the same, particularly in Part Three – Doing Policing.

T. Cook and A. Tattersall, *Blackstone's Senior Investigating Officers' Handbook* (Oxford: Oxford University Press, 2008) is written by two very experienced SIOs and describes approaches to the investigation of homicide and other serious crimes. Although intended mainly for practitioners carrying out the role of SIO and those aspiring to it, it provides a fascinating insight into the range of issues SIOs have to deal with and the level of detail they must pay attention to when making decisions.

K. Jansson, *Volume Crime Investigations: A Review of the Research Literature*, Home Office Online Report 44/05 (www.homeoffice.gov.uk, 2005) provides an excellent overview of the research on volume crime investigation processes.

There are many books on decision-making, particularly in the psychology and business literature, but none on decision-making in the context of criminal investigation. P. Stelfox and K. Pease, 'Cognition and Detection: Reluctant Bedfellows?', in M.J. Smith and N. Tilley (eds) *Crime Science: New Approaches to Preventing and Detecting Crime* (Cullompton: Willan Publishing, 2005) explores some of the difficulties of decision-making during criminal investigations. In M. Innes, 'Investigation Order and Major Crime Enquiries', in T. Newburn, T. Williamson and A. Wright (eds), *Handbook of Criminal Investigation* (Cullompton: Willan Publishing, 2007) the ways in which the structure of investigation and decision-making come together are considered.

As noted in the text, ethics should be a key consideration for practitioners when making decisions, and P. Neyroud, *Policing, Ethics and Human Rights* (Cullompton: Willan Publishing, 2001) is written by a practitioner and explores the range of ethical issues associated with the policing function.

Chapter 7

The supervision of criminal investigation

Introduction

The supervision of criminal investigations has often been thought of simply in terms of the relationship between investigators and their immediate supervisors. When things go wrong with a criminal investigation, it is often attributed to failings in front-line supervision. There is no doubt that the relationship between supervisors and investigators is extremely important but its effectiveness in ensuring the quality of criminal investigations is influenced by a far wider range of considerations. These include the governance and accountability arrangements of the police services; the way in which strategic priorities are set; the policy framework within which criminal investigations are carried out; how crimes are allocated; and the business processes that are available to manage them. Equally important are the performance management regimes put into place by police forces to ensure that the resources allocated to criminal investigation are achieving the policy aims and objectives set for them.

There is, then, a much wider picture to be painted of the supervision of criminal investigation than simply the relationship between investigators and their immediate supervisors. Within each police force there are a number of levels of management that are important. These levels are:

- Governance
- Executive management

- Business unit management
- Individual supervision.

This chapter aims to examine these levels of management and to establish how they influence the supervision of investigations.

Governance

The tripartite structure through which policing is governed was set by the Police Act 1996, which was amended by the Police Reform Act 2002. Responsibility for policing is shared between three parties: the Home Office, police authorities and chief constables. Between them, these three are responsible for setting national and local policing policies and objectives, funding police forces and ensuring that policing services are delivered efficiently and effectively. This tripartite system influences investigative practice by setting standards of investigation and carrying out audits and inspections to ensure they are met.

Standard, audit and inspection

Standards for criminal investigation are set by the policy framework that was discussed in Chapter 3. They come in a variety of forms, an example being the Home Office Crime Recording Standards, which determine when and how crimes are recorded. Each force also has policies setting out the standards they wish crimes to be investigated to. Some standards are made under legislation: the Code of Practice for Victims of Crime was issued under Section 32 of the Domestic Violence, Crime and Victims Act 2004 and details the standard of service that victims of crime should receive; the Code of Practice on the Use of the Police National Computer was issued under Section 2 of the Police Reform Act 2002 and details how the data in the PNC can be used. The standards that investigators will be most familiar with are the Codes of Practice issued under PACE 1984.

These standards are in addition to the obvious requirement for investigators to operate within the law and within the Police Discipline Regulations.

In addition to setting the standards, the tripartite members all play a role in ensuring that they are met. The Home Office funds Her Majesty's Inspector of Constabulary and the Independent Police Complaints Commission and can call on bodies such as the Audit

Commission to carry out inspections and audits when necessary. Chief constables and police authorities are responsible for carrying out internal inspections and audits of their forces and all forces have a Professional Standards Unit to investigate allegations of wrongdoing within the force.

Finally, although, as noted in Chapter 2, the role of the judiciary in overseeing criminal investigation has inevitably diminished because fewer cases are taken to court, they nonetheless still play an important role in providing public scrutiny of the quality of investigations, and this is an influential method of governance.

Objectives

The Police Reform Act 2002 amended the Police Act 1996 by adding a new Section 36A, which requires the Home Secretary to publish a National Policing Plan each year. The plan covers a rolling three-year period and sets out the strategic priorities for the police service for the next three-year period. The National Policing Board provides the Home Secretary with the main method of consulting with a range of stakeholders, including police authorities and chief constables, on the content of the National Policing Plan. The National Policing Plan is influenced by the National Strategic Assessment prepared by ACPO (see below) and influences the development of local policing plans by police authorities and forces. As an example, the 2005 to 2008 National Policing Plan set five key priorities for the police service. These were:

1 Reduce overall crime – including violent and drug-related crime – in line with the Government's Public Service Agreements (PSAs).

2 Provide a citizen-focused police service which responds to the needs of communities and individuals, especially victims and witnesses, and inspires public confidence in the police, particularly among minority ethnic communities.

3 Take action with partners to increase sanction detection rates and target prolific and other priority offenders.

4 Reduce people's concerns about crime, and anti-social behaviour and disorder.

5 Combat serious and organised crime, within and across force boundaries.

It can be seen that these are all in some way concerned with the investigation of crime and reflect the important role that crime investigation plays in delivering the strategic objectives of the police service. These objectives form the basis of each police authority's Local Policing Plan, which is developed in consultation with the force, local communities and partner agencies.

The national and local policing plans are informed each year by the ACPO National Strategic Assessment. Police forces carry out an annual strategic assessment of crime in their area and these are collated by ACPO which uses them, together with data from police forces in Scotland and other national agencies, to compile a national analysis of crime and policing in the UK.

Chief constables and police authorities use the National Policing Plan and the National Strategic Assessment to assist in making budget allocation decisions. These determine the level of resources that are available in each area of the force and the types and level of resources that will be available to investigate crime.

Executive management

Although the chief constable has overall responsibility for the organisation of the police force and the service it delivers, responsibility for specific areas of performance will generally be delegated to assistant chief constables (ACC). Allocating executive responsibility for criminal investigation can be difficult because it is so ubiquitous to the activities of a police force. Almost everything anyone does within a police force in some way involves or impacts on criminal investigation. As a general rule, an ACC will have overall responsibility for criminal investigation within a force. They will develop policy in relation to criminal investigation and will lead the force in carrying out strategic assessments and setting local objectives. They will also allocate resources for criminal investigation within the force. ACCs will often be supported by a head of CID or a head of crime operations, who will manage the force's central criminal investigation functions such as squads, but who will often also be the professional lead on criminal investigation within the force. Heads of CID are often therefore the most senior detective within the force and may carry a caseload of the most serious investigations in addition to their management functions.

The executive level of a force will generally also have responsibility for the units that support criminal investigation, such as scientific support units, intelligence units and criminal justice units. It is also responsible for implementing the business processes that support the management of criminal investigation within the force. There is no national process for managing criminal investigations. Volume crimes are likely to be managed by systems similar to the Volume Crime Management Model (VCMM) published in the ACPO *Practice Advice on the Management of Priority and Volume Crime* (2006) and homicide and major incidents are generally managed by the major incident room (MIR) system, both of which are discussed in more detail below. Those investigations falling in between these two ends of the spectrum, that is, those allocated to specialist units at the BCU or force level, are subject to a wider range of processes. They all have some common elements that are discussed below.

Allocation systems

There are two basic systems in use within forces for the allocation of crimes. Tasking and co-ordinating groups (TCG) are mainly concerned with instigating investigations based on the analysis of police intelligence, and crime screening systems are mainly concerned with allocating crimes that are reported to the police by members of the public.

Tasking and co-ordinating groups

These groups are the way in which police managers use the various elements of the National Intelligence Model (NIM) (see below) to allocate work. TCGs generally commission a strategic assessment in relation to their area of work and set a local strategy based on that and the local policing plan. TCGs meet periodically, usually once a week or once a fortnight, to monitor progress towards achieving the plan and to consider the tactical options for instigating operations and investigations. The tactical options will be contained in a document called a tactical assessment. The TCG will consider the opportunities contained in the tactical assessment and initiate investigations based on them. For example, street-level drug- dealing is a common problem on most BCUs and tackling it will often be a local objective. This will lead the TCG to require it to be included in the tactical assessments. The tactical assessment will analyse the available intelligence about street-level drug-dealing in the area. Where an opportunity to target a particular individual arises, for example because intelligence is received identifying where he is storing his drugs, this will be included as an investigative opportunity. Where the TCG considers the operation to be viable it will instigate an investigation by allocating it to a particular investigator or to a specialist unit.

The composition of TCGs is flexible, which enables them to cater for the unique features of the area or the specific remit of a particular unit. Groups are generally led by someone from the command team of the business unit and other members include those who manage resources, those who have responsibility for delivering operational plans, intelligence managers and analysts. Commanders are also likely to invite representatives of those partner agencies that can contribute to the resolution of policing problems.

Crime screening
The precise nature of crime screening systems differs between forces but most follow the common model described here. Following the initial response to a report of crime, a crime report is submitted, usually by the uniformed officer who first attended the scene. This report is inspected by a supervisor who quality assures the investigation carried out so far. This generally involves ensuring that all the information required for the report is present and that routine investigation tasks, such as interviewing the victim, looking for CCTV images and crime scene management, have been carried out.

A judgement is then made on the potential for the crime to be detected. Where there is material that could enable the case to be solved, the crime will be automatically allocated for follow-up investigations. If the case is one of volume crime or the enquiry is routine, for example arresting and interviewing an identified offender, it will usually be allocated to the reporting officer or a colleague. If the crime is serious or the investigation is complex, it is likely to be allocated to a specialist investigator, either in the CID or, if it falls within their remit, a specialist unit such as a child abuse or domestic violence unit.

Most crimes do not have material that would enable them to be solved at this stage, and are not allocated for further investigation. However, where they involve crime types that have been prioritised in the strategic objectives or where significant harm has occurred, such as a wounding, rape, homicide or large-scale theft, they will be allocated for further investigation.

Investigations that are filed at this or a later stage are not wasted because they form part of the intelligence analysis that informs the tasking and co-ordinating process and contributes to the strategic assessment. If new information comes to light in relation to a crime it is re-evaluated and judged again as to whether it is likely to be detected, at which stage it may be allocated for further investigation.

Volume crime management model

The VCMM identifies the resources that are required to successfully manage volume crime within a force and sets out the standards and processes that they should operate to. There is no national definition of a volume or priority crime because each force has different needs and priorities. The VCMM helps forces define what crimes they wish to treat as volume and priority crimes and then details what each of the resources involved should do during an investigation. The main focus is on good decision-making and ensuring that investigative actions are effective. These are listed under the following headings:

- Call handling and initial investigation
- Primary investigation and crime recording
- Crime management and administration (which includes allocation, discussed above)
- Secondary investigation
- Suspect management.

The VCMM enables forces to deal with large volumes of relatively minor crimes in a systematic way that maximises the chances of detecting them within the resource constraints set for that type of crime.

Major incident rooms (MIR)

Major incident rooms provide the business process by which forces investigate homicide and other serious crimes that require the deployment of large numbers of investigators and the management of large volumes of material. MIRs operate to a nationally agreed standard, which is contained in the ACPO *Guidance on Major Incident Room Standardised Administrative Procedures (MIRSAP)* (2005). This identifies the roles that are required in an MIR. Excluding the roles of senior investigating officer (SIO) and the team of investigators who carry out the enquiry, *MIRSAP* identified 21 roles that could be employed in an MIR. Not all of these are required in every case, and in some, one person can perform multiple roles. However, *MIRSAP* illustrates that the effective management of information and adherence to common standards is resource-intensive. It also contains templates of standard documents and details the processes through which material flows in an MIR to ensure that each piece of information is properly considered and handled.

MIRs are generally supported by the Home Office Large Major Enquiry System (HOLMES). This computer provides the following functions:

- *Document management*. Enables all documents to be monitored by the MIR and shows what is happening to each one at any point in the investigation.

- *Workflow management*. Enables the system to be tailored to the working practices in the MIR.

- *Graphical indexing*. Provides the facility for users to directly index from a typed copy of a document rather than re-keying the data.

- *Record management*. Enables data to be retrieved for research and analysis and provides a range of search facilities.

- *Task management*. Allows actions to be allocated and manages their progress.

- *Exhibit management*. Manages and tracks the movement of all relevant property throughout the investigation.

- *Research and analysis*. Provides links to commercial analytical software.

- *Disclosure management*. Helps to manage disclosure material.

- *Court preparation*. Enables a file to be produced for court.

The benefit of MIRs comes from the standardisation of practice that they bring about, rather than simply putting the material on to a computer. Even on those investigations where HOLMES is not used, which is frequently the case, the principles of *MIRSAP* are still followed.

Few forces have permanent MIRs because homicide and major investigations are relatively infrequent events. The usual practice is to have a central unit that provides the capability to set up an MIR near to the scene of an incident, usually in the nearest police station. These use portable HOLMES terminals, connected over a telephone network to a central server. Many homicides are solved relatively quickly and do not involve large amounts of information or many lines of enquiry. In these cases, many SIOs prefer to use card index systems, often called 'paper systems', as they believe that they are quicker to establish than HOLMES and are equally capable of managing small enquiries. These paper systems still follow the principles and practices laid out in *MIRSAP*.

Intelligence operations systems

Because HOLMES was originally conceived as a homicide and major incident investigation system and for many years was used solely for that purpose, other systems were developed for managing intelligence-led operations. Unlike HOLMES there was no central development or support for such systems and so they tended to be developed by a single force or commercially. No standard system has emerged that is in use by all forces, but most have functions that enable details of people, places, vehicles and other relevant information to be collated and analysed and for the actions of investigators to be managed. Because HOLMES also provides these functions and has become more user-friendly as it has developed, it has been increasingly used to manage intelligence-based operations as well as reactive ones, although other systems are still widely used.

As has been noted elsewhere, from the point of view of an investigator, the distinctions between a reactive investigation and an intelligence-led operation are not great and HOLMES is certainly capable of managing both equally well.

Kidnap and extortion

The investigation of crimes involving kidnap and extortion generally have as their aim the safe return of a hostage or the minimisation of a threat to do harm of some type, for example publishing compromising material or product contamination. This objective has often to be achieved against a deadline set by the offender and may even involve direct negotiations with an offender. This has led to the development of unique management systems for such cases which enable information to be assessed quickly, and for real-time decisions to be made in response to what are often fast-moving developments. Officers are trained in the use of these systems, which are deployed relatively rarely.

Reviews

A further business process, used mainly in relation to homicide and major incident investigations, but which can be adapted to any situation, is the formal review of the investigation by an independent investigator. These are normally carried out in accordance with the

ACPO *Guidance on Major Crime Reviews* (2008), which provides advice on the terms of reference for a review, the type of staff that should be used and the processes that should be followed.

Reviews are undertaken by an experienced independent investigator. They are generally commissioned by the ACC Crime or equivalent if the offence is still undetected after 28 days of investigation. They can be tailored to meet the needs of individual investigations and forces. A full review will examine everything done by the investigation to provide reassurance that no opportunities have been missed and that the techniques used have been implemented in accordance with national standards. Reviews are a very costly exercise and many focus on high-risk areas of an investigation to provide the chief constable with reassurance that they have been well managed.

Performance management

Performance management plays an important role in helping the police service to deliver the objectives that are set at a national and local level. Although the systems used in police forces differ they have a number of common characteristics. All generally rely on a range of performance measures that are used to monitor progress towards achieving the objectives. At a national level this data is collected and presented as comparative data, which enables forces to be ranked by their performance. This provides a powerful incentive for forces to achieve targets in an effort to maintain an acceptable ranking. Chief officers transfer this pressure down to operational units by allocating responsibility for achieving particular outcomes, measuring progress towards achieving them and holding individuals to account for delivery. Many operational units also do the same and so targets, and the responsibility for meeting them, are cascaded down throughout the service.

The data used for performance management is often drawn from the other business systems, discussed above, and they form part of the performance management structure of a force. Performance management has often been criticised within the police service by those who believe that it has skewed performance towards a narrow set of objectives and that the quality of investigative practice has been reduced as a consequence (Stelfox 2008). The mechanism by which this happens is not difficult to understand. The need to achieve short-term or low-cost goals leads managers to make choices that favour 'quick wins', with low cost and simplicity of implementation, even when the complex, the expensive and the hard to achieve may represent better practice and could lead to better long-term outcomes. In the absence of an incentive to adopt good investigative practice, the pressure to achieve targets may tip the balance towards poor practice. The implication for individual investigators is that they or their managers may focus on those cases that offer the best chance of meeting particular targets, rather than those that offer the best chance of achieving outcomes that are in the public good.

Another aspect of performance management is the pressure to deliver more services for the same resources. One way in which this is done is through the redesigning of investigative processes to identify those that must be carried out by a police officer and those that can be done by non-sworn staff. Breaking production processes down into sub-processes where skills or resources can be focused is a common way of improving performance in industry. It works particularly well in manufacturing but is more difficult to apply in service industries where customers like to feel that they are getting a personal service. They do not like to be passed from one sub-process to another. Everyone knows the frustration of dealing with a financial or utility company if their needs fall even slightly outside of the ordinary. Information processing systems that require a lot of unpredictable choices to be made are particularly difficult to apply this approach to. Research, medicine, journalism and other knowledge-based processes, where unpredictable choices have to be made, are still predominantly carried out by a single individual who makes the key decisions.

Criminal investigation requires a lot of contact with, and co-operation from, individuals. It also involves complex decision-making by investigators. This alerts us to the fact that sub-dividing it into discrete processes risks alienating victims and witnesses as well as making good-decision making more difficult.

These criticisms of performance management should not blind us to the fact that it can achieve a great deal in terms of focusing investigators on the objectives set by the organisation and reducing the costs of policing to the public purse. The point is that the systems put into place by the executive level of management should be capable of delivering these benefits without the negative effects often associated with performance management systems.

The business processes discussed in this section are all instigated by the executive level of the force for the purpose of managing criminal investigations. They are primarily used by those managing business units and by individual supervisors.

Managing a business unit

Below the executive level, police forces are generally broken down into business units. The main business units of any police force are its basic command units (BCU). These are used to divide the force into manageable areas and are generally under the command of a chief superintendent or superintendent. BCUs are often coterminous with local authority areas, which makes it easier for the police to work in co-operation with a range of local organisations. A BCU may be broken down into sub-divisions which are likely to be under the command of a superintendent or a chief inspector, generally known as the Sub-divisional Commander. In some forces, BCUs are further sub-divided into neighbourhoods under the command of a sergeant or inspector.

BCUs may have functional business units, such as domestic violence units, burglary squads, drug squads, street robbery units and so on. These are likely to be under the command of officers of inspector or sergeant ranks.

In addition to BCUs, police forces have a range of centralised units with special responsibility for particular types of investigation. These vary depending on the size of the force, the types of crime that it typically has to investigate and its priorities derived from a strategic assessment of the workload it is likely to face. Command of these functional units is likely to be with the head of CID or in some force the head of crime operations. Individual squads are then usually under the command of a superintendent, chief inspector or Inspector.

Whether at the BCU or force unit level, the management of a business unit is similar. The range of issues likely to be faced are:

- Resource management, including the acquisition of resources, which will include staff, budgets for investigative sub-processes such as forensic examinations and specialist and expert support, vehicles and office consumables.

- The management of staff, which includes training, professional development, discipline and welfare.

- Performance management of the case load of the business unit.

- Quality control.

- The management of local partnership arrangements, which give investigators access to the work of other relevant agencies.

Supervision

The direct supervision of criminal investigations is likely to be in the hands of officers of the rank of sergeant who are in charge of about five officers. These may be uniformed patrol officers or those in specialist squads. It should be borne in mind that many supervisors, particularly those in the specialist investigation roles such as the CID, will carry a caseload of serious and complex cases and will be themselves under the supervision of an officer of higher rank in the chain of command. Therefore those managing business units are usually carrying caseloads of their own as well as supervising the investigations of those under their command. However, the vast majority of supervision is carried out by sergeants supervising constables and others employed in the investigation process.

One of the main problems faced by anyone supervising a caseload of investigations is that of visibility. Criminal investigation generally takes place outside of police stations as investigators visit crime scenes, search locations and interview victims and witnesses. Unless a supervisor is actually present while these activities are taking place they cannot observe either the activity itself or the outcome that is achieved by it. This means that for the most part supervisors are reliant on the information provided to them by investigators to judge the quality of the work that has been carried out.

Supervisors usually seek to manage caseloads through regular review of the investigations that each section or individual within the unit is carrying. Various systems are used to record what cases have been allocated and the progress that has been made. At their simplest, these are registers of what has been allocated and the progress that the investigation has made, but more sophisticated methods are linked to larger performance management systems that provide information about personal, section and unit performance. Whatever the system used to record progress, supervisors will obtain the information they need either by a verbal interview at a weekly progress meeting or a written report from the lead investigators in a case. These will usually detail the action taken since the last meeting, the progress made and the prospects for furthering the investigation. This information enables supervisors to provide advice and support and to make resource decisions about individual cases. One of the most important of these resource decisions is when a case should be closed.

A key role of supervisors is to ensure that investigators have realistic caseloads. If this is not done, investigators can become overwhelmed by the sheer volume of cases. They may generate actions that have little chance of success on the basis that because a case is still open they should be doing something with it. Managing these actions will divert them from other more productive work on cases where real progress could be made. Judging when nothing further of value can be done in an investigation is never easy, but ensuring that cases are filed when the chances of detection are low is one of the most important roles that supervisors and manager play. To do this requires high levels of investigative skills.

The wide variation in information profiles and the willingness or otherwise of those with information to pass it to investigators means that it is probably pointless to talk in terms of an average length of time needed to thoroughly investigate a crime. Nonetheless, it seems obvious that investigators require sufficient time in which to carry out the investigations allocated to them and a lack of it is often cited as one reason why investigations fail. So caseload size, together with the other work allocated to investigators, is important.

Those compiling the ACPO *Practice Advice on the Management of Priority and Volume Crime* found that pilot sites limited the number of investigations they allocated to officers to an average of eight per officer (ACPO 2006b: 25). Although they felt that this reflected good management practice, there is no information on whether it led to improvements in detections by ensuring that investigators had sufficient time to carry out all the action required. A great deal would also depend on the volume of non-crime work that the officers were expected to carry out in addition to the eight investigations.

Major crime investigations are often cited as being expensive, in terms of both the money spent on services such as forensic science and pathology and investigators' time. Such enquiries are typically led by a senior investigating officer who manages a team of investigators and major incident room staff. The number of staff used on a major investigation varies enormously depending on the unique circumstances of the case and the priority given to its investigation. The level of resources also fluctuates over time in terms of both type and number of staff used. During the initial response a large number of uniformed patrol officers are likely to be deployed and they may be supported by officers from the local CID. As the investigation progresses these will be replaced by officers who make up the investigation team, primarily from the CID. But the scale of these enquiries and the higher profile they are given by the service means that those engaged on them are often carrying relatively few cases in comparison with those engaged on volume crime enquiries.

Some indication of the relative costs of criminal investigation is provided by Dubourg *et al.* (2005: 8). They estimated the police activity costs associated with various types of investigation, and these are shown in Table 7.1. Because an officer's time is the single largest component of any investigation, the figures provide an index as to the relative time spent by officers on the investigation of crimes within each category. The table clearly shows the enormous difference in the time spent on different types of cases and this impacts on the way in which supervisors allocate and supervise caseloads.

In addition to the direct supervision of investigations at whatever level, supervisors play an important role in mentoring and developing their staff. This particularly applies to uniformed sergeants, who must ensure that trainee police officers are exposed to a wide range of criminal investigations so that they develop their skills across a broad spectrum of crime types carried out in different situations. In doing this sergeants should provide support and suggest different approaches that may be applicable in novel situations. Even those supervising more experienced staff such as SIOs have to ensure that they are gaining the experience they need through exposure to different situations and to mentor them as they develop new skills or new ways of applying the skills they already have.

Table 7.1 Police activity costs

Crime category	£
Violence against the person	756
Homicide	14,910
Wounding	740
Serious wounding	5,917
Other wounding	412
Sexual offences	1,524
Common assault	119
Robbery	878
Burglary in a dwelling	576
Theft	134
Theft – not vehicle	191
Theft of vehicle	81
Theft from vehicle	31
Attempted vehicle theft	17
Criminal damage	76

The role of supervisor is not an easy one and requires those carrying out to have high levels both of management skills and of experience and knowledge as an investigator.

The investigative skills of managers and supervisors

The management model used in the police service is a bureaucratic one and assumes that those of higher rank are themselves competent investigators and are therefore in a position to know if the work done by those they are supervising is appropriate to the case and of the right quality. In recent years this model has been shown to be flawed. Her Majesty's Inspector of Constabulary (HMIC) has found that some managers do not understand the processes of criminal investigation and do not check that routine procedures are carried out adequately (Flannery 2004: 26). For example, the quality of supervision of rape investigations has been found to vary considerably from force to force (HMIC and HMCPSI 2007: 79). A number of public enquiries into failed investigations such as the Macpherson Inquiry into the Stephen Lawrence murder or the inquiry into the first investigation into the crimes of Harold Shipman have also revealed inadequate investigative skills among supervisors.

The bureaucratic model of supervision used within the police service appears therefore to be vulnerable if those promoted to the role of supervisor or manager do not have a high level of investigative practice. If they do not possess the knowledge, skills and experience required to carry out effective criminal investigations, they are unlikely to acquire them simply because they are promoted. Indeed, it is highly likely that such skills as they do possess on promotion will deteriorate thereafter simply because they will not use them as often in their new role. It can hardly be expected then that they are able to adequately supervise those under them or to assist in their professional development.

The extent to which inadequate investigative skills among supervisors is a problem is unknown but there is sufficient evidence to show that the assumption that supervisors are themselves competent investigators is at least questionable in some cases. As the Lawrence and Shipman cases illustrate well, this is not simply an issue for those of sergeant or inspector ranks, who are often the ones in most immediate line management of investigations; in those cases it was the failure of more senior officers to understand the issues involved that led to the problems.

The way in which poor skills among managers and supervisors can impact on the outcomes of criminal investigations is explored in more detail in the Chapter 8.

Conclusion

The effective supervision of criminal investigation is dependent on a number of factors: the governance structures put into place by the tripartite partners to policing and the way they use those structures to develop policy and objectives for those carrying out criminal investigations; the management processes put into place by individual forces at the executive, business unit and individual level; and the skills that individual managers and supervisors bring to the task.

This framework is important in determining how well investigators can perform. If they have the right support they will do better than if they do not. For example, the ACPO *Practice Advice on the Management of Priority and Volume Crime* (2006b: 7) found that organisational features meant that the overall police response to volume crime investigation was often not effective due to the following reasons:

- Lack of clarity as to when the investigation process begins
- Lack of continuity throughout the investigation
- Confused lines of command
- Limited and/or inadequate training
- Inexperienced investigators
- Excessive workload
- Lack of managerial support
- Lack of a performance regime
- No clear investigative direction given to officers.

Effective management and supervision is then of critical importance to the success of criminal investigation. The quality of individual investigators' investigative practice is, of course, central. They require the right knowledge, skills and understanding in order to successfully carry out criminal investigations. But given the inherent difficulty in supervising the work that they do, much of which is largely invisible to supervisors, it is important that they are motivated to do a good job irrespective of the level of supervision being applied to them.

There are a number of obvious steps that can be taken in this regard. Good leadership and a culture of carrying out good-quality investigations is possibly the most effective way of achieving this.

Another way of motivating investigators is through performance management regimes. These generally seek to measure the outputs of the investigation process, and where they are thought to be inadequate improve them by introducing better practice, sanctioning poor practice or rewarding good practice. Third, their tasking. It matters enormously what investigators are asked to do. If they are tasked with carrying out a high number of investigations of a type that are unlikely to be detected, they may well conclude that the investigation of crime is an unrewarding exercise that is doomed to failure. If, on the other hand, their caseload consists of those crimes where there is at least a chance of success, and it is managed in such a way as to give them the time required to do a thorough job, it is more likely that they will come to view the exercise as worthwhile.

The management and supervision of criminal investigation is therefore an important element in the police service's ability to achieve its objectives, but it cannot be defined simply as involving the relationship between front-line supervisors and investigators. Of equal if not more importance is the infrastructure within which that relationship takes place. This infrastructure is primarily determined by the partners of the tripartite governance structure of policing and the executive level of individual police forces.

Further reading

The tripartite governance of policing is explored in R. Reiner, *The Politics of the Police* (3rd edn, Oxford: Oxford University Press, 2000) and in T. Jones, 'The Governance and Accountability of Policing', in T. Newburn (ed.), *Handbook of Policing* (Cullompton: Willan Publishing, 2003).

Management within the police service has generally been explored from the perspective of chief officers and in R. Adlam and P. Villiers (eds), *Police Leadership in the Twenty First Century: Philosophy, Doctrine and Developments* (Winchester: Waterside, 2003) the editors, who teach leadership at the Police Staff College, examine the theoretical and practical aspects of leadership within the police service. C. Rogers, *Leadership Skills in Policing* (Oxford: Oxford University Press, 2008) looks at the skills required by leaders at all levels of the service. In relation to criminal investigation P. Neyroud and E. Disley, 'The Management, Supervision and Oversight of Criminal Investigation', in T. Newburn, T. Williamson and A. Wright (eds), *Handbook of Criminal Investigation* (Cullompton: Willan Publishing, 2007) provide an overview of the issues relevant to the investigation of crime. Although now a little dated, many of the issues highlighted in M. Maguire and C. Norris, *The Conduct and Supervision of Criminal Investigations. Royal Commission on Criminal Justice* (London: HMSO, 1992) are still relevant. A more contemporary picture is painted by HMIC, *Leading from the Frontline* (London: HMIC, 2008) which presents the results of a thematic inspection of the role of sergeants and covers many areas relevant to criminal investigation. The HMIC is a good source of material relevant to many aspects of management. For example, HMIC, *Modernizing the Police Service: A Thematic Inspection of Workforce Modernization – The Role, Management and Deployment of Police Staff in the Police Service of England and Wales* (London: HMIC, 2004) provides an insight into how managers in the police service are seeking to improve value for money through redesigning business processes and roles.

Although not specifically police related, G. Causer and M. Exworthy, 'Professionals as Managers Across the Public Sector', in M. Exworthy and S. Halford (eds), *Professionals and the New Managerialism in the Public Sector* (Buckingham: Open University Press, 1999) provides an insight into many issues that are common to all managers working in the public sector.

Chapter 8

How crimes get solved

Introduction

One reason for the abiding fascination that society has for criminal investigation may be the fact that, like sport, the outcome of a criminal investigation is never certain. Seemingly straightforward cases sometimes remain undetected and hugely complex cases are often solved. Overall, the majority of cases that are reported to the police for investigation remain unsolved and it is not at all clear why this is so. The study of criminal investigation has identified that information from the public is highly important in the detection of crime, but it is not known why such information is available in some cases and not others, or why some types of crime, such as homicide, have a generally high level of detection, while others, such as criminal damage, do not. It can be supposed that the skill with which investigative practice is applied in individual cases must play a part, and as in other walks of life; some investigators will be more skilled than others. This is obviously a factor, but even the most skilled investigators fail to detect many of the cases that are allocated to them. The answer to the question of why some crimes come to be detected while others remain unsolved, seems certain to lie in a complex interplay of factors. This chapter examines what these factors might be and how they come together to determine how crimes get solved.

First, the way in which detections are defined and patterns of detection are examined, before a consideration of the general and specific factors that are involved. A model of how crimes come to be detected is then proposed and tested against some common forms of crime.

Defining detections

All jurisdictions have rules that determine when a crime can be counted as detected. In England and Wales, these rules are contained in the *Home Office Counting Rules for Recorded Crime*, which are available online (www.homeoffice.gov.uk). In summary, they define a detection as occurring when one of the following applies:

- A person has been charged or summonsed for the crime (irrespective of any subsequent acquittal at Court).

- The offender has been cautioned by the police, given a reprimand or warning, under the Crime and Disorder Act 1998, given a penalty notice for disorder or a formal warning for cannabis possession.

- The offender asks a court to take the offence into consideration when being sentenced for another offence.

- Where no further action has been taken by the police against a known suspect, this is usually because:

  - The suspect dies before proceedings can be initiated.

  - The complainant or an essential witness is dead or refuses, or is permanently unable to give evidence.

  - The CPS or senior police officer decide not to prosecute because no useful purpose would be served (this is usually the case where the offender is already serving a lengthy prison sentence and would receive no additional sentence if prosecuted).

In the main, applying these rules causes little difficulty. From time to time abuses are uncovered where investigators, or their managers, have manipulated the rules to inflate the number of detections they appear to be achieving. Having offences 'taken into consideration' by a court (TIC) and taking no further action in relation to prisoners already serving prison sentences have been found to be particularly vulnerable in this respect. This is because both these methods of detection involve no separate punishment for the offender and so investigators have been able to coerce some into admitting offences they did not commit in return for favours. The extent of this practice is unknown and it is widely held to be more difficult in England and Wales since the introduction of measures to make the process more transparent.

The detection rate

The detection rate is the percentage of all recorded crimes that are shown as detected according to the rules outlined above. Because some types of detection do not lead to an offender being brought to justice, the government introduced a new measure in 2004, the sanctioned detection rate. A sanctioned detection is one where an offender has been charged or summonsed, has had a fixed penalty notice issued or has had the offence taken into consideration by a court. In other words, the offender has faced a sanction of some sort (Thomas and Feist 2004: 104).

In the five years between 2002 and 2006 the number of crimes detected, by whichever measure, by the police in England and Wales never rose much beyond a quarter of all crimes. Table 8.1 was compiled from the annual *Home Office Statistical Bulletin: Crime in England and Wales.*

Table 8.1 Detections for all crime types 2001–2006

	01/02	02/03	03/04	04/05	05/06	06/07
All detections	1,291,396	1,389,314	1,394,016	1,441412	1,515,978	1,475,436
Sanctioned detections				1,157,091	1,323,757	1,393,596
Detection rate	23	24	23			
Sanctioned detection rate				21	24	26
Crimes	5,525,361	5,898,560	5,934,580	5,640,573	5,556,513	5,428,273

A closer examination of the statistics shows that some types of crime had a consistently higher detection rate compared to others. Table 8.2 was composed from the same sources as Table 8.1 and shows the detection rates of a selected number of crime types.

It must be remembered that not all of those charged with an offence will be convicted of it. In 2007, 16 per cent of those charged with an offence that can be tried at a magistrates' court had the

Table 8.2 Detections rate for selected crime types 2001–2006

	01/02	02/03	03/04	04/05	05/06	06/07
Homicide	86	87	92	94	81	*
Wounding	59	55	52	41	44	*
Rape of a female	41	36	31	25	25	25
Robbery	17	18	18	17	17	18
Burglary	12	12	13	12	13	14
Unauthorised taking of a motor vehicle	13	13	13	12	13	16
Handling stolen goods	92	89	87	88	91	*
Trafficking in controlled drugs	93	93	91	88	89	*

*Changes in reporting format means that some figures are no longer comparable to previous years.

charges dropped before court or were found not guilty after a trial. For those offences that can be tried at Crown Court the figure was 22 per cent (CPS 2007: 86). The detection rate therefore tends to overstate the number of crimes where someone is eventually found guilty at court.

Patterns of detection

There is a general pattern to detections which has been termed the Triage Model (Eck 1982). Using data from US burglary and robbery investigations, Eck found that the investigation process implicitly divides crimes into three groups (1983: 224):

1 Those that can be solved because of the circumstances in which they are committed, for example offenders are identified by a witness or leave fingerprints at scenes (which he called the Circumstance Result Hypothesis).

2 Those that can be solved with a reasonable amount of investigative effort on the part of the police, for example by following up a description of the offender, or searching for those with similar MOs (which he called the Effort Result Hypothesis).

3 Those that cannot be solved because there is no information upon which the police can base an investigation.

Although Eck's triage model was developed in relation to offences of burglary and robbery, it seems to describe well the pattern that can be identified in the detection of most types of crime. For example, in his study of homicide investigation in England, Innes (2003) noted that cases could be divided into the 'self solvers', where all the information needed to detect that crime was available to investigators from the outset, and 'whodunits', where investigators had to work hard to locate and gather information, and some of these whodunits remain undetected. But, while the triage model explains a widely recognised pattern, it does not explain how individual crimes come to be detected or why some crime types have a higher detection rate than others. For that explanation we need to look at some general and some specific factors.

General factors

Three general factors determine the pattern of detection identified in the triage model: the law, information profiles, and priority.

Law

Chapter 3 explored how the points to prove differ between offences and how this impacts on the type of material that investigators must gather in order to prove that someone is guilty of an offence. The identity of the suspect and their connection to the offence must be proved in all cases. In practice it is easier to gather the material needed to satisfy the points to prove in some offences than in others. For example, the central point to prove in murder is that someone was unlawfully killed. There are so few circumstances when it is lawful to kill someone that the first of these presents very little difficulty in practice. By contrast, the central point to prove in rape is that sexual intercourse took place without the consent of the victim. Sexual intercourse with a consenting adult is not illegal and so merely proving that it took place is not enough; the difficult part is proving that it occurred without the consent of the victim. The material used to do this is mainly the testimonies of the victim and the suspect, which may provide conflicting accounts of consent. As such acts are rarely witnessed, it is often difficult to gather material that corroborates one or other of the accounts. There are occasions where forensic or medical material can provide support to one of the accounts, but these are not common and are rarely conclusive. As a consequence, rape is considered a difficult offence to detect.

It can be seen that the way in which legislation is drafted means that there are differences in the points that investigators have to prove, and these lead to differences in the type of material they must gather. These differences are one part of the explanation of why some crimes are more likely to be solved than others.

Information profiles

In Chapter 4 the relationship between the *modus operandi* of a crime and the information profile that it generates was examined. The type of behaviour that is considered criminal is very varied. For example, trafficking in controlled drugs involves a wholly different type of behaviour than stealing a car and the way in which individuals go about each one will differ greatly as well. These differences between types of offending and the way in which individuals go about committing them leads to big variations in the information profiles that are generated, and this impacts on the ease with which offences are detected. As a general but by no means universal rule, those offences where there is contact between victims and offenders will often lead to information about the offender's identity being generated. This could be because the victim already knows the offender or because they can at least provide investigators with a description and some contextual information that may enable them to be identified. On the other hand, many property offences, such as vehicle crime and burglary, do not usually involve a lot of contact between victims and offenders and so reports of these types of crime rarely contain any material concerning the identity of the offender.

Another factor that can affect the information profile is how spontaneous the crime is. Many assaults are spontaneous incidents that arise out of routine social interaction and so occur at times and in locations where offenders have little control over the presence of witnesses, CCTV cameras and other information sources that can lead to their identification. They may also adopt methods of attack that lead to the generation of forensic material that can help to identify them, for example picking up implements to use as weapons and leaving fingerprints on them. Vehicle crimes and burglaries may also be spontaneous in that offenders come across an opportunity and exploit it. But the dynamics of this spontaneous exploitation of an opportunity are quite different from those of an assault. Offenders are much more likely to assess if witnesses are present and to take other basic measures to reduce the information profile, such as wearing gloves or socks on their hands to reduce the chances of leaving fingerprints.

A very rough and ready rule can be posited, that if all other factors are equal, and as will be seen below they very often are not, spontaneous offending and a prior relationship between the victim and offender will lead to a richer information profile than when the offence is planned and there is no prior relationship between the victim and offender. A richer information profile does not mean simply more information, although that will be one element. There will also be more types of information, such as fingerprints, witness accounts, CCTV, forensics, and the information will be distributed more widely. This richness of information increases the investigative opportunities and makes it more likely that investigators will gather the information necessary to solve the case.

Priority

The resources to investigate crime are generally limited and so choices have to be made about which ones have priority. A number of mechanisms are used to do this and these were explored in Chapter 3. More resources are allocated to those crimes that are considered to be a higher priority, and where both the public and the police view of priority coincide, as in a homicide, investigators generally also receive a great deal more support in the form of information from the communities where the crimes occur. This higher level of resources and increased information makes it more likely that high-priority crimes are detected. By contrast, crimes that are not considered high priority by either the police or the public tend to receive few resources and little information, and as a consequence are less likely to be detected.

The *modus operandi* and information profiles, the way in which legislation is drafted and the policy that the government and police organisations adopt in relation to criminal investigation all play important roles in determining why some types of offence are detected more often than others. But even where the points to prove are relatively straightforward, the information profile rich, and the priority given to the investigation is high, as is the case for murder, some individual offences still remain undetected. In contrast some rapes, where the points to prove are difficult, the information profile often poor and the priority is less than homicide, do get detected. So while these general factors have some effect, there are clearly other influences in individual cases that can determine whether or not a crime is solved, and it is to these that we now turn.

Specific factors

The specific factors that influence the outcomes of individual cases relate to the behaviour of three key groups: offenders, witnesses and investigators. The way that each of these groups behaves after a crime is committed determines whether or not the material contained in the information profile is gathered by investigators. These three groups sit in a complex relationship with each other. Key to understanding how information moves between them is to think of them as either transmitters of information, or receivers of information.

In 1970, Willmer applied the principles of information theory to the investigation of crime. Information theory is concerned with the mathematical study of information and how it is transmitted. Willmer explored how this could be applied to the investigation of crime by examining how information was generated during the commission of an offence and how it came to be transmitted to the police. This led him to characterise the investigation processes as a battle over information between offenders, who will seek to minimise the amount of information they transmit, and the police, who will seek to maximise the amount they receive (Willmer 1970: 53). What is central to Willmer's model is the motivation of offenders to inhibit the transmission of information to the police. Not all are equally well motivated.

> When one looks at the whole spectrum of the criminal community it can be seen that at one extreme there are offenders who appear to make very little effort to minimise the signals they emit ... In complete contrast are [those who] plan and execute their crimes with great care and thoroughness to ensure that the police obtain as little useful information about their activities as possible. Between these extremes lie the vast majority of criminals. (Willmer 1970: 53)

The skill and ability of offenders to inhibit the transmission of information to the police will also vary and there will be occasions where chance plays a part (1970: 68).

Willmer considers the police to be the receivers of information. What is important from their point of view is to maximise the amount of information they receive about the crime by adopting the best investigative strategies and tactics.

Willmer offers a useful way of thinking about the factors that influence the outcomes of investigations: offender behaviour can be viewed in terms of the degree to which it facilitates or inhibits the transmission of information to investigators, while investigator behaviour can be viewed in terms of the degree to which it facilitates or inhibits the reception of information. Although Willmer did not consider the role of witnesses in his model, it can be seen that the same facilitator/inhibitor model can be used to consider the way in which their behaviour impacts on the detection of a crime.

Offenders

The amount of information offenders generate during the commission of the offence, and its relationship to detection, has already been discussed. Offenders can also influence detection by their behaviour after the offence, which can either inhibit the transmission of information to investigators or facilitate it.

Inhibiting behaviour

Offender behaviour after the offence can inhibit the transmission of information to investigators by the following means:

- Destroying material
- Controlling victims and witnesses
- Falsifying material
- Withholding material.

Destroying material

Even where they have generated large amounts of information during the commission of a crime, offenders may be able to destroy it. For example, it is not uncommon for offenders to attempt to clean scenes or to burn stolen vehicles with the intention of destroying forensic and fingerprint material.

Intimidating and controlling victims and witnesses

Intimidation and control of witnesses can take many forms; most involve putting them in fear of the consequences of transmitting information to investigators. It can be violence, social censure, family or relationship break-up. Whatever form it takes, it involves offenders controlling those with information about the crime in such a way as to prevent them from transmitting it to investigators.

Falsifying material

Offenders are able to falsify material in a number of ways, the most common being simply to lie about a particular issue to prevent a crime being discovered or to prevent themselves from being identified as the offender. Offenders can falsify material when they are in a position to control the flow of information to investigators. Those with power over their victims or the environment where the crime is committed are often in a strong position to do this. For example, those caring for children at home control the environment and have a great deal of power over those in their care. If they assault a child, they may seek medical assistance for the child but lie about the circumstances in which the injury occurred. They are able to do this because there are generally no witnesses and the child is either too young to give an account or can be persuaded to give a false account. When offenders work in closed institutions such as children's homes, prisons, police stations or army barracks, the opportunity to control both the environment and the victim in such a way as to falsify material is increased. However, it can occur in any context and can be accompanied by intimidation of victims and witnesses, as discussed above.

Offenders can falsify material to prevent themselves from being identified as the offender by lying about a significant fact, for example that they were not in a particular location at the time of the offence or were not wearing particular clothing. A more elaborate way is to construct a false alibi, which can range from the simple claim to have been at home watching television at the time of the offence, to the construction of a complex web of false witnesses who claim to have been with the offender in another location at the relevant time.

Falsifying information to prevent them from being identified as the offender generally takes place once people have been identified as a suspect. When interviewed they may choose to exercise their right not to answer questions put to them by investigators (see below). Or they may admit the offence. Between these two extremes are a great many opportunities to present false information. Someone who has committed a burglary and been caught with the stolen property may admit to handling it, knowing it to be stolen, but may deny being the burglar. They may admit an offence but put forward mitigation, for example that they wounded the victim but only because they were defending themselves from an attack by the victim.

What investigators will not know is who is lying and who is telling the truth. This should not matter, as investigators should explore all these responses thoroughly to gather information that will enable a court to test the credibility of the suspect's account. It should also be borne in mind that, like victims and witnesses, offenders may have genuinely faulty memories as a consequence of the cognitive processes discussed in Chapter 4.

Withholding material

One of the most obvious ways in which an offender can inhibit the transmission of information to investigators is by withholding it when interviewed as a suspect. In most countries, including England and Wales, this is a perfectly legal thing to do. A long-standing legal doctrine states that no one is obliged to incriminate themselves during an investigation. It is up to the prosecution to put its case together and if the offender does not wish to assist then that is their right. However, from a purely technical point of view, withholding information when interviewed can be viewed as inhibiting behaviour. It is naturally difficult to know how often offenders withhold information in this way. Gudjonsson (2007: 476) reports that about 60 per cent of suspects interviewed by the police confess to their involvement in the crime to some degree. What is not known is what proportion of the 40 per cent who do not confess are offenders who have made a decision to inhibit the transmission of information by not confessing, and how many are innocent and are either providing investigators with a true account or are remaining silent because they have decided that their best chance of being found innocent is to exercise their right to do so. However, there have been sufficient instances where offenders have denied offences, or have exercised their right to remain silent, but have subsequently pleaded or been found guilty, to identify withholding information in this way as a strategy for inhibiting the transmission of information.

Facilitating behaviour

Offenders can facilitate the transmission of information to investigators after the offence by admitting the offence to others or through the incompetent execution of some act which incriminates them.

Admitting the offence to others

Many offenders will tell someone of their involvement in a crime. They may confide in relatives, friends and associates, or own up to investigators when they are interviewed about the offence. One study into homicide investigation found that in 25 per cent of cases examined offenders were known to have confided in someone after the killing (Stelfox 2006: 79). Many of these cases involved offenders and victims who were known to each other and where the death was not the intended outcome of the assault. This may not be representative of crime in general and it is not known how often those who commit other types of offences confide in someone. But to the extent that it does happen it facilitates the transmission of information about the crime.

The main way in which offenders facilitate this transmission of information to investigators is when they are being interviewed as suspects. It is a commonly held misconception that offenders will try to inhibit the transmission of information when interviewed, whereas the reverse is the case. As noted above, Gudjonsson (2007: 476) reports that about 60 per cent do confess to their involvement in the crime.

Incompetence

Attempts to destroy information or inhibit its flow to investigators can be a high-risk strategy for offenders. In one case the offender murdered his girlfriend and set fire to her body. In an apparent attempt to distance himself from the scene he told several people false versions of where he had been at the time of the offence. However, the inconsistencies in these various versions were so great that he was immediately suspected of being the killer.

A more sophisticated attempt to reduce the amount of information generated by an offence was provided by the case of Harold Shipman, a local family doctor who killed 214 of his patients over a number of years. He adopted a variety of tactics for inhibiting the transmission of information about the crimes. Among these was attributing the cause of death of his victims to a pre-existing medical condition which was consistent with their sudden death and the circumstances in which they were found, most often in their own homes during the daytime. This cause of death was communicated to families in a persuasive manner and was recorded on the death certificate. He then altered the patients' computerised medical notes to make them consistent with the cause of death he had entered on the death certificate. So successful was he that his activities did not come to light for many years and to this extent his inhibiting behaviour could be considered to have been highly successful. However, unbeknown to him, his computer made an audit trail of the changes he made to patient records and, significantly, the dates on which he made them. This would not have been apparent to anyone making casual enquiries of the records. But, once it was suspected that he was committing homicides the audit trail created by the computer facilitated the transmission of information to the police and this enabled them to demonstrate that the falsifications to patient records had occurred after the deaths of victims, which was highly incriminating.

These cases illustrate two points. First, that the offender's competence in carrying out inhibiting behaviour is a factor that can influence the outcomes of investigations, and second, that even where suspects have a highly successful inhibiting strategy, it can under certain circumstances provide a rich source of information for investigators once it is uncovered.

Victim, witness and informant behaviour

Willmer did not include the role of witnesses in his model, but it can easily be seen how they gain their information, as witnesses either to the crime itself or some significant event before or after. The choices they then make about what to do with that information can either facilitate or inhibit the transmission of it to investigators. The importance of information from victims, witnesses and informants (often referred to in this context as 'the public') has been found to be crucial in bringing offenders to justice (Banton 1985; Bottomley and Coleman 1981; Burrows and Tarling 1987 for the UK literature; and Greenwood *et al*. 1977 for the US).

Obviously the main way in which victims and witnesses facilitate the detection of crime is by reporting it to the police in the first place. As a general rule, no one is obliged to report a crime to the police. There are some exceptions in relation to terrorism offences and money-laundering, but by and large the law takes the view that people are able to make a free choice on how to deal with crime they have been the victim of or have witnessed. No one knows how much crime is committed in any one year but what is certain is that a great deal of it is never reported to the police. This may be because of one of the following:

- *No one knows that a crime has been committed*. For example, it is known that a great deal of stock goes missing from shops and businesses each year, but on many occasions no one is aware of specific instances when it is stolen. It is known that employees often use company resources in ways that could be interpreted as criminal if a strict interpretation of the law was applied. Many employers either do not know this is happening or choose to ignore it. There is undoubtedly a great deal of crime of these types where victims are unaware of the individual offences and so are not in a position to report it.

• *Victims are aware of the offence, but choose not to report it.* A great deal of crime occurs between people who are known to each other and who choose not to involve the police in resolving what they believe to be a family or interpersonal problem rather than a crime. For example, parents who find a teenage child stealing from them are unlikely to involve the police. Another reason for not reporting a crime may be that the victim believes it to be trivial and not worth reporting. The most worrying cases of non-reporting are when a victim is in a relationship with the offender that does not give them the opportunity to report the crime, as with child abuse, or where they are put under pressure not to report it, as may happen with domestic abuse. It may also be that victims want to report a crime but have no confidence in the police, for example when the police relationship with a particular community is poor or where victims believe that investigators will not believe them or take their concerns seriously.

• *The crime is victimless.* Victimless crime is a term used to describe those occasions where the offence is against public policy rather than an individual, for example dealing in and using controlled drugs, and illegal gambling. All involved in such activities are generally behaving illegally and do not view themselves as victims (although many would argue that those addicted to drugs or who have a gambling problem are victims of the organised criminals involved). As a consequence, there is generally no one motivated to report the offence to the police.

When the police do know of crimes, either because they have been reported or because the police themselves have discovered them, information from the public is crucial to the investigation. While there is no doubt that the majority of witnesses provide information spontaneously and willingly to the police, it is known that in some instances many do not. The British Crime Survey (2000) found that only 15 per cent of witnesses to a serious fight or assault reported it to the police, while 12 per cent of respondents said that even if they were sure that an incident was a homicide they would not report it to the police (Spencer and Stern 2001: 36). The reasons for this reluctance were examined in recent research into witness participation in the criminal justice system, which concluded:

We know that, in practice, a complex range of factors determine whether a witness does in fact decide to come forward, of which the nature of the circumstances of the offence is only one. Research suggests that there are four additional reasons why witnesses can be reluctant to report what they know, to give a statement and give evidence in court. The witness may:

- fear retribution from the suspect or their associates
- be anxious about the experience they will have in the criminal justice system
- be hostile to or distrust the police and the way they may handle the case
- be unwilling through lack of interest or disinclination to allocate the time, or for practical reasons such as loss of pay while attending court.

Such reasons, whether considered or subconscious, may of course overlap: anxiety about reaction from the suspect or neighbours, coupled with unease about what would be expected in court, can be reinforced by the pressure of other commitments and lack of information about how to report the offence and what would be entailed. (Spencer and Stern 2001: 40)

Police experience is that many witnesses will not spontaneously come forward but will provide information if they are located and interviewed.

The criminological literature shows that many crimes are committed in circumstances where the offender knows the victim. It seems plausible that in these circumstances many of the witnesses may also know the offender and victim, and it may then be that family loyalty or friendship presents witnesses with a dilemma about whether or not to provide investigators with information. In some cases fear of the offender will no doubt be a factor. The literature suggests a further explanation, that some witnesses and informants will not necessarily view the incident as meriting criminal sanction and this may influence their choice of action in the event of being witness to a crime.

An insight into the circumstances in which such a situation might arise is provided by Brookman (2000: 231) who interviewed men serving prison sentences in the UK for homicide and for serious non-lethal violence. They described life histories where they had been subject to violence as children, predominantly by fathers and stepfathers, and had grown up in neighbourhoods where the use of violence was an established strategy for dealing with some types of conflict. As they grew older they were encouraged to adopt this strategy themselves by family members and peers. As adults they tended to socialise with others from similar backgrounds and in such situations a violent response to perceived threats carried a high social value. Such confrontations could occur in public spaces, pubs being a particularly common but not exclusive location. Alcohol often appeared to be a contributory factor. Brookman concluded:

> What seems to be of particular importance is the gathering of groups of young men and the role of an audience, all of which intensifies some men's need to respond to a challenge to masculinity. As such socialisation patterns would appear to play an important contributory role in some forms of masculine homicide. (Brookman 2000: 292)

Others have also noted the role an audience can play in encouraging violence in situations of social friction (Polk 1994: 68). This suggests two factors that may influence witnesses' choices. First, in some cases members of an audience may feel compromised in that they have encouraged or at least tacitly condoned the use of violence by the offender. Second, they may actually view the use of violence as an appropriate response to the situation and thus be less willing to co-operate with the police.

In addition to withholding information, witnesses having been located can inhibit the transmission of information by lying to investigators. It is not known how often this happens but it does occur. Whatever their motivation, witnesses who lie can create significant difficulties for investigators because they can distort investigators' knowledge of the event, and possibly lead them to take action that makes it less likely that the crime will be solved.

Investigator behaviour

Investigator behaviour can be viewed in terms of the degree to which it either facilitates or inhibits the receipt of information from offenders, victims and witnesses. This behaviour is influenced by the organisation within which investigators work and this was considered in Chapter 7. The organisational priorities, the resources that are made available to each investigation, the training investigators receive, the quality of their supervision and the general culture of their organisation – all will influence the work they do. However, the practice of particular investigators in individual cases will be highly significant. The knowledge, skills and abilities they bring to bear on a case will be highly influential in facilitating or inhibiting the receipt of information.

Failure on the part of investigators to receive the information transmitted by an offender can have a number of causes. First, and possibly the most obvious, the crime may be of a type that has been assigned a low priority and as a consequence does not have a high level of resources allocated to it (as discussed above). Even when crimes are allocated for further investigation, resources available to a particular unit or individual investigator may be limited and so a secondary screening process may be used whereby investigators and their managers decide which of the cases allocated to them will receive the most attention. Decisions are usually based on such factors as judgement about the opportunities to detect the crime and the relative priority a crime type has within the unit. In cases that are given a low priority and low resource allocations, investigators will simply not seek to be receivers of information, or their small resource allocations will mean that they can only apply a few basic techniques in the hope that they will lead to the quick recovery of material; but if they do not, no further investigative effort will be made.

The second way in which investigators can fail to receive information transmitted by offenders is through either failures of decision-making or the inadequate implementation of the techniques of investigation. These failings can occur at either organisational or personal levels. Organisational level failures generally result from inadequate procedures or insufficient resource allocation. Individual failings result from poor training, failure to update skills or lack of motivation. Organisational and individual failings appear to work in tandem, and often cases that have been the subject of public inquiries have revealed inadequate procedures and management leading to poor decision-making on the part of the individual. Public inquiries into failed investigations are very rare and so may not represent what is typical, but the combination of organisational and personal failings is found so frequently that they do seem to provide an insight into the types of problem that can occur. The two cases in Table 8.3 illustrate the point.

What these cases show is that where failed investigations have been subject to scrutiny, poor decision-making and the failure to adequately

Table 8.3 Organisational and personal failings

Case name	Organisational failing	Personal failing
Victoria Climbié	No formal system for screening and allocating cases.	Poor decision-making in failing to adequately assess the initial information and instigate initial enquiries.
	Poor training of investigators in child abuse cases.	Inadequate implementation of child protection procedures.
	Failure to supervise the investigators during the investigation.	Failure to interview key witnesses.
	Failure to check the investigators' conclusions before the case was closed.	Poor decision-making in closing the case before assessing the material that was available.
Harold Shipman	Case allocated to an officer with inadequate training and experience.	Failure to carry out investigative procedures adequately.
	Failure to supervise the officer during the investigations.	Poor decision-making in relation to the meaning of the material gathered.
	Failure to check the investigators' conclusions before the case was closed.	

implement investigative techniques rarely occurs in isolation from poor management and training. There are bound to be differences in the knowledge, skills and abilities of investigators, and as with all other occupational groups some individuals will be better at their jobs than others. Therefore, the way that investigative practice is applied in individual cases is bound to vary. This appears to become problematic where management structures that should ensure that cases are allocated to the appropriate investigator, and are properly supervised, are themselves inadequate or poorly implemented. Although poor practice and poor management are likely to impede the receipt of information by investigators, the combination of the two together appears to make it certain.

Modelling the factors that influence detection

There is no single reason why an individual crime is solved or not. The consideration of the factors discussed in this chapter shows that they are in a complex relationship with each other and that a number of factors have to come together to solve a crime. The factors, and the way in which they influence the likelihood of detection are shown in Table 8.4.

The matrix enables us to understand how in general some crimes are more likely to be detected than others. Whether or not an individual crime comes to be detected will depend on a complex interplay of all of the elements, and few crimes will fall particularly neatly to one side or the other of this matrix. In general, offences of murder fall to the left side of the matrix, whereas theft of motor vehicles falls to the right. As a consequence, the detection rate for murder is always above 80 per cent, while that for motor vehicle theft is always below 15 per cent. Despite this general trend, however, individual murders can remain undetected and a small percentage of vehicle crime is in

Table 8.4 Factors influencing the likelihood of detection

More likely to be detected	Legal	Less likely to be detected
Always illegal	*Actus reas*	Not always illegal
Easily established	*Mens rea*	Difficult to establish
	Information	
High	Volume	Low
Numerous	Types	Few
Wide	Distribution	Narrow
	Policy	
High	Priority	Low
High	Resources	Low
	Behaviours	
Facilitating	Offender	Inhibiting
Facilitating	Victim and witness	Inhibiting
Facilitating	Investigator	Inhibiting

fact detected. What appears to be most significant at this individual level is the behaviour of the various actors, rather than the legal drafting of the offence, the policy priority it has or its information profile. If offenders, victims and witnesses facilitate the transmission of information, and investigators facilitate its receipt, the offence is likely to be solved irrespective of the other factors.

Applying the model

The model in Table 8.4 can be tested against what is known about the detection of a number of offence types.

Murder

The detection rate for murder is usually around 85 per cent. This relatively high detection rate is due to a number of factors, including the straightforward legal provisions, the rich information profile that is usually associated with murder and the high priority it receives from both police and public.

The points to prove in an offence of murder are not complex. The main difficulties arise in relation to the intention of the offender. Offenders may admit to the killing but claim that the death of the victim was the unintended consequence of another act, such as an assault, or that at the time of the killing they were suffering from an abnormality of mind that diminishes their legal responsibility for it. Where these arguments are successful, offenders will be convicted of offences such as manslaughter or infanticide, which carry lighter sentences to reflect the lack of intent. Families of individual victims often feel that a conviction for these lesser offences is inappropriate, but the Home Office classes them all as homicide and so it makes little difference to the overall detection rate whether offenders are convicted of murder, manslaughter or infanticide.

The circumstances in which murder is committed vary considerably, and this is reflected in the different types of information profile generated by each one. For example, the spontaneous killing of a child by someone who should have been caring for it will lead to an information profile very different from that in the planned murder of a drug-dealer by a rival. Generally speaking, spontaneous offences that may be committed in front of witnesses or CCTV cameras have a higher probability of being detected than those that are planned. Most murders are the outcomes of spontaneous assaults rather than planned killings and so they can be expected to fall at the easier end of the spectrum of investigation. Both the public and the police generally treat murder as a high priority which means that the public are more prepared to provide material than may be the case in other offence types. Furthermore, the police allocate the level of expertise and resources needed to ensure that that material is received effectively and used well.

Rape

The rape of a female can be viewed as analogous to homicide in that both crimes are considered to be serious by both the public and the police, both involve contact between the offender and the victim that is likely to generate trace material, both can be either committed spontaneously or planned, and both can involve offenders who are either known to the victim or strangers. It might be supposed that the investigation of rape would generally be easier than that of homicide because the victims are able to provide investigators with a great deal of information about the offence, unlike homicide victims. However, despite these similarities and the seeming advantage of the victim's account, the detection rate for rape is far lower than that for homicide, at about 25 per cent each year.

The large difference in detection rates is explained by three main factors: legal; informational, and investigative practice. First, with few exceptions, sexual intercourse between consenting adults is not an offence; proving that intercourse took place is a necessary step but is of itself insufficient to prove rape. Many of those who are suspected of rape admit that intercourse with the victim did occur. The point at issue is whether or not the victim consented, which can be extremely difficult to prove to the standard of beyond reasonable doubt simply because there is often no other evidence apart from the accounts of the victim and the offender. Where a victim says they did not consent, and an offender says they did, it is difficult for courts to determine which version is correct. The legal doctrine that the accused must be given the benefit of any doubt means that in such circumstances they are likely to be acquitted. Changes in legal and investigative practice have attempted to ensure that as much relevant material is put before a court as possible to help them determine which version of events is correct but proving an absence of consent remains a difficult area. Evidence of the impact this has on the investigation of rape is provided by a joint inspection carried out by the HMIC and the HMCPSI into the reporting and prosecution of rape. This found that police reports show that in about 80 per cent of cases the identity of the suspect is known from the outset because they are named by the victim or are discovered through investigation (HMIC and HMCPSI 2007: 50). This indicates that the point at which rape investigations fail is not in identifying the suspect, but in gathering the evidence to prove the offence.

Second, some rapes, like some homicides, may be spontaneous in the sense that they are not premeditated and involve little planning. But, unlike homicide, in a spontaneous rape there will be in all probability no witnesses or CCTV cameras, and where the offence is premeditated and planned the offender will make certain there are no witnesses. As a result, the information profile of rape is very different from that of homicides, where there may be witnesses and CCTV images. With no other sources of information available, the information profile of rape generally consists of victim and offender accounts, which have been discussed above, and trace material. The value of trace material to the investigation depends largely on the level and type of contact between the victim and offender. But if the offender admits sexual intercourse, trace material has a very limited role to play in determining the question of consent.

The third factor involves the provision of facilities for the investigation of rape. Good practice is to provide specialist facilities and specially trained officers to investigate rape, which gives the unique level of support that is required in such cases. But the HMIC and HMCPSI (2007: 54) report found that there were wide variations between police forces in the provision of such resources. Even where they exist, rape rarely attracts the size of investigation team or level of expertise that is usually deployed to investigate a murder. This may reflect the fact that the identity of the suspect is known from the outset in many cases and so the level of activity required is somewhat less than in homicide investigations, but the fact remains that most rapes are investigated by single investigators working in a general CID office rather than dedicated teams, as would be the case in homicide.

Volume crime

The term 'volume crime' has come to be used by the police to describe those theft offences and minor assaults that form the greatest proportion of crime that is reported to them. ACPO does not provide a definitive list of the crimes that will fall into this category, mainly because the types of offences that are reported most often to the police vary from location to location, and also because within all types of crimes there are those that will be viewed more seriously by both the community and the police. As a consequence, ACPO defines volume crime as 'any crime which, through its sheer volume, has a significant impact on the community and the ability of the local police to tackle it'. Examples of the types of crime that may be included within this definition are street robbery, burglary, vehicle-related crime, criminal damage, minor assaults and anti-social behaviour, but the decision as to what types of crime will be considered to be volume crime is one that can only be taken locally. The main barrier to detection in these cases arises not only from the difficulties in individual cases, which were discussed above, but also from the attitude of communities and the police.

The Home Office does not count statistics for volume crime, but most forces include burglary of dwellings and vehicle theft in their definitions of volume crime and these generally have detection rates of around 13 per cent each. Investigators do not consider the legislation in relation to these two offences to be particularly problematic and the points to prove are straightforward enough. The main reason for the low detection rate appears to be that such crimes rarely involve any contact between victim and offenders and are not often directly witnessed. Furthermore, while it is acknowledged that both crimes are often committed spontaneously, offenders have the opportunity of selecting the time and method of committing individual crimes and can easily take measures to minimise the material they generate. The sheer volume of such offences also means that individual cases are not give a particularly high level of priority within the police service and unless there is material indicating the possibility of a detection at an early stage it is likely that offences of this type will not receive much attention once the initial investigation is over.

There is no doubt that the public take offences of this type seriously, but the lack of opportunity for communities to witness such crimes may impact on their ability to provide information to the police.

Handling stolen goods

In contrast to the original theft of property, handling stolen goods – that is, someone other than the thief being in possession of them knowing that they are stolen – enjoys a detection rate on a level with homicide. The high detection rate for this crime rests on the fact that offences are generally only recorded when the police find someone in possession of stolen goods. The 1994 British Crime Survey found that 11 per cent of respondents had bought stolen goods during the past year and so the chances of the police coming across them during other routine policing activity, such as searching suspects' homes, is relatively high. Such offences are rarely reported to the police in the same way that the original theft is and so the police mainly record crimes that have already been detected by them, thus giving a high detection rate. This category of crime is included here to illustrate the point that some types of crime have a high detection rate, not because the police are successful at investigating them, but simply because they only come to light when they are detected. The same is true for trafficking in controlled drugs, where there is a detection rate of around 90 per cent.

Conclusion

The application of the model proposed above to a small number of crime types illustrates that there is no single factor that explains why crimes come to be solved. What is significant in most cases is a combination of a number of factors, some general, some specific, that together create a situation that is either favourable or unfavourable to detection. Favourable factors are present more often in some types of crime than in others and this explains why crimes such as homicide have a generally higher detection rate than crimes such as burglary.

The main factors are the decisions taken by offenders, victims and witnesses to either facilitate or inhibit the transmission of information to the police. There are many ways in which they inhibit the transmission of information, and where they are successful they can even avoid the crime coming to the attention of the police in the first place. Where the crime is reported they can withhold information or supply partial or misleading versions of events to investigators.

The behaviour of investigators is also important. There is much they can do to create opportunities for those with knowledge of an offence to pass it to them and to uncover other data that is of use to an investigation. Their ability to do this will depend to a large extent on their investigative skills, and not all will be equally proficient. But the application of good investigative practice will improve the chances of any given crime being detected.

Further reading

During the 1970s and 1980s there was some interest among social scientists, particularly in the USA, in understanding how crimes came to be detected. An example of such research in England and Wales is D. Steer, *Uncovering Crime*, Royal Commission on Criminal Procedure Research Study No. 7 (London: HMSO, 1980). Interest then waned until the early years of this century when the Home Office sponsored work aimed at improving police performance in the investigation of crime. Examples of this work are J. Burrows, M. Hopkins, R. Hubbard, A. Robinson, M. Speed and N. Tilley, *Understanding the Attrition Process in Volume Crime Investigations*, Home Office Research Study 295 (London: Home Office, 2005). While the aim of this work is primarily at improving policy development and management, it provides practitioners with an insight into many of the factors relating to how outcomes are achieved during the investigation of volume crime cases.

The investigation of rape has also been the subject of much recent research as a consequence of concerns over the low detection and conviction rates achieved for such offences. For example, A. Feist, J. Ashe, J. Lawrence, D. McPhee and R. Wilson, *Investigating and Detecting Recorded Offences of Rape*, Home Office Online Report 18/07 (www.homeoffice.gov.uk, 2007) and L. Kelly, J. Lovett and L. Regan, *A Gap or a Chasm? Attrition in Reported Rape Cases*, Home Office Research Study 293 (London: Home Office, 2005).

The important role that information from victims, witnesses and informants plays in the detection of crime has been identified in the literature but there is little on the role that offenders play or on the relationship between investigative practice and outcomes. These are areas where practitioner research could make a significant contribution to the literature.

Chapter 9

Conclusion

In this final chapter, a number of the themes that have been running through this book are pulled together to examine the ways in which investigative practice might be improved in the future. These improvements might be qualitative, for example in the way victims are treated or the way in which evidence is presented to courts, or they might be quantitative, for example increased numbers of detections or the reduced cost of complex investigations such as homicide. The ways in which these could be brought about are examined in relation to the factors identified as being important in solving crime in the previous chapter.

Crime is committed in a wide variety of ways that have little in common other than they all involve behaviour deemed illegal by the legislature. Furthermore, even crimes of the same type can be committed in different ways and for different motives. Someone breaking into a house to steal property that is later sold to fund a drugs habit commits burglary, as does a man who enters his former partner's home with the intention of damaging property in revenge for her ending the relationship. The *modus operandi* of these offences is completely different, as is the motive of the offender; but they both commit burglary.

The diversity of behaviour that is criminal is mirrored in the diversity of those who commit it. While it has been found that most crime is committed by a relatively small group of persistent offenders, it is also true that many people commit crime at some time during their lives, particularly it seems during their teenage years. There are no social or economic barriers to who commits crimes. Most of those who are reflected in the recorded crime statistics come from lower socio-economic groups but many in those groups do not commit crime and many in higher groups do. There are enough police officers and solicitors in prison to illustrate the point that human frailty is not the preserve of some economic underclass; crime can be committed by anyone, even those who are well placed to know how their behaviour will harm others.

Society's response to crime is also diverse. Most people agree that some behaviour should be deemed criminal, but there is less consensus about which behaviour should be included and the response that the police and other criminal justice agencies should make to it. Even in the case of seemingly straightforward situations such as illegal killing, there are situations in which it is believed that convictions for murder or manslaughter are inappropriate. Examples include when householders kill intruders, when victims of chronic domestic abuse kill their attackers, and when carers kill or assist in the death of someone who is terminally ill. In this area, there is also an ongoing debate about whether those who kill while driving a car have the same moral and legal responsibilities as those who kill in other ways. At the moment they are often charged under road traffic legislation rather than with homicide offences. These differences in views about what type of behaviour the criminal law should concern itself with and how it should be applied in practice run through all types of crime. Whether crime is considered to be minor or serious is often based on opinion rather than the actual harm that the crime has caused to a particular victim or society as a whole.

Investigators and those managing them need to understand both the diversity and the complexity of behaviour that makes up the social phenomenon we call crime, together with the diversity of society's response to it. This will enable them to formulate improved policies and individual responses to crime; it will also alert them to the fact that society seeks a range of objectives from criminal investigation. There was a time, not so long ago, when criminal investigation was considered by the police as simply a means of bringing offenders to justice. No doubt investigators recognised the importance of issues such as victim care, community reassurance, intelligence-gathering and managing a variety of crime risks, but these were not considered to be objectives in themselves because they fell outside of the formal structure of evidence-gathering that defined investigative practice. There is now a realisation that these are legitimate objectives of criminal investigation in themselves and they have been incorporated into investigative practice through policy, and in some cases, such as victim care, through legislation.

Crime is, therefore, a complex social phenomenon and criminal investigation is an equally complex response to it which must work at all levels, from the local to the international, and must be capable of delivering a range of objectives. The police service's capacity to carry out criminal investigations across this wide spectrum consists almost entirely of the investigative practice of its staff, which provides them with the knowledge, skills and understanding they need in order to carry out effective criminal investigations.

Investigative practice itself is a relatively new concept within the police service and has developed in response to a number of triggers, which were discussed in Chapter 2. The investigative practice that has developed in recent years consists of a growing literature that is validated by practitioners, is transparent and is open to change. It provides investigators with the skills, knowledge and understanding they need to solve the many problems that can be presented by criminal investigation. It encompasses the full spectrum of the investigator's role and is not restricted to the legal and procedural issues, as evidenced by the roles that victim care, community reassurance risk management and the acquisition of intelligence now play.

The driver for improved investigative practice is the ACPO Professionalising Investigations Programme (PIP), which provides the framework for improved training and continued professional development, the testing of competence against National Occupational Standards (NOS) and the registration of competent investigators. This ensures that in future only those who have achieved a minimum standard of competence in investigative practice will be allowed to carry out criminal investigations on behalf of the police service.

These changes are profound and their implications are still being worked through by practitioners and policy-makers, but at their heart is the need to constantly adapt and change to the social, political and economic developments in society. These lead to ever-changing requirements for police services and this is as true of criminal investigation as it is of other areas of policing. Some of these changes occur slowly. For example, the problem of illegal drug use has a long history and the way in which criminal investigation is used as part of a range of government measures intended to reduce it has developed over an equally long period. Some problems, and the response to them, occur more quickly. For example, the use of the internet for commercial purposes has developed over a short number of years and the criminal investigation response to this problem is still being developed.

Previous chapters of this book have explored the factors that influence the way criminal investigation is practised. These are:

- The law and policy
- Information profiles
- The behaviour after the crime of:
    Offenders
    Victims, witnesses and informants
    Investigators

In the previous chapter, the way in which these factors determine the outcome of individual investigations was examined and it was found that no one factor will lead to success in criminal investigation. They sit in a complex relationship to each other and need to come together in ways that are favourable for a detection to be achieved in any given case.

In seeking to develop investigative practice to enable it to respond to the changing requirements that the police service have for criminal investigation, it is these factors that should receive attention. But in considering change, it should not be overlooked that a great many improvements have already been made over the years. It is difficult to provide evidence of qualitative changes to the way in which criminal investigations are carried out, but the changes to the legal framework of criminal investigation and to investigative practices such as interviewing are thought by many to have reduced the potential for the type of miscarriages of justice that came to light during the 1970s and 1980s. The potential for malpractice and corruption is ever-present in criminal investigation and it would be unwise to be too complacent, but there appears to be a genuine concern among investigators for the probity of the process and ethical practice. This provides an excellent foundation for moving forward.

Furthermore, the sometimes bleak picture of investigators' productivity can be viewed in a number of ways. Measuring investigator productivity is not easy, and the traditional way is through the detection rate, which is the percentage of recorded crime that the police detect each year. This is considered by most within the police service to be a poor measure of police investigative performance because it is affected by rises in offending that are unconnected to investigative outcomes. The detection rate in the early 1950s was about 47 per cent whereas by 2007 it had fallen to 26 per cent. However, the number of offences detected rose during the same period from just under 0.25 million to 1.4 million. So while the detection rate shows an absolute fall of about half, the number of detections increased by slightly under six times. There may be all sorts of reasons for this rise, from an increased number of easier-to- detect cases being reported to the police to developments in areas such as CCTV and forensic science. Whatever the cause, the figures illustrate that the absolute numbers of detections can be increased. The trick appears to be to make sure that the increase is in the type of crime that is of concern to the public and in areas that improve society's chances of managing future offending behaviour.

A further problem with the detection rate is that it focuses attention on only one outcome, that is, offenders brought to justice. Some success has been achieved in measuring the other outcomes sought from criminal investigation. Victim satisfaction surveys are commonly used by forces to gauge performance in that area, the number of intelligence inputs arising out of criminal investigation is counted by some forces, and there is a well-developed method for measuring the number of asset recoveries achieved by all forces.

The real problem in improving investigative performance is in increasing the outcomes achieved by individual investigators, irrespective of how they are counted. There was a slight rise in the number of detections per officer from 9.8 in 1995 to 10.4 in 2005 but the figure has remained static since then. Performance management regimes have been implemented in all forces in response to a government focus on targets for offenders brought to justice. These were discussed in Chapter 7, and mainly seek to improve outcomes by setting targets and holding investigators and their managers accountable for achieving them. Investigation processes have some-times been redesigned to reduce costs by the introduction of more specialisation or automation. There is no doubt that these measures have increased the overall number of offenders brought to justice in recent years but much of this improvement appears to have been achieved through targeting easy-to-detect crimes that can be dealt with by police cautions or other non-judicial disposals (Stelfox 2008). These practices have not been applied universally. Some performance management systems facilitate real improvements in detections, but where forces have simply set targets and put pressure on investigators to meet them or redesigned investigation processes with an eye only to reducing costs, improved management practices will need to be made if investigative performance is to improve. Once again, the focus needs to be on the type and quality of detections, rather than simply their number or the cost of achieving them. It is likely that this focus will be on the ways in which individual performance can be improved in harder-to-detect crime types such as rape and serious wounding, which generate high levels of public concern.

The scope for improvement in some of the factors examined in this book may be limited. Many legal changes have been made in recent years, especially in respect to offences related to terrorism and the procedures the police use to investigate it. But these changes have not been without controversy. Many believe that both the scope of the offences themselves and the powers that the police have to investigate them have upset the always delicate balance between the protection of society as a whole, and the rights of individuals. These measures are held by some to be wrong both in principle, that is, the rights of the individual should be infringed as little as possible, and in practice, that is, they do not make terrorist acts less likely. This debate will no doubt continue, but it points to the fact that while changes in the legal framework within which criminal investigation now takes place are possible, they are likely to be controversial and the evidence base for the improvements they will lead to is limited.

Policy changes are easier to bring about and much of the change in investigative practice in recent years has been achieved through improved policy; for example, the PIP programme, improvements in relation to victim and witness care, and improvements in relation to intelligence management and use were all driven by policy change. These will undoubtedly continue and it seems likely that the majority of improvements in investigative practice will come from policy on improved standards of investigation and ways in which information is used within the police service.

Improvements in information profiles have been brought about by the huge explosion in the use of passive data systems in recent years. This has meant that when crimes are committed, there are now far more opportunities for offenders to be caught on CCTV cameras or to have their presence in a particular place proved by some electronic data generated by a mobile phone, an ATM or their use of a credit card. Such data can also be used to investigate relationships between people through telephone records or payments made between them. As with legislation, these changes have not been universally welcomed. Some believe that the use of passive data has gone too far and that the police access to it is too easy. It seems likely, however, that new ways of providing government and business services will be highly dependent on large electronic systems and that the police will continue to seek as much access to these as possible to gather material that is useful to investigations. Where the line will be drawn over this access is as yet unclear.

Less controversial but equally effective ways of enhancing the information profile of individual offences continue to be developed. The traditional method of writing a postcode on valuable property to help investigators identify it in the event of theft has been joined by more sophisticated products that coat property in uniquely identifiable liquids that are invisible to the naked eye, making positive identification of items easier. Money-laundering has provided an example of how legislation can be used to increase the information generated by an offence. Regulations place an obligation on financial institutions to report details of certain types of activities; this is intended to alert investigators to the potential that they may involve criminal activity. Scientific, technical and legal changes can therefore be made that may increase the amount of material in the information profile of any offence.

The greatest potential for improving outcomes in criminal investigation must surely lie in changing the behaviour of offender, victims and witnesses after the event. Changing offender behaviour before the event so they do not commit the crime in the first place is, of course, even more desirable, but that is another issue. It is known that many offences are not reported to the police at all, and even when they are, witnesses may not provide the information they have to the police. The majority of offenders who are arrested as suspects and interviewed do provide useful information to the police; if more did so, the number of detections would obviously improve considerably. Wider social attitudes to offending appear to be at the heart of this issue and there seems no doubt that a great part of the success in such areas as homicide investigation is due to the willingness of the public to spontaneously provide information in such cases. Where people feel less concerned about the crime type it is probable that they will be less likely to report it or to provide the police with information about it. Notwithstanding this, all the evidence points to the importance of information from the public in detecting crime and improvements in this area appear to offer the best prospect of making improvements overall. Above and beyond changing general social attitudes to improve reporting rates and the spontaneous transmission of information to the police, it seems that the most effective way in which offenders, victims and witnesses can be encouraged to provide more information is by locating them quickly after a crime has been committed and communicating with them effectively about it. Improving the rate at which this occurs involves improving investigative practice.

Changes to the law, enhancing information profiles and improving the flow of information from those involved in crime, either as victims, witnesses or offenders, are all important ways in which criminal investigation can be improved. These changes will not lead to improvements in the outcomes of criminal investigation unless investigators know how to apply the techniques of investigation in such a way as to ensure that the available material is properly gathered and to make good decisions about how to use it to further the investigation. Whichever way one looks at it, the success or otherwise of criminal investigation is dependent on the knowledge, skills and understanding that investigators have. These elements are the basis of investigators' training and continued professional development and it is only by improving them that improvements in criminal investigation can be made.

The model of professionalisation that is emerging in relation to criminal investigation already has some strong elements. The service has a capacity to develop professional practice in ACPO, the National Policing Improvement Agency and the Home Office. The National Occupational Standards produced by Skills for Justice are an established means of setting a performance benchmark for investigators, and they have been incorporated into PIP. PIP itself provides a comprehensive means by which investigators can be trained and can develop their investigative techniques in operational settings.

Some elements of the professionalisation process are not so well developed. A comprehensive body of professional practice should be supported by a strong evidence base, continual evaluation of existing practice and ongoing review of the knowledge, skills and understanding needed by practitioners. What is required is the capacity to carry out research and development that will produce a specialist literature upon which evidence-based practice and policy can be developed. These elements should combine with those already discussed to provide a cycle of continually improving professional practice within the service, as shown in Figure 9.1.

The two final elements of this cycle, ongoing evaluation and the capacity to produce a research literature, are not well developed in relation to criminal investigation. If the benefits of professionalisation are to be fully realised, capacity will need to be developed in these two areas. The police service is not alone in this, as Nutley *et al.* (2002: 4) observe: 'Whichever part of the public sector one is

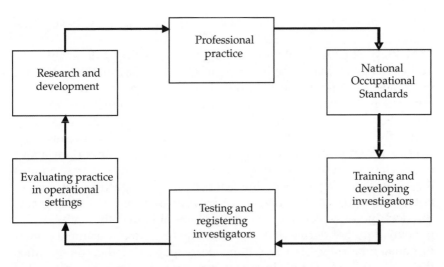

Figure 9.1 The cycle of improving professional practice

concerned with, one observation is clear: the current state of research based knowledge is insufficient to inform many areas of policy and practice.'

Some of this capacity does exist, however. For example, the Home Office and ACPO both commission research into various areas of policing, but the co-ordination required for the creation of an evidence base to inform policy and the development of best practice is missing from the equation. How this gap in the cycle of professional practice might be filled is beyond the scope of this chapter, but it seems likely that it must involve forging stronger links between the service and those universities that have developed expertise in the study of policing. These institutions are already involved in the kind of evaluation, research and development that is required and are experienced at working closely with the police service. But there is often a discrepancy between what is of interest to researchers and what the police service needs (Laycock 2001: 2). Bringing the interests of these two groups into closer alignment would go a long way towards filling the gap in the professional practice cycle. But university research is not cheap and one of the major challenges of professionalisation may be finding ways of funding the level of research required to support it. Furthermore, ways will need to be found to enable more multi-disciplinary research to be carried out. Investigative practice is far too complex for significant improvements to be made to it within a single academic discipline. Practitioner researchers must also be far more involved than they have often been.

Making improvements in investigative practice will enable the police service to maximise progress in the other factors that influence outcomes in criminal investigation. These improvements are important not simply because they increase investigator productivity or help the police service to better manage the harm crime does to society, although those are important in themselves, but also because the way in which crime is investigated says something important about the society in which we live. Investigative practice that facilitates the willing participation of the widest possible spectrum of society not only improves the chances of solving more crime, it reinforces the doctrine of policing by consent. This holds that the mandate for policing does not derive only from the law or from government policy, of equal importance is the willing participation of the communities that are policed. Good investigative practice can encourage this participation.

But the most important statement that investigative practice can make about the type of society in which we live is in the way in which suspects and offenders are treated. Most jurisdictions have legislation that seeks to protect the basic rights of those who are suspected of committing crimes. Compliance with these standards should be a given, but investigative practice should go further. It should equip investigators to exercise discretion intelligently, to use their legal powers considerately and to ensure that those with whom they deal feel that they have been treated fairly. This is not always easy to achieve in practice because many of those they deal with as suspects will have inflicted considerable harm on others and may be aggressive, confrontational or just downright unpleasant. The mark of professionalism is to apply the highest possible standard of investigative practice when dealing with such people.

If society, government and the police wish criminal investigation to make a positive contribution to the well-being of society, the professionalisation agenda within the police service and the development of improved investigative practice must continue to be driven forward.

Further reading

The connection between the skills required of those working for the police service, how those skills are trained and developed and the quality of service delivery this gives rise to feature heavily in the government's 2008 Green Paper, *From the Neighbourhood to the National: Policing our Communities Together*. These themes are echoed in HMIC, *Leading from the Frontline* (London: HMIC, 2008), which acknowledges the role that sergeants have in developing their staff and ensuring that standards of service delivery are maintained, and R. Flanagan, *The Review of Policing: Final Report* (London: Home Office, 2008). Although not dealing specifically with the development of investigative practice, these documents provide a good insight into where it sits in relation to other developments within the police service.

Finally, a paper written about the police in another jurisdiction and about crime prevention, not its investigation, is suggested reading. G. Laycock, 'Research for Police, Who Needs It?', *Issues and Trends*, 211 (Canberra: Australian Institute of Criminology, www.aic.gov. au/, 2001). The author has many years' experience of the policy and practice of policing and sums up the challenges faced in developing evidenced-based investigative practice.

References

ACPO (2001) *Investigative Interview Strategy*. London: ACPO.

ACPO (2005a) *Guidance on Major Incident Room Standardised Administrative Procedures (MIRSAP)*. Wyboston: NPIA.

ACPO (2005b) *Practice Advice on Core Investigative Doctrine*. Wyboston: NPIA.

ACPO (2005c) *Practice Advice on Search Management and Procedures*. Wyboston: NPIA.

ACPO (2006a) *Murder Investigation Manual*. Wyboston: NPIA.

ACPO (2006b) *Practice Advice on the Management of Priority and Volume Crime*. Wyboston: NPIA.

ACPO (2007) *Practice Advice on the Resources and the People Assets of the National Intelligence Model*. Wyboston: NPIA.

Adhami, E. and Browne, D. P. (1996) *Major Crime Enquiries: Improving Expert Support for Detectives*, Home Office Police Research Group Special Interest Series Paper 9. London: Home Office.

Allgood, J. (1984) 'A Degree of Professionalism', *Police Review*, 6 April: 676–7.

Banton, M. (1985) *Investigating Robbery*. Aldershot: Gower.

Barrett, E. C. (2005) 'Psychological Research and Police Investigations: Does the Research Meet the Needs?', in L. Alison (ed.) *The Forensic Psychologist's Casebook: Psychological Profiling and Criminal Investigation*. Cullompton: Willan Publishing.

Beckley, A. (2004) 'Professionalisation of the Police Service', *Police Research and Management*, 6: 89–100.

Benner, P. E. (1984) *From Novice to Expert: Excellence and Power in Clinical Nursing Practice*. London: Addison-Wesley.

Bernhard, L. A. and Walsh, M. (1995) *Leadership: The Key to the Professionalization of Nursing*. St Louis, MO: Mosby.

Bottomley, K. and Coleman, C. (1981) *Understanding Crime Rates*. Farnborough: Gower.

Bowling, B. and Phillips, C. (2002) *Racism, Crime and Justice*. London: Longman.

Brookman, F. (2000) 'Dying For Control: Men, Murder and Sub-Lethal Violence in England and Wales', unpublished PhD thesis, Cardiff University.

Brookman, F. (2005) *Understanding Homicide*. London: Sage.

Bull, R. and Milne, R. (2004) 'Attempts to Improve Police Interviewing of Suspects', in G. D. Lassiter (ed.) *Interrogation, Confessions and Entrapment*. New York: Kluwer/Plenum.

Burrows, J. and Tarling, R. (1982) *Clearing up Crime*, Home Office Research Study 73. London: HMSO.

Burrows, J. and Tarling, R. (1987) 'The Investigation of Crime in England and Wales', *British Journal of Criminology*, 27: 234.

Byford, L. (1981) 'The Yorkshire Ripper Case: Review of the Police Investigation of the Case', unpublished report for Her Majesty's Inspector of Constabulary.

CPS (2004) *The Code for Crown Prosecutors*. London: CPS.

CPS (2007) *Annual Report and Resource Accounts 2006–2007*. London, CPS.

Dale, A. (1994) 'Professionalism and the Police', *Police Journal*, 67: 209–18.

Davies, M. (1994) *The Essential Social Worker: An Introduction to Professional Practice in the 1990s*. Aldershot: Arena.

Davis, M. (2002) *Profession, Code and Ethics*. Aldershot: Ashgate.

Dubourg, R., Hamed, J. and Thorns, J. (2005) *The Economic and Social Costs of Crime Against Individuals and Households 2003/04*, Home Office Online Report 30/05.

Eck, E. J. (1983) *Solving Crimes: The Investigation of Burglary and Robbery*. Washington, DC: Police Executive Research Forum.

Emsley, C. (1996) *The English Police: A Political and Social History*, 2nd edn. London: Longman.

English, J. and Card, R. (2005) *Police Law*, 9th edn. Oxford: Blackstone.

Exworthy, M. and Halford, S. (1999) *Professionals and the New Managerialism in the Public Sector*. Buckingham: Open University Press.

Flanagan, R. (2008) *The Review of Policing: Final Report*. London: HMIC.

Flannery, K. (2004) 'Watching the Detectives', *Police Professional*, July: 25–7.

Flynn, R. (1999) 'Managerialism, Professionalism and Quasi-markets', in M. Exworthy and S. Halford (eds) *Professionals and the New Managerialism in the Public Sector*. Buckingham: Open University Press.

Garland, D. (2002) 'Of Crimes and Criminals: The Development of Criminology in Britain', in M. Maguire, R. Morgan and R. Reiner (eds) *The Oxford Handbook of Criminology*, 3rd edn. Oxford: Oxford University Press.

Greenwood, P. W., Chaiken, J. and Petersilia, J. (1977) *The Criminal Investigation Process*. Lexington, MA: D.C. Heath.

Gudjonsson, G. H. (2007) 'Investigative Interviewing', in T. Newburn, T. Williamson and A. Wright (eds) *Handbook of Criminal Investigation*. Cullompton: Willan Publishing.

Harfield, C. and Harfield, K. (2005) *Covert Investigation*. Oxford: Oxford University Press.

Hitchens, P. (2003) *A Brief History of Crime*. London: Atlantic.

HMIC (2000) *Policing London*. London: HMIC.

HMIC (2004) *Modernising the Police Service: A Thematic Inspection of Workforce Modernisation – The Role, Management and Deployment of Police Staff in the Police Service of England and Wales*. London: HMIC.

HMIC and HMCPSI (2007) *Without Consent: A Report on the Joint Review of the Investigation and Prosecution of Rape Offences*. London.

Home Office (2001) *Policing a New Century: A Blueprint for Reform*. London: Home Office.

Home Office (2005a) *National Policing Plan 2005–2008*. London: Home Office.

Home Office (2005b) *Offending in England and Wales: First Results from the 2003 Crime and Justice Survey*. London: Home Office.

Innes, M. R. (2003) *Investigating Murder: Detective Work and the Police Response to Criminal Homicide*. Oxford: Oxford University Press.

Irvine, B. and Dunningham, C. (1993) *Human Factors in the Quality Control of CID Investigations*, Royal Commission on Criminal Justice Research Study 21. London: HMSO.

Johnston, D. and Hutton, G. (2005) *Evidence and Procedure*. Oxford: Blackstone.

Kelly, L., Lovett, J. and Regan, L. (2005) *A Gap or a Chasm? Attrition in Reported Rape Cases*, Home Office Research Study 293. London: Home Office.

Laurenson, S. (1995) *Health Service Developments and the Scope of Professional Nursing Practice: A Survey of Developing Clinical Roles within NHS Trusts in Scotland*. Edinburgh: National Nursing, Midwifery and Health Visiting Advisory Committee.

Laycock, G. (2001) 'Research for Police, Who Needs it?', *Issues and Trends*,

211. Canberra: Australian Institute of Criminology.

Laycock, G. (2005) 'Defining Crime Science', in M. J. Smith and N. Tilley (eds) *Crime Science: New Approaches to Preventing and Detecting Crime*. Cullompton: Willan Publishing.

Macpherson, W. M. (1999) *The Stephen Lawrence Inquiry: Report of an Inquiry by Sir William Macpherson of Cluny*. London: Stationery Office.

Maguire, M. (2003) 'Crime Investigation and Crime Control', in T. Newburn (ed.) *Handbook of Policing*. Cullompton: Willan Publishing.

Malin, N. (ed.) (2000) *Professionalism, Boundaries and the Workplace*. London: Routledge.

May, R. (1999) *Criminal Evidence*, 4th edn. London: Sweet and Maxwell.

Milne, R. and Bull, R. (1999) *Investigative Interviewing: Psychology and Practice*. Chichester: John Wiley.

NCPE (2005) *Professionalising Investigation Programme Information Pack*. Wyboston: NCPE.

Neyroud, P. W. and Beckley, A. (2001) *Policing, Ethics and Human Rights*. Cullompton: Willan Publishing.

Nicol, C., Innes, M., Gee, D. and Feist, A. (2004) *Reviewing Murder Investigations: An Analysis of Progress Reviews from Six Police Forces*. London: Home Office.

Nutley, S., Davies, H. and Walter, I. (2002) *Evidence Based Policy and Practice: Cross Sector Lessons from the UK*. London: ESRC.

Ormerod, T. C., Barrett, E. C. and Taylor, P. J. (2005) 'Investigative Sense-making in Criminal Contexts', in J. M. C. Schraagen (ed.) *Proceedings of the Seventh International NDM Conference*. Amsterdam, June.

PA Consulting (2001) *Diary of a Police Officer*, Home Office Police Research Series Paper 149. London: Home Office.

Perrier, D. C. (1978) 'Police Professionalism', *Canadian Police College Journal*, 2: 209–14.

Phillips, D. (2003) The Route to Professionalism', *Policing Today*, 9: 5–6.

Polk, K. (1994) *When Men Kill: Scenarios of Male Violence*. Cambridge. Cambridge University Press.

Reiner, R. (2000) *The Politics of the Police*, 3rd edn. Oxford: Oxford University Press.

Saunders, E. (2001) 'The Decision-making Processes used in Operational Policing and Serious Crime Investigation', unpublished PhD thesis, Warwick University.

Small, M. W. (1991) 'Police Professionalism: Problems and Issues in Upgrading an Occupation', *Police Journal*, 64: 314–20.

Smith, J. (2003) *The Shipman Inquiry Second Report: The Police Investigation of March 1998*. London: Stationery Office.

Smith, N. and Flanagan, C. (2000) *The Effective Detective: Identifying the Skills of an Effective SIO*, Police Research Series Paper 122. London: Home Office.

Spencer, S. and Stern, B. (2001) *Reluctant Witness*. London: Institute for Public Policy Research.

Steer, D. (1980) *Uncovering Crime: The Police Role*, Royal Commission on Criminal Procedure Research Study 7. London: HMSO.

Stelfox, P. (2006) 'The Role of Confidants in Homicide Investigations', *Journal of Homicide and Major Incident Investigation*, 2(1), Spring: 79–91.

Stelfox, P. (2007) 'Professionalising Criminal Investigation', in T. Newburn, T. Williamson and A. Wright (eds) *Handbook of Criminal Investigation*. Cullompton: Willan Publishing.

Stelfox, P. (2008) 'Investigative Practice and Performance Management: Making the Marriage Work', *Policing: A Journal of Policy and Practice*, 2(3): 303–10.

Stelfox, P. and Pease, K. (2005) 'Cognition and Detection: Reluctant Bedfellows?', in M. J. Smith and N. Tilley (eds) *Crime Science: New Approaches to Preventing and Detecting Crime*. Cullompton: Willan Publishing.

Thomas, N. and Feist, A. (2004) 'The Detection of Crime', in T. Dodd, S. Nicholas, D. Povey and A. Walker (eds) *Crime in England and Wales 2003/2004*. London: Home Office.

West, A. (2001) 'A Proposal for an Investigative Science Course: Any Takers?', *Police Research and Management*, 5: 13–22.

Williamson, T. (2007) *'Psychology and Criminal Investigation'*, in T. Newburn, T. Williamson and A. Wright (eds) *Handbook of Criminal Investigation*. Cullompton, Willan Publishing.

Willmer, M. A. P. (1970) *Crime and Information Theory*. Edinburgh: Edinburgh University Press.

Wilson, G. (2004) *The Beat Officer's Companion*. Coulsdon: Jane's Police Review.

Zander, M. (1979) 'The Investigation of Crime: A Study of Cases Tried at the Old Bailey', *Criminal Law Review*: 203–19.

Index

Added to a page number 'f' denotes a figure, 't' denotes a table and 'n' denotes notes.